The End of Comparative Philosophy and the Task of Comparative Thinking

SUNY series in Chinese Philosophy and Culture

Roger T. Ames, *editor*

The End of Comparative Philosophy and the Task of Comparative Thinking

Heidegger, Derrida, and Daoism

STEVEN BURIK

SUNY PRESS

Published by
STATE UNIVERSITY OF NEW YORK PRESS
Albany

Printed in the United States of America

For information, contact
State University of New York Press, Albany, NY
www.sunypress.edu

Production by Dana Foote
Marketing by Anne M. Valentine

Library of Congress Cataloging-in-Publication Data

Burik, Steven, 1970–
The end of comparative philosophy and the task of comparative thinking : Heidegger, Derrida, and Daoism / Steven Burik.
p. cm. — (SUNY series in Chinese philosophy and culture)
Includes bibliographical references and index.
ISBN 978-1-4384-2733-1 (hardcover : alk. paper)
ISBN 978-1-4384-2734-8 (paperback : alk. paper)
1. Philosophy, Comparative. 2. Heidegger, Martin, 1889–1976. 3. Derrida, Jacques. 4. Philosophy, Taoist. I. Title.
B799.B87 2009
181'.114—dc22 2008048479

10 9 8 7 6 5 4 3 2 1

Contents

Acknowledgments

A great number of people have given me advice and support during the writing of this book. I thank them hereby. Most specifically, I would like to thank Roger Ames and Eliot Deutsch of the University of Hawai'i at Manoa for their valuable contributions to first drafts of this book. I would also like to thank Sor-hoon Tan of the National University of Singapore for her valuable guidance and patience in seeing me through this effort. Furthermore I would like to thank Francis Alleblas for the use of her artwork "Tree" on the cover of this book. And I would like to thank Mark and Eunice Nowacki from LogicMills in Singapore for their support in getting this book ready.

Introduction

> Monotonization of the world. Strong spiritual impression of all travels of the last years, despite the individual happiness: a pale drab of monotonization of the world. Everything is becoming similar in its outward appearances, leveling out in a uniform cultural scheme. The individual customs of peoples are wearing off, the way of dress is becoming uniform, ethics international. Ever more nations seem fused together, people living and working in the same way, cities looking alike. Ever more the fine aroma of the specificness of cultures evaporates, ever more vengeful the colors peel off, and beneath the cracked layers of varnish the steel-colored pistons of the mechanical bustle, the modern world-machine, become visible.[1]

> Being at one is godlike and good; whence, then, this craze among men that there exists only One, why should all be one?[2]

Comparative philosophy is a relatively young discipline in philosophy. On one hand, the realization of the fundamental limitations of Western style (mainstream) philosophy, with its demands for adherence to strict logic and rationalism, as well as the increasing awareness that every single form of philosophy, and even scientific research, carries with it (the burden of) a cultural component and foresight, have resulted in more and more Western philosophers taking an interest in the ways of thinking of other (than Western) cultures, which were looked down upon earlier in Orientalist ways. On the other hand, non-Western cultures have felt the growing need to assess and integrate their respective forms of thinking in the greater philosophical discourse. Non-Western cultures are not only realizing the importance of coming to terms with the West in a more profound way by advocating their own traditions in the philosophical discourse, but they are also aware that their own philosophies and cultures per se are very much worth further exploring and comparing with other non-Western ways of thinking.

Let me start with an explanation of my views on what comparative philosophy should and should not be, at least if it is sincere in trying to be truly intercultural. Comparative philosophy cannot stop at the finding and explanation of similarities and differences between thinking from different cultures, however valuable these findings are. As a discipline, it should locate itself between these differences, while aware of the impossibility of a purely neutral viewpoint, and in that sense I use the term *intercultural*. Being between different cultures suggests not the Western metaphysical ideal of objectivity, but it does suggest the openness toward what is other and the willingness to step outside one's own comfortable sphere.

In the last decades, comparative philosophy has seen great development. I think recent scholarship in comparative philosophy and other areas exhibits very little anymore of Edward Said's "Orientalism"[3] in the sense of a feeling of Western superiority or imperialism, but that does not mean this scholarship is now completely neutral. Rather, my argument is that the language of many intercultural encounters, including philosophical ones, still displays and favors a prejudiced and one-sided way of thinking, even if often not consciously, and that this one-sidedness is presented as neutrality or objectivity. Said showed convincingly that there is a certain mindset at work in a lot of scholarly work which involves the encounter between different cultures. This mindset to him is the result of colonial imperialism, which gave rise to the idea of the supremacy of certain (mainly Western) civilizations or cultures over others. According to Said, even in this present era much of what he considers to be Orientalism still dominates scholarship on other-than-Western cultures. Said's notion of Orientalism made problematic certain questions of how to (re-)present other cultures, or of what constitutes another culture. His main idea is that most representations are biased in that they tend to see the other culture as inferior, and promote and justify the dominance of the representer's culture over that of the other.

Heidegger has argued in a similar vein that disciplines like ethnology already "operate with definite preliminary conceptions and interpretations of human Dasein in general,"[4] and while Heidegger does not have the political implications in mind that Said has uncovered, we can read in this the idea that the West tends to impose its structures and conceptions on other cultures.

Such a thing has often happened in comparative philosophy, whereby Western ideas, concepts, and thought structures were superimposed on other cultures with the idea that these were a more truthful approach to what "they" were really thinking. It is here that Western languages play a crucial role, as most intercultural exchanges in philosophy are "done" in Western languages. It is thus argued that the language of current comparative philosophy shows an inclination or tendency toward a form of Orientalism, very subtle but still present indeed in the ways of communication and the focus of scholarly research, and which, thought through, has certain philosophical and even political implications which arise from misunderstanding or misrepresenting other cultures.

Contrary to such misrepresentations, to accommodate different ways of thinking into one discourse without that discourse favoring one of these ways above the other, and thus to make productive meetings possible, should be one of the main tasks of comparative philosophy. This task is by no means an easy one, and it remains to be seen whether this is at all possible without getting caught in some political, linguistic, metaphysical, or other prejudice. This is one of the main questions of this book. I explore the possibility of a different reading of the protagonists that seeks to avoid the standard metaphysical implications. The comparative way of thinking wishes to acknowledge and promote the *equivalence* of *different* cultures, whereby otherness and diversity are valued above equality and unity. Equivalence does not mean equality, for to "make equal" carries with it the connotation of getting rid of differences, whereas the term equivalence, although not without its own limitations, conveys better the idea of respect for differences. In this sense the language of Western philosophy has been notorious for its equalizing effects because of its thinking in terms of generalizations, ideas of identity and unity valued over difference and change. It is also a fact that most if not all Western languages have been so influenced by the metaphysical way of thinking that it is hard to even bring up the idea of some different way of thinking. Therefore a new way of seeing language is vital for the project of comparative philosophy. It is clear that comparative thinking should not be a proponent of some obscure world syncretism or of a "melting of horizons" that would annihilate all differences and with that the richness of diversity, in favor of unity or identity, a world culture. We should avoid trying to make things identical (what Heidegger calls *das Gleiche*), but we should treat them as being similar in a different way, which translates Heidegger's notion "the same" (*das Selbe*). As he says: "But the same is not the merely identical. In the merely identical, the difference disappears. In the same the difference appears. . . ."[5]

It is problematic to think of a "common" ground in this respect. Although Heidegger has referred to such a thing on occasions, he simultaneously hinted that this common ground could be nothing but a hidden one.[6] One focus of this book is to look for the way this common ground is to be thought of, and what it would entail. If anything, it should admit of differences as equally originary. Similarities at some level should not function as above, or more important than, differences.

The idea of comparative philosophy which guides me in this book thus has the following characteristics: Comparative philosophy should focus on two things: similarities and differences between ways of thinking. It should however not content itself with merely pointing to these similarities and differences but should instead seek to make them productive in the sense that through these similarities and differences we come to understand better first of all what we are comparing, and second the way in which we compare these philosophies, and that means also our contemporary philosophies and presuppositions of how we perceive our world. I do not believe in one overarching theory or methodology of comparative philosophy. In that sense my approach is hermeneutic, in that it recognizes the necessity of perspectives. There are however a couple of ideas which comparative philosophy should adhere to. It should seek a dialogue, between two different cultural perspectives (and it must be noticed that the Western philosophical tradition, although often one of the interlocutors, is not necessarily always involved), that is based on equivalence. This dialogic approach means that comparative philosophy should try as much as possible to position itself in-between the different cultures. How this in-between is to be perceived is addressed in this book. But at least it is not meant to overcome differences, but to acknowledge and appreciate them in a realization of the complementarity of perspectives. Raimundo Panikkar argues for example that comparative philosophy should be understood as "diatopical hermeneutics,"[7] by which he means a search for understanding in a dialogue between different spaces.

My understanding of comparative philosophy also entails that theory and practice of comparative philosophy cannot be separated. This is meant in a double sense. First of all, it means that it is impossible to abstract a purely theoretical methodology, which would somehow stand above, and be applicable to, all instances of comparative philosophy. Second, it means that as such, any comparison is of necessity related to the theory of comparative philosophy in that it is only in the comparisons that we can locate any theory or method. In other words, the interlocutors *of* the comparative dialogue to a large extent dictate the guiding theory behind that particular dialogue. So this book is as much an exercise *in* comparative philosophy as it is *about* comparative philosophy. In other words, we can only learn about comparative philosophy by doing it, by actively crossing over to different ways of thinking. Since I believe and hope to prove that a nonmetaphysical understanding of Daoism is feasible, in effect this means that comparing Heidegger and Derrida to Daoism will entail a nonmetaphysical and nondialectic approach or rather what Heidegger has called *Auseinandersetzung*. This approach is the only possible way to take seriously the fact that there is no neutral overall birds-eye view from which we could objectively look down at the compared ways of thinking.[8]

Last, but maybe most important, understanding comparative philosophy as a constantly renewing dialogue entails that language is a crucial factor. Any comparative philosophical enterprise has to be cautious of the language it uses. Certain conceptual schemes are so embedded in Western languages that it is hard to avoid or circumvent them within these languages, but this is exactly what we need to do in order for different conceptual schemes[9] to be brought forward in comparative philosophy. With this in mind what this book aims for is an inquiry into the philosophies of Heidegger, Derrida, and classical Daoism, and through this I hope to show that the ideas of language propagated in these ways of thinking can aid the project of comparative philosophy specifically, and philosophy generally, in trying to overcome its suffocating ties to the metaphysical way of thinking that has dominated Western philosophy for the last twenty-five hundred years and is still dominating and frustrating our efforts in intercultural encounters. This dominance of metaphysics in philosophy becomes evident if we look more closely at Heidegger's and Derrida's writings on these subjects, which also show how Western languages in general have been influenced by philosophical ideas and language, and have thereby become biased through this metaphysical dominance. In the same way, I show how many interpretations of the Daoist classics have inserted this same bias in an effort to appropriate Daoism into the wider philosophical discourse. In arguing against what I would call these metaphysical interpretations I am not suggesting that there is some other, true meaning of what these Daoist classics mean.[10] On the contrary, I am suggesting that the search for such a strict unified meaning is futile considering the inherent vagueness of the compositions and the language used. This does not mean, however, that Daoism is open to an "anything goes" attitude, a relativism, or skepticism. Obviously, some interpretations make much more sense than others. The importance of my approach lies more in the idea that comparative philosophy should also further our understanding of the problems we face today, and that means that a purely historical approach or a one-sidedly metaphysical approach is unsuitable. We need to look at the possible contributions of the thought of Heidegger, Derrida, and Daoism to a better understanding of this world, and that means an attitude that is more open to different interpretations of the texts of these three protagonists.

There are then a number of questions which this book tries to address, and the main one is to what extent differences in languages and the backgrounds of particular languages used by Heidegger, Derrida, and Daoism are influenced by and do influence not only philosophy in general and culturally different ways of thinking in particular, but especially the ongoing efforts in comparative philosophy, and thus in what way do these differences in languages have an effect on intercultural understanding?

To further explain this main question a number of related questions are asked: What exactly is the influence of language and its use in the thinking of Heidegger, Derrida, and Daoism? Are there similarities in their ideas or use of language, and if so, what do these amount to if we apply them to intercultural encounters, dialogues, and the like? And are there serious differences in their linguistic views, which would warrant caution in trying to apply similarities?

In relation to this, how should we see the ongoing practice of intercultural understanding in mostly Western languages? We could see this in two ways: as an obstacle or impediment to intercultural understanding, or as a necessary medium *of* comparative philosophy. Another question worth asking here would be if a change to other-than-Western languages for comparative philosophy would not run the same risks.

Does the recognition of important differences in language and in ways of thinking lead to a position of relativism or not? What are the communication possibilities? Is it possible to take an objective stand and maintain that serious and unprejudiced communication is possible, or do we have to admit to the hermeneutic fact brought to our attention by Gadamer that no dialogue or discourse is ever so neutral, that prejudice or perspective is inevitable, but that we can turn this into a positive aspect of understanding? What are the consequences of such a view?

What can be said of the existence of ideas *about* intercultural encounters in Heidegger, Derrida, and Daoism? Aside (or maybe not) from the language, can we find ideas which expressly relate to other cultures, or from which we can construct ideas on how these three protagonists would look at universalism or cultural differences and the way to deal with them?

The idea of "Nothingness"[11] is prominent in Heidegger and Daoism, and to a lesser extent in Derrida as well. What is the status of this Nothingness, as it seems often to be seen as something beyond language? How does language relate to this Nothingness, and how is it seen to function within and without language?

How exactly is language seen here? Does it consist solely of the spoken and written word, or should we extend the meaning of language by including different sign structures, like art, music, and poetry? As we shall see, poetry has a special function for Heidegger, and we will have to rethink in what way we extend what we mean by language. Do we just widen the scope of language, or do we have to radically rethink the whole concept of language and its functions? If we do, what are the consequences for philosophy?

Given the findings, what in the end should comparative philosophy stand for and what should it practically consist of? What are its possibilities?

All these questions are not easy ones, and I do not pretend to have an answer to each of them. But they are used as a guideline as this book attempts to shed some light on the questions of the problem of how language and interpretation go together in comparative philosophy. Heidegger, Derrida, and Daoism put together might be able to change our ways of thinking about these problems, in anticipation of a different way of thinking. Guiding this attempt will be the notion of a dialogue between them, thought through from different perspectives such as *logos, polemos, physis*, differance, trace, supplement, and *dao* 道, *tian* 天, *men* 門, *ziran* 自然, *wuwei* 無為.[12] Starting with Heidegger's approach to comparative philosophy, I then bring in Derrida as both a proponent of this approach and its critic, and proceed to see whether his philosophy allows a comparative variant and whether his critiques directed at language offer a viable alternative to the traditional thinking of identity and opposition that still dominates philosophy today. From the other side, Daoism is put in intercultural perspective as well, and its interpretations by Western language translators and philosophers are scrutinized. Heidegger and Derrida have shown us that the metaphysical idea of language as naming can be seen as an attempt at identification and stabilization, fixing reference, to which my interpretation of Daoism would offer an alternative view, resulting from the horizons expanded by Heidegger and Derrida, but most of all in accordance with the "original" openness of Daoism.

The reader will have to keep in mind that this is a work about three different philosophies, in three (or more) different languages. To accommodate these into English is not something to be seen as a side effect. It is rather one of the main problems. To give but one example beforehand, the dynamic or process character of Heidegger's work, especially his verbal thinking, is hardly translatable into English, as any translation of Heideggerian easily becomes static through the use of nouns. Think of *Wesen*, usually rendered as "essence," or sometimes as "root unfolding." It is easy to misread "essence" in a metaphysical way as substantial and thereby neglect the "esse" in it. And, as a rather bad starting point, I could quote Heinrich Petzet, Heidegger's long-term friend, who on the occasion of being presented with the English translation of *Sein und Zeit* complained that "almost every sentence either missed an essential point or failed to consider a perhaps-significant nuance of meaning. This was confirmed when we [Heidegger and Petzet] went through the translation sample together."[13] I try to alert the reader to these problems throughout the book, but I nevertheless venture forth. The main focus is thus on language and on the *logos* of dialogue, and on the supposed Nothingness as the guiding principle, but these are rethought from three different sides in a way which runs counter to usual interpretations.

To conclude this introduction, we need to be aware that while the dialogue is the most important means for comparative thinking, language is also the foremost danger in this area. The development of ideas about translation and its importance in philosophy of language seems to warrant a closer look at translation(s). W. v. O. Quine's theory of the indeterminacy of translation[14] is that there are always different possible translations, and that it is only a matter of elegance or usefulness which translation is chosen. There are no objectively true translations. Quine uses this theory to argue that meaning itself is relative or indeterminate, because there is no objective language which will capture *the* meaning of things. Donald Davidson[15] seems to avoid this at first, but he can only do so by *assuming* some basic truth on which he grounds his theory of meaning. Certain constraints are introduced to get an idea of this truth. But Davidson can only defend these constraints by introducing the "principle of charity," which basically assumes that we assign our own beliefs and ideas of truth onto speakers of other languages and cultures, holding our Western notions as universal truth conditions. And even if we do not extrapolate our own beliefs, others are at least supposed to be *intelligible* to us, which can only mean we assume that they think like us, in similar categories, and from there we arrive at meaning. But even with this theory Davidson cannot deny some degree of indeterminacy of interpretation, translation, and thereby meaning.

There is thus a translation problem in philosophy of language, and I take this indeterminacy of language up using Heidegger and Derrida, who have both, although in different ways, done very much for a different appreciation of the role of language in philosophy. There are different sorts of language used in different areas of philosophy. There is, for example, a certain use of language in analytic philosophy, and a different one in continental philosophy, and yet a different one in Daoism. So there are not only translation problems between languages, but also between different ways of thinking within one language. English can be used in a specific way for analytic philosophy, but also for continental philosophy, where it is used in a different way. Philosophical languages can then not be simply equated or sided with natural languages; different philosophies imply a specific use of languages. Different use, different meaning. What I focus on is mainly continental philosophy in relation to classical Chinese philosophy in translation, where different ways of thinking try to find a way of expression in one language. The question is whether such a one language, in this case English, is able to provide enough space for such differences to emerge.

The point of all this is that I realize that in the ideal circumstances I would have to have proficiency in the classical Chinese language. But nevertheless I think that even without this proficiency and with just some acquaintance with classical Chinese, I can still make a valuable contribution. I am not doing a language study; my main concern is how language is used, how it functions in (intercultural) dialogue, what the metaphysical assumptions behind it are, if there are any, and how language is seen to relate to the world and reality. In my view this can be done by studying works *on* Chinese language, and by studying the way translators, commentators, philosophers, and interpreters have dealt with the problems they encountered. This brings out the profound differences between the classical Chinese language and Western languages, and thereby the difference in ways of thinking in Daoism in an equally thorough fashion. The point is that I think it is possible, without fluency in classical Chinese, to nevertheless raise interesting questions about the Daoist way of thinking by looking at the differences in translations and interpretations and the reasons that translators and philosophers have given for defending these differences. These questions might then be addressed by those with sufficient knowledge of classical Chinese. It is also the case that as this is a work in the English language, it appeals more directly to English-speaking readers, and one of its main points is to show the difficulties that arise especially in the space *between* cultures. By taking into account as many differing translations and interpretations as possible, I hope to make up for the lack of proficiency in classical Chinese.

Another reason why I believe I can make a valuable contribution is that one of the things I hope to show is exactly how being able to read (classical) Chinese does not necessarily entail getting closer to the meaning of the Daoist classics. Ability in a foreign language is always influenced by certain ways of thinking, and the scholars with proficiency in classical Chinese are known to widely differ on many aspects of the language and the philosophy behind it. But even without such proficiency, the main aim of this book is to promote intercultural understanding. This understanding is much needed today, and it is unrealistic to assume or expect proficiency in multiple languages to be a necessary requirement for the expansion of such understanding. I hope to show in conclusion that comparative thinking is possible despite the inherent dangers of interpretation, translation, and language.

CHAPTER ONE

Heidegger and the Other Commencement

HEIDEGGER'S GREEK CONNECTION

> . . . that every reflection upon that which now is can take its rise and thrive only if, through a dialogue with the Greek thinkers and their language, it strikes root into the ground of our historical existence. That dialogue still awaits its beginning. It is scarcely prepared for at all, and yet it itself remains for us the precondition of the inevitable dialogue with the East Asian world.[1]

Martin Heidegger himself started or at least prepared both of the above-mentioned dialogues. The first one, the dialogue with Greek thinking, was one of Heidegger's main concerns from early on to late in his career, especially as a means to help the overcoming of Western metaphysics. I use the term "metaphysics" and related terms with the following fundamental characteristics: the distinction between the sensuous and the non-sensuous since the time of Plato. The outcome of this distinction can be seen throughout the history of Western philosophy, as the abstracting and theorizing influences of the later Greeks, the theologizing influences of medieval times, and scientification in more modern times of the originary thinking of Being. In general this distinction has led to further distinctions such as between form and matter, essence and attributes, substance and properties, mind and body, truth and appearance, and so on. Related to these general distinctions there arose the hierarchical view that one side of the distinction was worthy, good, and true, while the other was at best a hindrance with which one had to live, or at worst something evil that was to be eradicated if we were ever to find the Truth.

The transformation that thus took place throughout the history of thinking brought about and was brought about by a change of the functioning of language, in a reciprocal way, and the dominant theory has since become our standard way of seeing and experiencing the world, with little or no tolerance toward views which differ profoundly. The ancient Greeks were precisely different from this dominant metaphysical tradition in that they were *before* metaphysics, so what Heidegger saw in them was an opportunity for finding a different way of thinking which could challenge the dominating philosophy of his own time.

It would be hard to overestimate the influence of early Greek thinking on Heidegger's work. In nearly all his writings there is usually at least a mention or reference to an ancient Greek word or saying. As Heidegger obviously felt that the language of certain Presocratics was worth thinking over against the usual interpretations that are normally given, it is only logical that I too should venture into this. Because Heidegger thought that by looking more closely at the way in which the Greeks actually thought, or rather in how Heidegger reinterpreted them, we could find what is really worthy of thought. This *Wiederholung* of Greek thinking is very important for the project of comparative philosophy in two ways. First of all, Heidegger thought the *Auseinandersetzung*[2] with the Greeks a necessary precondition for the possibility of an encounter with the East Asian world. His argument for this was that he thought that modern philosophy had become corrupted by the narrowness of the metaphysical and purely rational way of thinking, making it unsuitable for an encounter with very different thinking. This different thinking was exactly what Heidegger expected to find in East Asian thought. The narrow metaphysical outlook and the insistence on its rightness in certain places that prevailed in the West would prevent any encounter that would not try to explain things according to Western ideas and values. Heidegger also thought that in East Asian thinking he would find, along with a way of thinking that was not influenced by metaphysics as we know it in the Western world, languages or at least views on language that were equally unspoiled.

The second reason why the dialogue or *Auseinandersetzung* or confrontation with the Greeks is important is that Heidegger's translations and readings of the (ancient) Greeks is exemplary of the way he wishes us to approach that which is "foreign" or "other," in a thoughtful confrontation that leaves what is con-fronted as it reveals itself, from itself, and to give this "other" the space to do so. In other, slightly less Heideggerian words, the way to approach what is other is to let it speak for itself. The real difficulty is how to achieve this. Of course, ancient Greek civilization has long vanished, and the same goes for the world of the Daoist classics, so, even if given the chance, how could they be speaking for themselves? In spite of this obvious discrepancy, Heidegger thinks there are opportunities to think these ways of thinking in a more originary way, to make them speak again or rather to make them speak to us. In what follows, I focus largely on Heidegger's rethinking of the Presocratics, whom he saw as the representatives of thinking before it was overtaken by metaphysics. Insofar as philosophy has become metaphysical, he considered the Presocratics not philosophers but "greater thinkers,"[3] who thought before *Seinsvergessenheit*, the forgetfulness of Being, made its entry into thinking, turning it into philosophy as metaphysics.

It should however be made clear that Heidegger was not some sort of nostalgic thinker who longed for the good old days of philosophical astonishment. Superficial reading of his work could lead one to take this position. After all, did he not on many occasions lash out at modern technology, the modern subject and its rational approach to all objects? He did indeed, but not because he was principally opposed to these things, but because he saw their increasing dominance and exclusive claim to truthfulness, and wanted to counterbalance this by putting them in their proper place. To this extent he argued for example for a reinterpretation of τέχνη (techne) and λόγος (logos), the Greek etymological grounds for the notion of technology.

Basically a lot of Heidegger's work is based on reinterpretations of the ancient Greeks and their language in order to come to a new understanding of what is going on today. It is in this light that we must see his ongoing efforts at reading "what the Greeks have thought in an even more Greek manner"[4] than the Greeks did themselves. This *Wiederholung* does not mean reading in the sense of a nostalgic return to what was, but it is rather a task that lies ahead of us, for the better understanding of what is now through what has been, by thinking it through *ursprünglicher* or more originary[5] than the Greeks could themselves, means thinking through what remained unthought by them. This means that the ancient Greeks inhabited this originary world, but they did not think it as such. It is this thinking through that would then be Heidegger's contribution to thinking as it lies before us. In a way we should read the sentence "thinking through" in a double sense—first, that we are returning to the Greeks and what they thought and left unthought in this way of thinking, and second, that we get to think because of something else, which somehow shows itself to us and calls for our thinking. The German *von* in much of Heidegger's work has the same connotations, in that it can mean both "from" and "of," and even "on," so that we get to think "from" the Greeks, by our renewed thinking "of" them.[6]

Heidegger uses the very same strategy in his con-frontation with Asia, so it is crucial to understand his *Wiederholung* of Greek thinking first. Heidegger's efforts at rethinking and rereading the Presocratics were often in direct opposition to those of classical philology. It should be noted however that Heidegger was himself very well versed in ancient Greek and that the point of his enterprise was precisely to upset and uproot the tradition both of philosophy and philology by offering different ways of reading these Presocratic works. Heidegger argued that traditional philology "is always already situated within a linguistic and conceptual structure which it does not question."[7] This linguistic and conceptual structure Heidegger thought of as ontotheological philosophy or metaphysics, which has been mentioned already. In order to fight this single-minded domination of metaphysics, Heidegger therefore needed to challenge the philosophical foundations of philology, as it remained closed to different interpretations because of its liaisons with philosophy as metaphysics. This is of considerable importance for the encounter with East Asia, as traditional philological translations and interpretations have influenced the efforts of Western philosophers seeking to understand Asian ways of thinking for ages.

There are three of these challenges to normal philological and philosophical interpretation which come readily to mind to anyone familiar with Heidegger's work. These are his interpretations of Anaximander, Parmenides, and Heraclitus. I now look into all three of them to see where their importance for comparative philosophy lies, starting with the earliest one, Anaximander. All three interpretations or readings by Heidegger involve similar thinking and ultimately make roughly the same point, but it is still useful to treat them separately in order to understand the full impact Heidegger's interpretations of the Greeks had on his encounters[8] with East Asia, and mainly with Daoism.

Anaximander

In *Der Spruch des Anaximander*[9] Heidegger inquires into what is being said in one of the oldest known pieces of Western philosophy:

> ἐξ'ων δὲ ἡ γένεσίς ἐστι τοῖς οὐσι, καὶ τὴν φθορὰ εἰς ταῦα γίνεσθαι χατὰ τὸ χρεών. Διδόναι γὰρ αὐτὰ δίχην χαὶ τίσιν ἀλλήλοις τῆς ἀδιχίας χατὰ τὴν τοῦ χρόνου τάξιν.[10]

Looking at a number of different translations Heidegger comes to the conclusion that they are all influenced by later thinking, and that they thus do injustice to the *Spruch* or fragment itself, in that they impose concepts and ideas of a later time on an earlier thinking. This happens seemingly automatically when we translate, because we use terms which are familiar to us, but which need not at all have the same familiarity or usage for the Greeks. Heidegger says that even in calling the early Greek thinkers *Pre*-socratics later philosophers have made this mistake: "The unexpressed standard for considering and judging the early thinkers is the philosophy of Plato and Aristotle. These are taken as the Greek philosophers who set the standard both before and after themselves."[11] The idea is that it was right to measure the Presocratics by standards of Plato because these earlier thinkers were supposedly thinking the same as the later ones, but not yet correct, or still fragmented.[12] This sort of reading from one's own point of view[13] has happened throughout the history of metaphysics, as Heidegger argues, from the early medieval Christian interpretations of what we should rather now call the early Greeks, to Hegel and even Nietzsche.

Against these sorts of interpretations Heidegger exhorts his readers to look more closely at the text itself and what it could be saying from itself. However, this does not mean that Heidegger is arguing for a more literal translation, since we must not understand "literal" in the normal sense. As he says: "But when a translation is only literal it is not necessarily faithful. It is faithful only when its terms are words which speak from the language of the matter itself."[14] Translating the original German sentence of this quote alone could lead us into trouble. The difference between *Wörter* and *Worte* is subtle, and it goes together with the difference between *wörtlich* and *wortgetreu*. Both these latter terms are usually translated by "literal," although Krell and Capuzzi translate *wortgetreu* with "faithful." A problem with this translation is that "faithful" is first of all closely associated with religion, which is something Heidegger would not approve of, and then a more "literal" translation would rather be "word-loyal." "Faithful" also does not hint at the difference between *Wörter* and *Worte*, which makes for the subtle wordplay of the quotation in question. But even from the translation of the aforementioned fragment it is clear that Heidegger makes a distinction between "literal" and "true to the word." "True to the word" would be a translation that would speak *aus der Sprache der Sache*, that is, pertaining to the true "matter" of thinking. Heeding this "matter" of thinking would first of all require readers to relinquish the practice of looking at older thinking through the lenses of more recent ideas and concepts. The *Wirrnis*[15] (confusion) that has arisen through this practice, which has dominated Western philosophy, has first of all to be addressed. This is not done by just giving better or truer translations of the original Greek, but by rethinking our relation to the Greeks in a more originary way, which means by coming to a real dialogue with them.

What has to be done then is to think through Anaximander from a different perspective, or maybe even to give up the idea of perspective if that is at all possible, looking for what is yet unthought in these words. To do this, it is necessary to jump over (or maybe, as we shall see later, into) a trench or abyss[16] to another way of thinking. In doing this Heidegger offers his own version of the *Spruch*, but before I give that, it is better to first give the usual, standard translation of Anaximander's fragment:

> And from what source things arise, to that they return of necessity when they are destroyed; for they suffer punishment and make reparation to one another for their injustice according to the order of time.[17]

Heidegger's translation runs very different, having reinterpreted most of the words and even questioned the validity of attributing part of the *Spruch* to Anaximander, so that only the part . . . χατὰ τὸ χρεών. Διδόναι γὰρ αὐτὰ δίχην χαὶ τίσιν ἀλλήλοις τῆς ἀδιχίας remains certain. Although the rest of the fragment might not be from Anaximander himself, Heidegger still considers the whole fragment as Anaximandrian, considering the other parts as "secondary testimony"[18] to Anaximander's thinking. He comes to the following German translation:

> Von woheraus aber der Hervorgang ist dem jeweilig Anwesenden auch die Entgängnis in dieses (als in das Selbe) geht hervor entlang dem Brauch; gehören nämlich lassen sie Fug somit auch Ruch eines dem anderen (im Verwinden) des Un-Fugs entsprechend der Zuweisung des Zeitigen durch die Zeit.[19]

The differences between this and the usual translation are obvious and very significant. In English the translation of Heidegger's version would be:

> The place from out of which emergence comes is, for everything that emerges, also the place of disappearance into this (as into the same)—in accordance with exigence (brook); for they let enjoining and thereby also reck belong to each other (in the getting over) of disjoining, responding to the directive of time's coming into its own.[20]

Another translation in English, only of the part which was thought to be originally from Anaximander and on which Heidegger focuses, runs as follows:

> . . . along the lines of usage; for they let order and thereby also reck belong to one another (in the surmounting) of disorder.[21]

If only one thing, these heroic efforts at translation in English from Heidegger's difficult German and the discrepancies between them show how radically different his interpretations really are. Heidegger's readings think from a very different perspective, trying to undo what he thinks is a false sense of security and complacency with what we consider "normal." In the passage that Heidegger is concerned with the most, he translates Tò Χρεών with *Brauch* and translates δίχη and τίσις with *Fug* and *Ruch*. It is interesting to see what he says right after that, and I will have to quote at some length:

> We cannot demonstrate the adequacy of the translation by scholarly means; nor should we simply accept it through faith in some authority or other. Scholarly proof will not carry us far enough, and faith has no place in thinking. We can only reflect on the translation by thinking through the saying. But thinking is the poetizing of the truth of Being in the historic dialogue between thinkers. For this reason the fragment will never engage us so long we only explain it historiologically and philologically. Curious enough, the saying first resonates when we set aside the claims of our own familiar ways of representing things. . . .[22]

Only when we set aside our claims to rightness can we engage what is "other." For Heidegger this means that we discard the dominance of metaphysics in favor of a different thinking. This is also exactly what comparative philosophy has to do. The notion of *Brauch* and its relation to language tell us another important thing. Although the most common translation of *Brauch* is "custom," it also means "use," "usage," and "need" (exigence), and by employing this notion *Brauch* Heidegger aims to show us how language as Saying (*Sage*) is both something we use and need for our understanding of the world. There is no understanding without (the need for and use of) language. We need language, but we need to rethink the way we see and use it.

To come back to the English translations, the two versions offer some significant differences. *Brauch* is, as we have just seen, translated as "exigence/brook" and "usage," for *Fug* "enjoining" and "order" and for *Ruch* there is consensus on "reck," not very easily used or understood words. But maybe Heidegger would not object to these different translations, as his own German was especially meant to retain the broad meaning of the original Greek. It is by retaining the openness and broadness of these words that Heidegger can pursue the interconnectedness or "belonging together in difference" of all things, something that he is always eager to show.[23] It is therefore probably not a question of whether Heidegger's translations are better than others, because there is really no consensus on standards by which to judge them in that respect. The meaning of these words is so broad that Heidegger says that words like these "cannot be enclosed within the boundaries of particular disciplines. "Broad" does not mean here extensive, in the sense of something flattened or thinned out, but rather far-reaching, rich containing much thought."[24] Heidegger's translations do not bring us nearer to the original meaning; they are however supposed to bring us nearer to thinking, and they do so largely by challenging preconceptions of how Being has been understood. Heidegger shows that when we follow his readings, this will at least alert us to how the *Seinsvergessenheit* has come to be. He can then use his translations to show that Anaximander already intimated with τὸ χρεών what Parmenides and Heraclitus were trying to say with Μοῖρα and Λόγος, respectively, which is to think Being as presencing (*Anwesen*), in the sense of coming into presence, lingering a while, and returning into absence.

> Each presence is present, as long as it dwells, dwelling it arises and passes away, dwelling it exists as the enjoining of the transition from origin to departure. This ever dwelling existence of transition is the proper continuity of presence. This however does not consist of mere persistence.[25]

So we now see that Heidegger tries to read the fragment of Anaximander as a fragment on Being, not really a fragment about humanity. He does not read the fragment from a human perspective; he lets it speak from something else. In this reading he seeks to upset the metaphysical opposition between Subject and Object, of representational or propositional thinking, and come to an understanding which would make the saying "resonate" in the sense of giving us a different thinking relation to our world. By doing so, his interpretation differs, and this also allows him to undo the false pretension that Parmenides and Heraclitus were opponents. In fact, Parmenides (Being) and Heraclitus (transformation, transition) belong together.[26] By reading Being in the nearness of "*weilen*," which can be understood both as "sojourn" and "abiding," but which I have translated here as "dwelling," Heidegger sees presencing as a coming from and returning to absence, and thus the continuity (*Beständigkeit*) of Being and Nothing is thought to reside exactly in transformation, transition, change (*Übergang*), and I argue later that this way of thinking has strong similarities with a different-from-traditional reading of Daoism.

The three most important things that can be summarized from Heidegger's efforts on Anaximander are first to be very cautious with language and translations, second to see the idea of Being as transformation, and third to heed the matter of thinking in a thoughtful dialogue with what is different to us, which largely means not to extrapolate familiar terms to explain unfamiliar things, in this case *ancient Greek philosophy*, and we can see now that these three words themselves still stand in need of rethinking, thus opening them up to comparative philosophy, where it is crucial not to impose conceptual structures that are foreign to a different language or culture.

Parmenides

Heidegger's second engagement with early Greek thinking is his interpretation of Parmenides. In *Vorträge und Aufsätze*[27] he takes the fragment known as τὸ γὰρ αὐτὸ νοεῖν ἐστίν τε καὶ εἶναι or "the same is thinking and being" as his guide. Far from the normal interpretation which says that thinking is also a being, that is, thinking cannot be nothing, Heidegger again offers his own version, not so much in a translation this time, but more in an inquiry into the key words that make up this sentence of the fragment. Again he warns against imposing later concepts and thought structures on earlier thinking, and he says that an authentic inquiry should be a dialogue that asks not about things that seem familiar, but rather looks into "the obscure passages" in a "thoughtful translation of early Greek speech."[28] With the help of fragment 8, which is lengthier but deals with the same problematic, Heidegger reconsiders the text to say something of the belonging together in difference (being the "same") of what he calls *In-die-Acht-nehmen* and *Anwesen* (presencing, emerging, or even unfolding). Especially the idea of "belonging-together-in-difference" with which Heidegger translates τὸ αὐτὸ, or "the same," *das Selbe*, which we have already encountered, cannot be stressed enough in relation to comparative philosophy. This is exactly what I understand Heidegger's strategy in comparative philosophy to be about: to treat different cultures as belonging together through difference and diversity.

The fragment in its translation by Heidegger is important for another reason. This is because νοεῖν is not translated as "thinking," which is the normal translation but which has led to the metaphysical readings of much early philosophy. Instead he translates it with *In-die-Acht-nehmen*, which in English could be rendered as "taking in, facing up to, respectful perceiving" and this is an effort to demolish the metaphysical reading of thinking as *Vorstellen*, as representational thinking, and to turn to a different kind of thinking like *Andenken* and poetic thinking, of which I speak later. It is this approach which runs through Heidegger's encounters with the early Greeks. If thinking is thus transformed from being merely metaphysical, representational, and conceptual thinking to something different or at least wider and more encompassing, this bodes well for an eventual encounter with thinking in non-Western cultures, where these specific features get less attention.

Heraclitus

Heidegger's reading of Heraclitus is much more thorough. He gave two lecture courses on Heraclitus,[29] and transposed some of this material in several writings. He also frequently made references to Heraclitus in other works, so there is a wealth of source material available. In it we can find fundamental reinterpretations of *logos*, *physis*, *aletheia*, *polemos*, and language. Heidegger wants to upset the traditional view that Heraclitus was the foremost proponent of a philosophy of becoming or change, as opposed to Parmenides, who is seen as the philosopher of a permanent Being. Heidegger reinterprets Λόγος (*logos*) here from the verb λέγειν (to gather, to say) as "the Laying that gathers" (*die lesende Lege*),[30] thinking with this term that which consists of gathering together and letting things be in letting them lie before us. We should be mindful here of other words like *Auseinandersetzung* and *das Selbe*, "con-frontation" and "the same," respectively, to realize how this gathering together and letting be of differences can go together. In other places Heidegger also translates *logos* as "gathering."[31] He thereby tries to release *logos* from its metaphysical translations, such as reason, ratio, God, and so forth. He retains the idea that *logos* means "saying" or "speaking," "discourse," but gives his other interpretation as something even more or equally originary. The connection between language and *logos* is thus brought to a deeper understanding. This *logos* was what the ancient Greeks lived in, their language was alive in this way, but they never thought through this situation themselves. As Heidegger says:

> Ὁ Λόγος, thought as the Laying that gathers, would be the essence of saying [*die Sage*] as thought by the Greeks. Language would be saying. Language would be the gathering letting-lie-before of what is present in its presencing. In fact, the Greeks *dwelt* in this essential determination of language. But they never *thought* it—Heraclitus included.[32]

Thus thought, the ancient Greeks lived language as saying from Being, as *logos* is the name for the Being of beings, but they did not think it thus. Heidegger thinks this *logos* as "gathering in letting be," but we should guard against seeing this as a metaphysical principle guiding all things. "Gathering" is not to be read as a noun, it should much more be read in a verbal sense, as it hints at a temporal phenomenon, a process more than a principle. Seen in this way *logos* would then rather mean the "temporary gathering of things in their difference through language."

In another essay on Heraclitus Heidegger goes over the notion of *aletheia*, usually translated as "truth." Heidegger rejects this translation, giving his rendering of "unconcealment" instead. Heraclitus thought concealing and unconcealing together, as Heidegger shows from fragment 123, φύσις κρύπτεσθαι φιλεῖ. Usually translated as "nature loves to hide itself," Heidegger retranslates: "Rising (out of self-concealing) bestows favour upon self-concealing,"[33] and explains how *physis* as rising or coming to unconcealment and concealment are mutually related, belong together, again *das Selbe*, the "same."[34] Heidegger had already established in his work on Nietzsche that for "the Greeks, *physis* is the first and the essential name for beings themselves and as a whole. For them the being is what flourishes on its own, in no way compelled, what rises and comes forward, and what goes back into itself and passes away. It is the rule that rises and resides in itself."[35] In another part of the same volume Heidegger seems to suggest that *physis* thought in a Greek way was the "original configuration"[36] or unity of Being and becoming. *Aletheia*, *physis*, and *logos* then show a closeness in belonging together in this unconcealing and concealing.

Related to this interplay of unconcealing and concealing the notions of *Auseinandersetzung*, or con-frontation, or πόλεμος (*polemos*), plays an important part in my arguments, especially when we read these notions in their intercultural sense. Heraclitus is well known for having allegedly said in fragment 53 that "war is the father of all things." Heidegger thinks again that this interpretation is mistaken or at least one-sided. There is again a more originary way of looking at the fragment, which starts with πόλεμος πάντων μὲν πατήρ ἐστι. Heidegger translates "Confrontation (*Auseinandersetzung*) is indeed the begetter of all (that comes to presence). . . ."[37] This is already a huge difference from normal translations, but even more important is the continuing sentence which is usually left out: . . . πάντων δὲ βασιλεύς, which Heidegger translates as ". . . but (also) the dominant preserver of all."[38] So far from trying to say that war is the father of all things, Heidegger says that con-frontation, as *Auseinandersetzung*, is the begetter and keeper of all things. Difference and the interaction of differences thus become extremely important. But we should also think of con-frontation as *our* con-frontation with the world. Our *Auseinandersetzung* through language gives meaning to us, and in that sense we should be aware of how we con-front the world. Heidegger's answer of course has to do with letting be and letting things show from themselves. Heidegger even explicitly names *polemos* as "*die Lichtung*"[39] (the clearing), making it resonate with another of his key terms in explaining his later thinking.

From this it can safely be assumed that *Auseinandersetzung* is one of the most important terms Heidegger uses, together with *logos, aletheia, physis,* and other such key words from the ancient Greek language. There are numerous places where he speaks of these ancient terms in their relatedness, going so far as to say they are the same. *Logos* is *polemos*, is *aletheia*, is *physis*, is *moira*. These are all interrelated and eventually point to that which cannot be spoken of, Being. As Heidegger says:

> . . . the Λόγος which Heraclitus thinks as the fundamental character of presencing, the Μοῖρα which Parmenides thinks as the fundamental character of presencing, the Χρεών which Anaximander thinks is essential in presencing—all these name the Same. In the concealed richness of the Same the unity of the unifying One, the Ἓν, is thought by each thinker in his own way.[40]

The Ἓν stands for Being, which is always the "matter" of thinking. Heidegger is convinced however that certain ways of thinking hear, resonate, or respond to Being better than others, and I have tried to show here that he was also of the opinion that the early Greeks thought more originary than later thinkers. Starting with Plato, things got confused: one side of the coin, thinking, took over at the expense of Being, effectively destroying the "belonging together." This was exacerbated significantly by the translations of Greek into Latin in later times, which according to Heidegger were so foreign to the Greek ideas that they destroyed the Greek meaning, as the Romans brought to philosophy a fundamentally different attitude, not sharing the same ideas and background that had made the Greek world what it was.[41] Yet Heidegger is not pessimistic about translation per se, for as he says again in *Holzwege*:

> Could a mere translation have precipitated all this? We may yet learn what can come to pass in translation. The truly fateful encounter with historic language is a silent event. But in it the destiny of Being speaks. Into what language is the land of evening translated?[42]

First I want to look at the English translation, which is inadequate since it fails to capture the wordplay of the German, which has *geschichtlich*, *geschicklich*, and *Geschick*. It also fails to notice that the final question is not in the passive, but in the active tense, so it would be more appropriate to translate it "Into what language does the Evening-land translate?" This would better capture the fact that it is *our* translations which are wrong or one-sided and need to be looked at afresh. The encounter with other languages then needs to be a silent one, in which there is a thoughtful adherence to the sameness thought in a Heideggerian way, as well as to the differences of different cultures. In this encounter, translation (*Übersetzung* as setting across of a different way of thinking) plays a crucial role. It is vital to the project of comparative philosophy that this is acknowledged and that people who translate works from other cultures keep an open mind toward different possibilities and different forms that such encounters can take. Heidegger's work on the early Greek thinkers and his translations or reinterpretations of some of their fragments have shown that such different meetings are possible, but have to remain vigilant against being overrun by metaphysical speculations, which are not wrong in themselves, but are only one option amongst many others yet unexplored. One of the other options Heidegger chose to look into is the relation of poetics or poetry with thinking.

HEIDEGGER AND THE POETS

> What is difficult to grasp about this work [Nietzsche's *Zarathustra*] is not only its "content," if it has such, but also its very character as a work. Of course, we are quick to propose a ready-made explanation: here philosophical thoughts are presented poetically. Yet what we are now to call *thinking* and *poetizing* dare not consist of the usual notions, inasmuch as the work defines both of these anew, or rather, simply announces them.[43]

Heidegger has extensively dealt with poetry in his search for a different thinking that would overcome to a certain extent the "forgetfulness" of metaphysics. It is no secret that Heidegger saw the present metaphysical-technological configuration of the West in terms of a decline. This is not to say however that Heidegger wished to return to some purer state of thinking which supposedly existed before this decline. It is to say that he used different approaches to establish a certain resistance toward the dominating forces of philosophy, which exclude any form of thinking which cannot be incorporated into its rigid frameworks. These forms of different thinking Heidegger found in the early Greek thinkers, in poetry or poetic thinkers and thinking, and in some forms of East Asian thinking, where Heidegger looked especially toward Daoism. Apparently he found important similarities between Daoism and early Greek and poetic thinking, or at least his approaches toward these show similarities. Therefore the second most important feature in understanding Heidegger's efforts at establishing an intercultural dialogue, after his engagement with the Greeks and related to it, involves his thinking about the poets, and his reinterpretation of philosophy as "poetic thinking." This is of importance to comparative philosophy for two reasons. First is to show how Heidegger wished to engage the poets he dealt with, and from that derive a similar approach that he takes in encountering other cultures. Second, the way in which Heidegger identifies, locates, and uses the ways of thinking which he finds in poetic works is interesting because it goes to show that not all thinking has to be along the lines of Western philosophy as it has evolved into ontotheology and thus into what Heidegger calls the technological way of thinking with its reductive totalization that brings to a forced unity all that is different. There are more forms that thinking can take, or rather, thinking can happen in different forms. But it should be remembered that Heidegger did not first engage the early Greeks and the poets in order to then extract from that an intercultural thinking. It is more to the point to say that the three different approaches were equal avenues to explore the possibility of an "other commencement"[44] of thinking, which would be different from metaphysics.

To expose the extent to which Heidegger engaged poetry, I look at his work on Friedrich Hölderlin, Georg Trakl, Stefan George, and Rainer Maria Rilke. It is especially in the way that language comes to speak through these poets that Heidegger finds them worthy of being called "the thinking poets." Heidegger's focus on poetry however does not mean that all poetry is automatically related to thinking, or has some fundamental insights to show us. Only certain poets have achieved this "height," and it is in their work and more specifically in Heidegger's interpretations of them that we can find hints on how Heidegger wants to engage other cultures. Especially Heidegger's work on Hölderlin reveals a lot about the approach to what is *das Fremde*, or what is "other" or "foreign."

Poetry and Thinking

So what exactly does Heidegger see in these poets, and what is the relationship of this poetry to thinking or philosophy? First of all, it is important not to understand poetry as mere poesy, or the poetic use of words or language to create some idea. Poetry (*Dichten*) has a much deeper and broader meaning for Heidegger. All language and thinking has its essence (*Wesen*) in poetry. This is not to confuse poetry and philosophy, and not to think that some more poetic form of philosophy or a more philosophical form of poetry is needed as a kind of fusion between the two. As Heidegger says:

> All philosophical thinking—and precisely the most rigorous and prosaic—is in itself poetic. It nonetheless never springs from the art of poetry.

> A work of poetry, a work like Hölderlin's hymns, can for its part be thoughtful in the highest degree. It is nonetheless never philosophy.[45]

Poetry and thinking are very close, yet they are not to be confused, and one is not the logical ancestor or descendant of the other. Heidegger is very strict in this separation, and we will see why. For his idea is that only things that are different can have such a close relationship:

> We must discard the view that the neighbourhood of poetry and thinking is nothing more than a garrulous cloudy mixture of two kinds of saying in which each makes clumsy borrowings from the other. Here and there it may seem that way. But in truth, poetry and thinking are in virtue of their nature held apart by a delicate yet luminous difference.[46]

It is this difference that somehow speaks from an indefinable common ground that is the focus of Heidegger's engagements with the various poets. Again and again he stresses this, maintaining that any similarity, equality, unity, or common ground is to be read *only* through or from this difference. In fact, we could say that this difference or diversity is the only form the common ground can have, as it is this difference that is constitutive for a dialogue between thinking and poetry to succeed, for only as long as this difference is firmly held in place can there be a real exchange of ideas, in which both talk about the same thing. Or, to put it in Heidegger's words:

> The poetical Said and the thinking Said are never identical (*das gleiche*). Yet both one and the other can say the same (*dasselbe*) in different ways. This however, only succeeds when the abyss between them is kept clear and resolute.[47]

Again it is important to understand clearly the difference between *das Selbe* and *das Gleiche*, or the "same" and the "identical." The "same" is not some metaphysical construct; it is not an overarching concept, but only functions because of difference. Heidegger says:

> The same never coincides with the equal, not even in the empty indifferent oneness of what is merely identical. The equal or identical always moves toward the absence of difference, so that everything may be reduced to a common denominator. The same, by contrast, is the belonging together of what differs, through a gathering by way of the difference. We can only say "the same" if we think difference.[48]

The "identical" then is part of a typical metaphysical striving for identity, generalization, and unity. Heidegger employs Hölderlin to explain the difference between "same" and "identical": "Being at one is godlike and good; whence, then, this craze among men that there should exist only One, why should all be one?"[49] Hölderlin named this short fragment the "Root of All Evil,"[50] and Heidegger certainly shared this concern. Things that are "the same" should not be forced to become identical. And sameness only exists as a function of difference. Differences, or the play of differences, must be understood as the more originary. This naturally brings me back to one of the key terms of this book, *Auseinandersetzung*, or con-frontation. It is only in the sense of *Auseinandersetzung* that has been discussed previously that we can understand Heidegger's engagement with the poets he so carefully chose. It is a keeping apart in togetherness, or a thoughtful appropriation that leaves the other as it is itself, that is again his aim, as it was with his *Auseinandersetzung* with the Greeks. This gathering in difference can be understood as promoting the idea of the interconnectedness, the relationality of all things, which nevertheless should not be reduced to an ultimate guiding principle. We shall see later how a similar thinking is espoused in Daoism if we read it through different lenses.

Poetry and Language

Throughout his career Heidegger has valued the importance of language. Already in *Sein und Zeit*, the important paragraph 32 which discusses the fact that we always encounter things *as* something, and that we thus always have some preconceived notions in our perceptions, shows the importance and necessity of language in our experience of the world.[51] The hermeneutics that Heidegger thinks of acknowledges the fact that language is "how we think." Later on, language is called "the house of Being"[52] and both *Weg* (way) and *Ereignis* (event of appropriation), two key terms in Heidegger's later work, are closely intertwined with language. We can safely say that language was, together with Being, one of Heidegger's most important focuses, since he understood that language is inevitable in our understanding, and in our experiencing and thinking of the world. Experience and thinking can only gain meaning through language, understood in the sense of signification structures.

Thus the second important aspect in Heidegger's engagement with poetry and his efforts at establishing or at least preparing the "other thinking" through poetic thinking is found in his reinterpretation of language, as it is used in poetry. Heidegger finds that the normal functions of language, such as information exchange, everyday social language functions, and even the more "spiritual" sides of language, which are often used by poets, cannot explain what happens in poetry, or rather in certain poetry and certain poets. He therefore again tries to introduce new readings of these works, readings that are not at all obvious to "normal" interpretations. When Heidegger says that it is language that speaks through humans, and not humans who speak, this still resembles normal interpretations of being inspired by and influenced by language. Yet Heidegger goes much further by saying that what happens in some poetry is really much more originary and fundamental than a reinterpretation of language by poets. Saying that poetry is derivative of normal language is therefore at fault, or as Heidegger puts it: "Poetry proper is never merely a higher mode (*melos*) of everyday language. It is rather the reverse: everyday language is a forgotten and therefore used-up poem, from which there hardly resounds a call any longer."[53] Language has become something it was not before; it has flattened and emptied through its history of metaphysics. The *Verfallen* (Falling) of everyday language, everyday man, and everyday opinions are all (negative) derivations of a more originary and fundamental region in which language spoke (or speaks, as it is not only in the past that we can still find this) from itself, as it did with the Greeks. Heidegger finds this more originary region in poetry. As he says: "Language itself is poetry in the essential sense."[54] Poetry is of course here taken "in so broad a sense and at the same time in such intimate unity of being with language and word, that we must leave open whether art, in all its modes from architecture to poesy, exhausts the nature of poetry."[55]

Heidegger's interpretation sees the work of (some) poets as the "deployment of certain key words which call for the thinker's reflective analysis."[56] Heidegger's analysis brings out the "other" meaning of these works through giving other meanings to their key words.[57] These other meanings are not necessarily better or more truthful, but at least also possible and call for a rethinking of language, which is Heidegger's main concern. With regard to Heidegger's intercultural steps it is important to notice that he took the same approach in his encounters with the East, for example when he, together with his Japanese guest, reinterpreted the word for "language" in Japanese,[58] or when he used the notion of *dao* as pointing to something roughly equivalent to his own version of "*Weg*" or "way."[59] In the next section of this chapter these similarities are dealt with more thoroughly.

Language then has some other meaning; it is not as rigid as our everyday definitions seem to suggest. There is a certain "unsaid" in language which to Heidegger is more important than the obvious definite meaning which we usually ascribe to words. This multiplicity of meanings of important words is hinted at in Heidegger's readings of the poets he deals with, for as he says in an essay on a work by Georg Trakl:

> This language is essentially ambiguous (*mehrdeutig*), in its own fashion. We shall hear nothing of what the poem says so long as we bring to it only this or that dull sense of unambiguous (*eindeutigen*) meaning. [. . .] Yet this multiple ambiguousness of the poetic saying does not scatter in vague equivocations (*ins unbestimmte Vieldeutige*). The ambiguous tone of Trakl's poetry arises out of a gathering, that is, out of a unison which, meant for itself alone, always remains unsayable. The ambiguity of this poetic saying is not lax imprecision, but rather the rigor of him who leaves what is as it is. . . .[60]

In German *mehrdeutig* has not only the negative meaning of ambiguity, but also means "open to more than one interpretation," or could be said to argue for some kind of "polysemy" inherent in language. The translation of *mehrdeutig* with "ambiguous" leaves this point in the air, the more as "ambiguity" is usually referred to as negative, especially in the stricter regions of philosophy where identity and unity are the most important features. The translation also fails to capture the sense of *mehr-deutig* that relates to more than one meaning without becoming vague (*viel-deutig*). If we leave aside translation problems for the moment, the point is that Heidegger wishes to retain a sense of openness and unfinishedness that to him is evident in thoughtful poetry. Because where there is really no final and definite meaning, we should not impose one artificially, as is often done with poems where we are supposed to find "the" meaning in them. It is much better to leave what is as it is, and Heidegger thinks there is a way to do this without sinking into a passive relativism of the "anything goes" kind. That Heidegger was aware of this we can clearly see in the passage cited previously, where he sharply distinguishes between *mehrdeutig* and *vieldeutig*. We must now take a closer look at Heidegger's *Auseinandersetzung* with Hölderlin and explore the polysemy and issues of translation which Heidegger's readings of Hölderlin bring about.

Hölderlin, the Foreign, and Translation

Heidegger's engagement with Hölderlin can bring us very useful clues to understanding his ideas about comparative philosophy and what it should stand for. It also gives us access to the thinking about a different perspective on language which Heidegger derived from Hölderlin's poetry. These ideas have to do with polysemy (*Mehrdeutigkeit*),[61] which, as we saw, Heidegger does not equate with vagueness. We must also bear in mind that Heidegger did not concern himself with literary scholarship on Hölderlin, and that his reading of Hölderlin is not necessarily what the latter thought of his own work himself, but first of all Heidegger's effort to wrestle Hölderlin from the narrow bonds of philology, so as to open his words to a wider understanding, of which the intercultural aspect is an important part.

I first look at the ideas of the approach to the "other" or the "foreign" (*Das Fremde*) which Heidegger extracted from Hölderlin, and after that explore the ideas on language. Florian Vetsch has compiled three steps in the intercultural encounter which Heidegger took to be crucial and which he himself deduced from Hölderlin:

> 1) Before his departure to the foreign, the future wanderer is still caught in his own surroundings.
> 2) The journey begins, and the wanderer encounters the foreign.
> 3) The wanderer returns, but remains thoughtful of the foreign; in this something new shows itself.[62]

This goes to show that for Heidegger, the *Auseinandersetzung* with the foreign has two aims; the first is a learning of what the foreign has to offer. To establish this, the "self" has to (temporarily) forget its own, not in the sense of losing oneself in a taking over of "other" habits and ideas, but in opening up a space for different ideas to be allowed access. If we remain closed, any "wandering" will be futile. As Heidegger puts it:

> . . . where it remains only a matter of refuting, or even of annihilating the foreign, what necessarily gets lost is the possibility of a passage through the foreign, and thereby the possibility of a return home into one's own, and thereby that which is one's own itself.[63]

This is the second aim of the *Auseinandersetzung*. The passage through the foreign is crucial for an understanding of what is one's own. But again the "wandering" has to be of a very specific character, and we come back to the *Auseinandersetzung* and the Same, because ". . . only where the foreign is known and acknowledged in its essential oppositional character (*Gegensätzlichkeit*) does there exist the possibility of a genuine relationship (*Beziehung*), that is, of a uniting that is not a confused mixing but a conjoining in distinction (*Unterscheidung*)."[64] It is thus not a matter of learning another culture as a "sum of learnable data,"[65] which you can then take home, but to learn to see another culture as a living, historically moving, open-ended totality, which is not readily at one's disposal, but always open to renewed conversation.[66] This is also a part of the *Auseinandersetzung*. In this way the relation between different cultures is then literally a never-ending story.

It is also vital to fully understand the complexity of the relation between the "own" or "homely" and the "other," "foreign" or "unhomely," as it unfolds in Heidegger's *Hölderlin's Hymn "The Ister."* It has already been noted that it is not a mere appropriation or incorporation of the other that is meant here. The other *as* other is not to be overcome in this way; it is the encounter that matters, so that ". . . the law of the encounter (*Auseinandersetzung*) between the foreign and one's own is the fundamental truth of history."[67] The coming home is not then a return to a kind of safe haven, but it is precisely *in* the encounter itself that the wanderer finds himself. We could also say that the third step of the intercultural encounter is not so much then a return to one's own, but a lingering in the encounter, a taking home of the encounter, to remain in the *Auseinandersetzung*. This is where, in the third step, "something new" happens. And this is exactly what the poets' works show us, especially Hölderlin's. As Heidegger says in a section on the *Antigone* in *Hölderlin's Hymn "The Ister"*: "What is worthy of poetizing in this poetic work is nothing other than becoming homely in being unhomely."[68] And elsewhere in the same volume on Hölderlin he says that "The appropriation of one's own *is* only as the encounter (*Auseinandersetzung*) and guest-like dialogue with the foreign."[69] Note that encounter in these passages is always the *Auseinandersetzung* that has been discussed.

We know Hölderlin himself worked extensively at an *Auseinandersetzung* with the ancient Greek tragedies through his poetry and other writings, and it is from there that Heidegger takes his clues as to his own intercultural ideas. The understanding that "[w]e have still scarcely begun to think the mysterious relations to the East that have come to word in Hölderlin's poetry"[70] and the realization that the greatness of the ancient Greek world arose only through the encounter with the East (albeit Asia Minor) committed Heidegger to look for different ways of thinking, not just in a *Wiederholung* or de(con)struction of the Western tradition, but more and more in a turning toward the ways of thinking in East Asia. It is then Hölderlin who in this way encouraged Heidegger further on the trail to the "East" and on the ways of engaging what is other.

The second feature of Heidegger's Hölderlin interpretation concerns language. In his later writings, Heidegger no longer sees poetry "in terms of the poet's originary power of disclosure, of maintaining things in being, of the grounding, lighting, or opening up of a world; *Dichten* now has to be understood as the way of entering into the mode of being of *Gelassenheit*, the letting-go of things."[71] So poetry, according to this account of Gerald Bruns, opens not so much Being, but a particular way of Being, which is *Gelassenheit* or "releasement" toward the unsaid. It is in poetry that we can find hints of this unsaid, and therefore Heidegger considers the language of poetry so important. Yet we must take care not to see this unsaid as a last (or first) principle, toward which poetry would then point us. The unsaid never appears as such, for then it would be a thing and thus nameable and handed back over again to metaphysics. As with *aletheia*, appearance and disappearance, or unconcealment and concealment, go hand in hand. There is no one without the other, so the unsaid always remains beyond our grasp, or rather only exists in the interplay of concealment and unconcealment, and this is what poetry shows us, as it introduces us to the fact that language fails us when we try to grasp it, where on the other hand it is our only option. For this reason metaphysics dismisses poetry, as metaphysics is unable to deal with something that escapes its grasp by being unnameable. But to Heidegger this "*Ohnmacht*" (incapability) of metaphysics is not a negative thing, as he says in the *Letter on Humanism*: "If man is to find his way once again in the nearness of Being he must first learn to exist in the nameless."[72] This is what Hölderlin and Trakl have taught Heidegger, or what he took their words to mean. This namelessness is interesting with regard to Daoism, for the obvious reason that *dao* is also considered to be nameless. I come back to this in the next section.

To exist in the nameless would not mean to give up speaking or language as a whole, but to shift attention from the word as a term for something else to the word as word, and to see that language is in Heidegger's words "uncanny"[73] because along with unconcealment it always involves concealment as well. Thus metaphysics comes to a closure, but as Bruns notes: "the inability to bring one's subject under conceptual control, fixing it propositionally, is not the end of thinking; on the contrary, it were better to say that the breakdown of concepts and the failure of words is an opening that takes us out of the realm where representation and calculation are all that matter to thinking."[74] Metaphysics as a discipline of propositional and representational thinking which focuses on finding the final word or the final principle thus breaks down, for with the nameless comes the nothing, and in the words of Robert Bernasconi, "*Nothing* is not a word for Being. . . . The nothing corresponds to the thinker's experience of the lack of a word for Being. This speechlessness, this breaking of the sequence of words for Being, comes to be understood historically as marking the end of the succession of words for Being within metaphysics."[75] Heidegger later on even resorted to crossing out the word "Being." The fact that we cannot find a word for Being does not mean that Being is something beyond language, but it does suggest that language as used by metaphysics falls short of thinking Being. We need a different understanding of language, one that incorporates equivocality or polysemy.

Some interesting implications arise because of this equivocality or polysemy of language, and because of the impossibility of naming in the sense of ascribing a single meaning to a word. Again Hölderlin is

Heidegger's main source for showing this inherent polysemy in poetic work. In *Hölderlin's Hymn "The Ister,"* Heidegger says it in the following way: "The Greek poetic work is intrinsically equivocal (*mehrdeutig*), because what is to be poetized is equivocal in the truth of its essence (*Wesens*)."[76] We only end up with a real translation problem if we keep looking for singular, definite meanings, where none are to be found. Elsewhere in the *Ister* work Heidegger devotes a few pages to the problem of translation alone. Because he sees translation as interpretation, his own interpretation of Hölderlin is already as such a translation *within* one language, in this case German. Translation is interpretation and vice versa, every interpretation is also a translating. This does not mean that we should hand over the understanding of translation "to just any opinion," but rather "making something understandable means awakening our understanding to the fact that the blind obstinacy of habitual opinion must be shattered and abandoned if the truth of a work is to unveil itself."[77] "Translating" this idea to comparative philosophy means that with regard to language it is crucial to "shatter" our own presuppositions in translating a work from a different culture. Heidegger was very aware of this problematic character of translation, and his work on the poets seeks to confront and address these problems, as did his work on the early Greeks. As he says: "the difficulty of a translation is never merely a technical issue but concerns the relation of human beings to the essence (*Wesen*) of the word and to the worthiness of language. Tell me what you think of translation, and I will tell you who you are."[78] This unusually strong individual message of Heidegger only strengthens the idea that translation, and foremost language, were among the pivotal concerns of Heidegger, especially in his later work. But even in the *Letter on Humanism* Heidegger calls language, as we have seen, the "house of Being," and continues to argue how "the metaphysical-animal explanation of language cover[s] up the essence of language in the history of Being (*seinsgeschichtliches Wesen*). According to this essence, language is the house of Being, which is appropriated (*ereignet*) by/from (*vom*) Being and pervaded by Being. And so it is proper to think the essence (*Wesen*) of language from its correspondence (*Entsprechung*) to Being and indeed as this correspondence, that is, as the home of human being's essence."[79] Although hard to retrace through this inadequate translation, Heidegger says that language is essential to the human experience of Being. Being only comes through language.

But we must then proceed to ask what Heidegger did consider to be "good" translations, since every translation is in itself violence and interpretation. We have already seen in the previous section on the translation of the early Greek thinkers that Heidegger thought a translation had to be an *Über*-setzung, in that it has to transport the way of thinking of what is to be translated, instead of an Über-*setzung*, which seeks to set what is foreign in familiar terms. Because translation is interpretation, and therefore a thoughtful dialogue,[80] it in the end aims at a return to the self, but as we have seen, this return is to be found in the encounter itself. Genuine translation is always a con-frontation, and this means translation is, according to Heidegger, "an awakening, clarification (*Klärung*), and unfolding of one's own language with the help of an encounter (*Auseinandersetzung*) with the foreign language."[81]

We have seen in the past two sections that both the early Greek thinkers and some (German) poets have had great influence on Heidegger's thinking, especially on his thinking of language and its meaning. The most important conclusion we can draw from Heidegger's approach is that we can only become what we are through and in a sustained encounter with what is genuinely "other," and that this encounter involves great caution in thinking about language. Heidegger's feelings on language can be summarized in the following citation:

> We do not wish to assault language in order to force it into the grip of ideas already fixed beforehand. We do not wish to reduce the nature of language to a concept, so that this concept may provide a generally useful view of language that will lay to rest all further notions about it. To discuss language, to place it, means to bring to its place of being (*Ort ihres Wesens*) not so much language as ourselves: our own gathering into the appropriation (*Versammlung in das Ereignis*).[82]

This view of language has direct consequences for his thinking encounter with different cultures, where, as has already been briefly noticed, he employs the same strategies and understanding. It is time now to take a closer look at Heidegger's more direct comparative thinking.

HEIDEGGER AND THE "EAST"

> Who can be still and out of stillness and through it move something on to the Way so that it comes to shine forth?[83]

In this section I explore Heidegger's efforts to set up a dialogue with the East Asian world, a dialogue which he has been preparing for as inevitable. I first give a general outline of Heidegger's thinking and some of his key concepts and their meanings. This is then used as a background as I proceed to investigate his views on comparative philosophy.

Heidegger's main contribution to philosophy has been the notion of Being (*Sein*) as opposed to beings (*Seienden*). This he called the Ontological Difference: Beings, including human beings, are things that *are*, while *Being* itself *is* nothing, for if it were something, then it would be a being. All beings share the characteristic of *Being*, that is, they are, but we cannot reduce *Being* to the category of beings. *Being* is often referred to as "happening," "becoming," or "presencing" (*Anwesen*), or taken as "event." Yet *Being* can not be properly named; it is in fact unnameable since with every naming Being would again be reduced to a something. This thought implies a fundamental criticism of Western philosophy and its dualistic approach. The Western metaphysical tradition has always concerned itself with beings, and with God, the Spirit, the Idea, etc. as the highest or most real of the beings. It has thus neglected Being as a temporal phenomenon that permeates the entire world. Heidegger's main concern is the destruction of this "Forgetfulness of Being," with the aim of preparing a new way of thinking. Being, and not beings, should be the "source" of thinking. Philosophy has forgotten this source (which is not a real source, for it cannot be named and is no-thing) and this, according to Heidegger, is the main reason for the pitiful state the West is in now. The manipulation of beings has been the main concern of Western philosophy, resulting in the technological way of thinking blocking out all other ways. Logic and reason have not just become the *main*, but the *only* criteria. Heidegger stresses that when pushed too far, this way of thinking will lead to its own self-destruction as it effectively blocks all creativity outside its field. What Heidegger wants is not to leave this tradition behind and replace it with another thinking tradition or a new way of thinking, but to put it in perspective as a phase of the history of Being and to put it in its proper place among other ways of thinking.

Heidegger then proceeds to hint at what he calls "the other way of thinking" or the "other commencement." Although he remains vague as to what this actually consists of, he points in a number of directions. This vagueness is also a characteristic of his thinking which he calls "formal signalling." This means he does not provide the content of his ideas; he just points in directions and leaves it to us whether we are willing and ready to receive this message and to act on it.

The later Heidegger then puts man in a position where he is not ruler, but mere part of the greater universe. This constellation he calls the "Fourfold" (*Geviert*).[84] It consists of the unity of and relations between the mortals, the divinities, the heavens, and the earth. As this is a very difficult piece of Heidegger's thinking on which there is much unclarity, I do not linger on it here but just use it at some point when describing Heidegger's intercultural efforts.

Early[85] Heidegger and Comparative Philosophy

Now against this background we can take a closer look at Heidegger's work regarding comparative philosophy. Although Heidegger's main concern was with the destruction of Western metaphysics, there are a number of places where he explicitly talks about other cultures and our relation to them. To start with a not-so-positive review, Heidegger's earlier work cannot properly be called intercultural or comparatively inclined at all. In his earlier works it seems that Heidegger could more probably be considered as a very Eurocentric thinker, the very opposite of intercultural. He does not get himself involved in other cultures. And even in some of his later work, there are instances where we can apparently read this Eurocentric inclination, and Heidegger even goes so far as to state that only in the West there is what we call "philosophy," and that for example India and China do not have philosophy.[86] It seems Heidegger wants nothing to do with other cultures, as can be heard in the warning that in everydayness, Dasein "confines its interests to the multiformity (*Vielgestaltigkeit*) of possible types, directions, and standpoints of philosophical activity in the most exotic and alien of cultures; and by this very interest it seeks to veil the fact that it has no ground of its own to stand on (*Bodenlosigkeit*)."[87] Heidegger advocates that a solution to the problems of the West should come *from* the West. Not very promising from a comparative perspective, and even within the West Heidegger has his preferences. As we saw, only some early Greek thinkers and some German thinkers and poets, such as Heidegger himself and Hölderlin and Rilke, can properly be called "thinkers" according to him.

Aside from this, throughout his career Heidegger mostly considered the English and French languages completely inadequate for philosophical purposes, with a couple of exceptions here and there. As we already saw in the introduction, Heidegger was not too enthusiastic about the possibility of English translations of his work, and generally of the philosophical reach of English as compared to German.[88] Also, in an interview in the late 1960s with the leading German magazine *Der Spiegel*, Heidegger is quoted saying: "When the French begin to think, they start speaking German."[89] It is not hard to imagine that Heidegger was not very much loved in at least some English and French academic circles. So far he has demonstrated himself to be a very stubborn and one-sided thinker, which is contrary to what comparative philosophy aims to establish. But this picture may be distorted, and Heidegger explains himself. The reason that both French and English are inadequate is that they originate in or to a large extent follow Latin, and not Greek. As we saw, Heidegger is convinced that with the violent translation of ancient Greek into Latin in the course of history, so much of the original meaning was lost that the ground of Western philosophy was swept away and philosophy in general began its rapid deterioration and "forgetfulness of Being." German supposedly suffers less from this since it is a Germanic language.

The very important issue of translatability in comparative philosophy again rears its head. It is noted by everyone who has ever tried it that it is extremely difficult to translate work from Heidegger's original German. And so it is in general with every form of translation. Translation is by its very nature a violent thing and it is almost always impossible to capture in one word the full meaning of another word. If this is already so between languages in Western cultures with a largely common ancestry and historical background, how is it ever possible to translate key concepts or notions of entirely different cultures from our own? Yet an intercultural dialogue must assume some form of translatability, if we are to understand what "the other" means. I come back to this point later.

Up to now Heidegger does not seem to be a very interculturally inclined philosopher. His major work from the earlier period, *Sein und Zeit*, retains a strong Western prejudice and outlook, although (and maybe because) Heidegger tries to give with the Daseinsanalysis a universal account of the structures of mankind. His focus in *Sein und Zeit* on the Ontological Difference between beings and Being has left Heidegger oblivious to the essential differences between beings (read cultures), or, as Safranski has formulated it, "the Ontology of Difference."[90] So the Daseinsanalysis, although it seeks to provide a universal existential analysis, proceeds from one point of view, without realizing it is by no means obvious that this is the right or universal view. That means that *Sein und Zeit* is written from the standpoint of the Western individual in the early twentieth century, who through increasing secularization and mediocrity, has been left with the frightening prospect of a meaningless, empty, and finite existence. To see what this means we can think of Heidegger's term "Anxiety" (*Angst*), a state in which the individual's references fall away and the Dasein is left with literally "Nothing." Or we can think of "Being-unto-Death" (*Sein zum Tode*), which is the position that tries to take seriously the finiteness of existence Dasein realizes when the "Afterworld" of the religions has fallen away. This position is the task of Dasein to actively take the finite existence on its shoulders. There are more examples, but the bottom line is that *Sein und Zeit* shows its origin and thus presents a

Western, individualistic point of view, where we could easily claim that such a view is far from being universal.

Still, while we have seen Heidegger so far as an anti-intercultural thinker, there is one paragraph in *Sein und Zeit* where he speaks positively about "primitive" cultures and describes these cultures as having a more originary relation with the world of phenomena than the West.[91] This more originary relation is exactly what Heidegger was looking for throughout his work. Regardless of the term "primitive," which is now considered derogatory,[92] this is the one place in his early works where Heidegger takes an interculturally more positive position.

Later Heidegger and Comparative Philosophy

After the less-than-favorable position I have bestowed on Heidegger from a comparative perspective, I now turn to his later work. Having briefly been associated with the Nazis during the early 1930s, Heidegger soon distances himself from them,[93] and by the end of World War II his thinking has undergone some fundamental changes. Although his efforts at deconstructing Western metaphysics continue relentlessly, these now lead him even more to the awareness of the fundamental limits to Western style philosophy. He also becomes during this period right after the war increasingly isolated, due to the fact that, because of his brief association with the Nazis, he is not allowed to teach by the Allied Forces. He finds himself again in comparison with Laozi, the supposed author of the *Daodejing*. Perhaps this personal confrontation is one of the reasons why Heidegger in the late 1940s and early 1950s becomes increasingly aware, as has been mentioned before, of the fact that his major source of thinking, the ancient Greeks, were only able to achieve such greatness as they did in a direct confrontation with Asia (although Asia Minor). However, we should note here that the psychologism that lies in equating Heidegger's comparative thinking with his personal experiences is out of place and merely a heuristic device. Yet philosophically it is the case that Heidegger finds himself more and more isolated in the West and looks for different ways of thinking.

All this leads Heidegger to a search for a possible other "commencement" (*Anfang*) of thinking and to prepare for the arrival of this other commencement. It is important to notice that Heidegger uses the word *Anfang*, which I have translated with "commencement," in a different way than the word "beginning." With the other commencement of thinking Heidegger is not searching for some ancient starting point in history, perhaps in Asia or Africa, from which thinking evolved through Greece and Rome, to finally achieve its end or destination in Germany, as Hegel seemed to think. Heidegger's other commencement is not a point of time in the past in our own or some other culture, but a task that lies ahead of us. The other commencement refers to the other way of thinking Heidegger is trying to develop and to the "Forgetfulness of Being" that has dominated thought ever since Plato. The other *Anfang* has to find ways to try to bring Being to light, without thereby losing its "essence" or turning it into a being.

With the working title "The End of Philosophy and the Task of Thinking" (*Das Ende der Philosophie und die Aufgabe des Denkens*)[94] Heidegger now denounces his stance of *Sein und Zeit*, and actively seeks contact with other cultures to enlarge the thinking world. He looks to other cultures for ways of thinking that can assist him in his efforts of preparing the other way of thinking. For example, he says: "Who knows one day in Russia or in China ancient ways of thinking come to the fore that can help us in our struggle against Metaphysics."[95]

The working title explicitly refers to the end of philosophy, which Heidegger has by then come to see as something profoundly Western. With this Heidegger's statement that neither India nor China has philosophy[96] comes to stand in a different light. Heidegger wishes to express the idea that philosophy is but one way of thinking (i.e., the Western one that has been characterized before by terms as ontotheology, metaphysics, logic, and reason) and that there may be greater "thinkers" in other parts of the world than there are philosophers in the West. Thinking is much more than just philosophy.

Through several encounters with Chinese and Japanese thinkers, by the early 1950s Heidegger is acutely aware of "the inevitable dialogue with the East Asian world."[97] But how does Heidegger perceive this intercultural dialogue or encounter? A dialogue like this has to take place between the Self (*das Eigene*) and the Other (*das Andere*). Here the Self should be read as one's own culture, the Other as the different culture. As we saw earlier, for Heidegger the encounter with the Other has as its final goal a return of the Self to the Self. This means that there are two ways of encounter that Heidegger is *not* looking for. The first is a simple "melting of horizons," for this could only be the obscure world syncretism that is not directed at differences but at a unity in which all differences dissolve, thereby doing great injustice to the different ways of thinking. The second way of encounter Heidegger thinks is not right has two options. It is either the stubborn reluctance or refusal of the Self to encounter the Other, thereby denying the value of the encounter with something different from itself, or it is the complete losing of the Self *in* the Other, in the way adventurers or people that completely change their lives and "go native" do. To Heidegger, the first option makes it impossible for the Self to become truly itself as we have seen that going through the Other is essential for the Self becoming itself. Of the second option Heidegger says that it merely substitutes one culture for another; there is no real dialogue.

Both these ways do not set up any serious dialogue between cultures, and thus what Heidegger is looking for is another way of encounter which has been identified as "*Auseinandersetzung*." We have seen that this German word is hard to translate adequately. If we stretch the English language just a little, the best option would probably be "con-frontation," and this is the option I have been using. Although usually thought of as a negative term in the sense of a clash between two identities unwilling to change, if we read this word more carefully we find the implication that we expose ourselves to the Other, and vice versa, which means we start the dialogue as much as possible without prejudice, or at least aware of our prejudices and open to different ways of thinking, and we create an atmosphere of mutual coming together in difference, in which things can show themselves as they are. But "con-frontation" also means that we position ourselves as different from the Other. The *Auseinandersetzung* is an encounter of the Self and the Other, and we must learn to let go of the assertively polemic connotations which often accompany the word "confrontation," or rather, read them in a different way. Heidegger has argued already that *polemos* is not just polemic, it is really "clearing" (*Lichtung*),[98] one of the key terms of his later thinking, which is the opening that provides for the unconcealment of things. The starting point and the end point of an *Auseinandersetzung* must be difference. This roughly means that we should neither lose ourselves completely in similarities nor remain stubbornly by our own convictions, never questioning them. Heidegger grounds the intercultural dialogue on difference and proceeds to set the encounter in the three stages we have seen earlier:

1. Before the encounter the Self is naturally turned inward; its own cultural truths and values are therefore not questioned.
2. The actual encounter takes place, and truth and value of the Self are temporarily placed in the background, not forgotten but in a kind of suspended animation. In the encounter the Other is more important, for it is there that we hear other truths and values.
3. Afterward, the Self returns to its own sphere, but is changed by the encounter. The experience of "Otherness" has pervaded the Self, which thereby becomes aware of the original unity of the Self and the Other, a unity which could be conceived

> of as *Being*, if we leave this nameless. We could also think of equivalents in other cultures, maybe things like *satori* in Zen Buddhism or the unnameable *dao* 道. At the same time however, equally important, the Self also becomes aware of the unbridgeable differences between itself and the Other. With this double awareness, the Self is now truly it-Self, as it realizes it has of all times been related in an originary way to "Otherness" already, and without knowing this relation of unity and diversity, it was really not it-Self.

Seen in this light, Heidegger can be acquitted of the criticism of Emmanuel Levinas that he is oblivious to the "Other." Levinas has made extensive studies of the relations between the Self and the Other,[99] and although Heidegger does not say a lot about the direct relations between individuals, it can by no means be argued that he has neglected the "Other." But for Heidegger, the "Other" is not as for Levinas the other human being as individual, it is rather the "other" way of thinking Heidegger wishes to explore.

Having now shown the structures of how Heidegger would like to see the intercultural encounter, one of the finest examples of this encounter is Heidegger's own "From a dialogue of language / between a Japanese and an inquirer" (*Aus einem Gespräch von der Sprache / zwischen einem Japaner und einem Fragenden*).[100] For inquiring into Heidegger's comparative thinking it is necessary to delve deeper into this conversation. Heidegger presents himself not as a philosopher or a Westerner, but as someone who asks questions, an inquirer. In the dialogue itself no arguments are made, no positions are taken or defended, but there is a mutual reaching out to each other in order to learn from each other's ways.[101] "Way" (*Weg*) is a very important concept in Heidegger's thoughts. Thinkers are always on the way; there is no fixed abode to stay or positions that are always correct; there is only the eternal going of the way. In this light we have to see our own cultural truths and values; they are provisional. Ways can go in different directions, and there is no one way which is the only right or true one. We do not necessarily try to replace our own truths with truths of another culture, for both ways are provisional. Being aware of this is half the way on a never-ending road that leads to nowhere in particular. In comparative philosophy, it is not *where* we go, but *that* we go and *how* we go. To go to the Other, or the readiness to go, is much more important than any eventual destination, which sounds too much like a final, metaphysical truth. Thus Heidegger's dialogue with the Japanese scholar teaches us an attitude of openness. Besides this, the dialogue also brings to light another important aspect of Heidegger's thinking, something he calls the "danger" (*die Gefahr*). This danger is the ongoing Westernization and thus the technologization of the world and our worldview. We can see this where the ancient Japanese traditions seem to be fading into obscurity, and the Japanese guest is unable to translate into a Western language Japanese key concepts. That means Heidegger is acutely aware that this same danger is also to be found in language. We already saw that translation is difficult, if not impossible, and as the practice is that most conversations are in a Western language, the thoughts and traditions that come with Western languages are not easily avoided. The problem is how to avoid getting trapped in the dominant Western ways of thinking while recognizing that the language of the intercultural dialogue is usually or often Western, and even the word "dialogue" is an inheritance of a Western form of conversation.

I do not think I have to further explain the term "Westernization." Heidegger is especially concerned with it as it is a consequence of the attitude of mastery pervasive in science and technology. Often disguised as development, Westernization is visible all around us. Ancient cultural traditions, truths, and values are evermore bulldozed aside to make way for the technological and economic worldview of the West. It invades every part of our lives, and non-Western cultures seem to have little choice but to follow or be left behind (economically and technologically, that is) for good. The most important problem with this is that Westernization often brings more welfare in the short term, and that the negative side effects are not easily or directly noticed. The technological worldview, of which the key words are calculation, economic efficiency, economic achievement, and so on, produces such dangers as environmental problems, huge differences in distribution of wealth, not to mention neo-imperialism and what is popularly known as the "coca-colonization" of the world. One could object that these problems have their origin and major impact in the West, but Heidegger answers this by saying that although that might be true, these problems have gone beyond the West to threaten the entire world and are therefore no longer purely Western, but truly universal problems.

The similar but more important danger for Heidegger as a thinker lies, as we have noticed, in language. Western languages, says Heidegger, are so infested with metaphysics, representation, and the specifically Western form of logical rationality, that in fact every intercultural dialogue in a Western language risks the danger of corrupting the thoughts of other cultures. Even German cannot escape this, although Heidegger was more hopeful of its possibilities. The problem has more to do with the metaphysical tradition and modern technological thinking:

> Who would want to dispute that these German words are firmly rooted locutions? Today nothing in us takes root anymore. Why? Because the possibility of a thoughtful conversation with a tradition that invigorates and nurtures us is lacking, because we instead consign our speaking to electronic thinking and calculating machines, an occurrence that will lead modern technology and science to completely new procedures and unforeseeable results that probably will push reflective thinking aside as something useless and hence superfluous.[102]

These limitations and the ensuing one-sidedness of Western philosophy show themselves in translation. Translation in itself is always corruption, as we saw was the case with the translation of ancient Greek into Latin, which started the impoverishment of Western thinking. There are no easy ways to escape these dangers that constantly threaten us, but Heidegger tries to do so nonetheless by urging us into another idea and usage of language. In the dialogue with the Japanese he perceives language as "Saying" (*Sage*). Although Saying is in close proximity to speech, for Heidegger the essence of language lies as much in being silent and listening as it does in speaking. *Logos*, the Greek word that was wrongly translated into the Latin "Ratio," or rationality, actually means speaking, speech, the use of language in a correct way. So if man is the rational animal, we can change this "false" translation into: man, the animal that has *logos*, speech. Seen together with the earlier notion of *logos* as "gathering," mankind in its deepest reality is dia-*logos*, dialogue. We can speak and listen. Heidegger's attitude to language also shows his hostility toward dualism. We as subjects are no longer the beginning or center, but it is language that speaks through us and it remains for us to try to be willing and able to listen and hear the message of what is said. It is not the formal definitions of words that we want to hear; rather, we want to understand what is being said.

If we relate this to intercultural thinking, Heidegger is urging us to try to retrieve what is actually said in other cultural expressions and not to look at verbal contents only. It is in this sense that translation is extremely important. For as long as we seek to find literal translations of words, we will not notice that we are working from our own metaphysical background. In order to upset that background, which is necessary if we want to convey profoundly different ways of thinking in our own languages, we must make an effort at real *Auseinandersetzung*. And this *Auseinandersetzung* means then that we look for ways to "transport" (*übersetzen*) different ways of thinking, and not seek to accommodate words or concepts of these ways of thinking into our own idiomatic structures. Since different conceptual schemes can not be accommodated into our own metaphysical schemes, we need to upset these preconceived notions, and that means we need to look for different forms of translating and different forms of understanding language.

With this the poetic thinking comes back into play. For it is not only in essays and scientific journals that we find knowledge; it can be found, if looked for, in other cultural expressions as art, poetry, and literature and in dance, ceremony, or ritual as well. But this will not be the clean-cut knowledge we are used to, so we have to be careful how to approach it. In the dialogue with the Japanese, Heidegger is very cautious about the ways in which to communicate. We cannot learn from other cultures if we adhere to strict definitions. In comparative philosophy, therefore, we are not to be hindered by conventions on translation or on what is commonly called "knowledge." We saw that Heidegger did not let himself be hindered by conventions in his reinterpretation of the Early Greeks or of the poets he found "thoughtful." As receivers of other ways of knowing and thinking, we have to keep a very open mind and stretch our definitions. In this way, the dialogue with the Japanese is a good example of intercultural philosophy. In this dialogue, Heidegger not only asks the ancient wisdom of another culture to try to express itself as it is, but the dialogue as an exploration of the possibilities of intercultural encounters also shows us the dangers involved and the fact that theory and practice cannot be separated. The dialogue is theory and practice in one, especially in its realization of the dangers of language.

Besides this dialogue with another culture, Heidegger has worked in other ways on what he called the "other thinking," which has taken many forms, but is always aimed at overthrowing the dominance of metaphysics. I now proceed to explain a few of the key notions of this "other thinking" which can be related to comparative philosophy. The first one is the already-mentioned "Fourfold" (*Geviert*).[103] Fourfold is the unity of and relations between mortals, divinities, heaven, and earth. Mortals are those who actively accept their finite existence and who are aware of the finiteness and temporality of all earthly existence. The divinities are the "beckoning messengers of divinity." It is very controversial and difficult to understand what Heidegger means by this, especially since he was a fierce opponent of the influence of religion on philosophy. He seems to mean that divinity is an essential part of the world, which means that he is trying to say that the world is not just the superficiality of things we see, but that all things have a deeper or at least a different meaning that we cannot imagine with our scientifically oriented way of knowing. So, with the term "divinities," Heidegger asks that we have to keep an open mind toward the mystery of the world. Heaven is the constantly developing movement of night and day, sun and moon, weather and wind. It refers to the cosmos and to time, but placed in a far more encompassing reach than science gives these concepts. The earth Heidegger typifies as the "serving bearer of fruit, plant and animal." With regard to the earth's serving and bearing character, Heidegger states that that is in principal its essence, but that in the present time the earth is being exploited, polluted, and threatened, so it cannot any more perform its natural function. Mortals, divinities, heaven, and earth are very much interrelated. In fact, Heidegger perceives these four as a unity of existence, thus directly criticizing dualistic philosophy and implying a more cosmological way of thinking. Fourfold does not place man opposite the world, but implies that he is a part of it and that he needs to play an active role in keeping its unity, not forgetting he is but a part of the greater whole.

Another aspect of the other way of thinking is "Releasement" (*Gelassenheit*).[104] Releasement, or detachment, is an attitude to be taken toward things. It is not a passive detachment, but an attitude that lies beyond the opposition passive versus active. Releasement is keeping an open mind toward the mystery of the world and of existence. It is aimed at creating an openness in which things can be what they are, it is a letting-things-be as they are, and not, as in dualistic philosophy, to oppose or try to master them and see them as something usable. Things *are*, and it is this *Being* of things that Heidegger tries to give room, in letting them *be* without naming them, since naming them usually involves stigmatizing and fixating them relative to man and other things.

Then there is the aforementioned "aesthetic" or "poetic" thinking. This is not to be confused with thinking *about* art or poetry, but as I have said it is also a way of thinking that tries to bring us closer to the world we live in. It is a more originary and truthful way of thinking, where again it has to be reminded that truth, for Heidegger, is unconcealment, so that this way of thinking tries to perceive of the world as disclosing itself in a way that is more direct and original than metaphysics and science make us believe. It is up to us whether we can hear this disclosure, whether we are ready and willing to change our attitudes. Heidegger himself has remained very reluctant to say what this other thinking would actually in reality consist of. All he wants is to prepare us for a different relation to our world. It is up to us to put these thoughts into existence, and of course, existence differs. There is more than one way these thoughts can be understood, there are different ways. Yet he seems to be pointing to a more experiential way of thinking that aims to reunite us with the deeper (or rather different) meaning of the universe, and I believe that this is one of the reasons Heidegger turned to the East. To Heidegger the fundamental experiences of man are those that place him firmly in this world, for example "Anxiety" (*Angst*) as an experience of "Nothing," and therefore of *Being*. Heidegger has frequently argued that "experience" should become a far more encompassing concept and not just be seen as an experience of an object by a subject.[105] Experience is the form of thinking. The concepts of Fourfold and Releasement can easily be thought of as advocating a more experiential thinking, close to some forms of mysticism, if we do not forget that it is not something otherworldly that Heidegger aims to unite us with, but that thinking and experience are meant to bring man closer to the reality and interrelatedness of existence.

The intercultural approach of this other thinking is very obvious. Everywhere Heidegger hints at the importance of different ways of thinking, no one way is better than another. His work does have a lot of relations with mysticism, yet again we have to stress that Heidegger has maintained that he wanted nothing to do with mysticism, as he considered it an attempt to escape from the finite world, and it is this finite world that he takes to be our final base. In this way Heidegger can be said to have developed a "mysticism after the death of God." The mystical influences in his work are not aimed at releasing us from this world into a state of bliss, but at seeing it for what it really is: a finite world, yes, but with a lot more meaning in it than has been advocated by science and rationality. Interculturally, this means Western philosophy has to let go of its prejudice of scientific truth and pretence to objectivity, and has to admit that even in our finite world, meaning can not be reduced to scientific meaning.

CONCLUDING HEIDEGGER

Having put Heidegger's thoughts into relation with comparative philosophy, we might ask what the implications of this way of thinking are. With regard to language and communication, we can say that as long as comparative dialogues are held in a Western language without explicit awareness of the dangers this brings with it, little progress will be made in the direction of trying to retrieve the thoughts behind expressions and key concepts of cultures profoundly different from the West. In other cultures languages may have other functions than the exchange of information. We can also relate this to the motives behind comparative philosophy. It appears that much of what is referred to as comparative philosophy might actually be Western in origin, motive, or discourse. It is the West that is now seeking to start a dialogue, and it remains to be seen whether this attitude of wanting a dialogue is itself inter- or cross-cultural at all. Heidegger urges us to take different cultures "as they come," and not to try to read too much into them that is just not there. Too much of "other thinking" is still bent and curbed until it fits our Western discourse, and that which does not fit in or has no equivalent in something known to us, is dismissed and not allowed to participate in the dialogue. As long as this remains the case, there might be little incentive for another culture to participate when it knows beforehand that it cannot express itself anyway. This is where Heidegger has argued that we have to change our ideas of language and meaning to be able to start a truly intercultural dialogue.

But Heidegger has also protested fiercely against total cultural relativism. All thinking everywhere is based on the universal source of thought, *Being*, the unity on which the distinction of Self and Other is based and to which it has to return. But because *Being* itself *is* nothing, it is not something we can identify and thus as such it will remain forever in the background, retreating further the harder we try to expose "it," because "it" is non-existent, it is nothing other than the play of differences. *Being* cannot be identified, but *Being* can come to unconcealment in the differences, if we are ready and willing to look and hear. Keeping this in mind, we must come to a constructive dialogue that can provide a counterforce to the ongoing threats of Westernization both within philosophy and in the wider world. We must constantly be on guard against Western, but also against Eastern, prejudice and presuppositions if we wish for a rich and diverse source of thinking. For that is what the diversity of cultures also is: an unnameable source from which thinking can be derived. So if we allow the Western point of view to become the dominating or even the only true one, we lose in many ways.

The West still dictates, albeit hardly traceable and very subtle, the rules of dialogue and exchange. Although thinking itself is universal, the ways of thinking are so diverse that we cannot afford to lose sight of this differentiality. Thinking goes on all across the planet, and that is what Heidegger meant when he stated that we need a "planetary thinking"[106]—not in the sense of one way of thinking for the whole planet, but in a realization that there are different ways of thinking around.

What I have tried to show in this chapter is three things. First is that Heidegger's thinking is useful in seeing both the possibilities and the dangers of comparative philosophy, which stem mainly from language. Second is that the nothingness, or clearing, or openness between differences need not be understood as a transcendental or metaphysical guiding principle, but must, according to Heidegger himself, be purely understood from the interplay of differences itself. Third is that even with the best intentions, comparative philosophy is still easily dominated by Western traditional scholarship. And as Heidegger himself met with great resistance from the establishment, so a truly intercultural dialogue also faces great difficulties. But I am convinced that *if* we are serious in our comparative efforts, the only way open to us is to face the decision to widen the range of philosophy. And, as Heidegger saw well, then we had better leave behind the heavy burden of the term "philosophy" altogether. If I can venture a conclusion of this chapter, this might be what Heidegger can offer us as the most important task of comparative thinking: paving the way for different kinds of thinking, from one universal philosophy to different kinds of planetary thinking.

CHAPTER TWO

Derrida

Otherness, Context, and Openness

> I must nonetheless formulate in a somewhat dogmatic way [. . .] a very dry necessity whose consequences could affect our entire problematic: *what is proper to a culture is to not be identical to itself.* Not to not have an identity, but not to be able to identify itself, to be able to say "me" or "we"; to be able to take the form of a subject only in the non-identity to itself or, if you prefer, only in the difference *with itself [avec soi].* There is no culture or cultural identity without this difference *with itself.*[1]

In order to get a better understanding of the relevance of Jacques Derrida's work for the field of comparative philosophy, it is important to have a closer look first at Derrida's efforts in reinterpreting what he sees as the mostly Western, metaphysical tradition of philosophy. These efforts are found in his attacks on phono- and logocentrism. Together with these attacks come his criticisms and reinterpretations of the oppositional structure of much of Western philosophy, where thinking has always seemed to develop in some form of dualism, in which opposites or dichotomies emerge, and of which good/evil, mind/body, being/nothing, presence/absence, essence/appearance, and identity/difference can be examples. This way of thinking is in itself questionable, meaning that such clear-cut distinctions are never really possible, and Derrida's work is meant to show that the drawing of the borders, limits, or dividing lines between the subsequent opposites of the distinctions are always open to various deconstructions. Furthermore the hierarchy imposed on and within these dichotomies, whereby one side of the oppositions or differential structures is favored above the other, is also arbitrary or untenable according to Derrida. He questions this longstanding tradition through such nonconcepts as deconstruction, differance, tracing, supplement, iterability, and so on, and it is precisely this questioning which we have to look at before we can turn more directly to the project: "Derrida and comparative philosophy." For it is really *in* the dislodging and deconstructive enterprises that Derrida's ideas about something beyond or other than philosophy in the logocentric sense can be located.

Another reason for inquiring into Derrida's relation to Western, metaphysical philosophy[2] before looking into his relations with other ways of thinking is that direct references in Derrida's work to non-Western or nonmetaphysical philosophy are not only sparse, but problematic and ambiguous in themselves. This is especially so if we for a moment ignore the numerous references to Algeria (Derrida's birthplace), or to the Jewish, Christian, and Islamic world.[3] In dealing with these traditions, Derrida tries to show that they are essentially speaking from the same roots, as they can be traced to the Abrahamic background, and are thus squarely located within the metaphysical tradition. Although Derrida locates numerous differences within these views and in their relations, the essence is that all three share the same metaphysical background and direction. There is very little mention in any of his works of anything beyond the Middle East, or of Sub-Saharan Africa, East Asia, or any other non-Western place for that matter. In *Acts of Religion* Derrida goes further in showing that the whole notion of religiousness is seemingly reserved for the Abrahamic traditions. When he deconstructs the religious vocabulary and finds it to be Western and Christianized, this then in turn is taken to explain the "globalatinization,"[4] meaning the universalizing intentionality of these religions, through their language. As he puts it: "In any case, the history of the word 'religion' should in principle forbid every non-Christian from using the name 'religion.'"[5] However, Derrida does not further explore the consequences of these ideas *for* other ways of thinking, and neither does he ever incorporate other ways of thinking *into* his own critique of Western metaphysics. So in a very surprising fashion, since Derrida is noted for criticizing the tradition of Western metaphysics and for arguing for the interconnectedness and relationality of what seem to be separate identities at first glance, he leaves out any serious approach to other cultures and ways of thinking which might show him some possible forms of nonlogocentric thinking. We must keep this in mind when trying to locate Derrida in comparative philosophy, and thus realize that it is mostly not any actual encounters of Derrida with other cultures, but the way of thinking he has developed, which is interesting in that it might shed more light on the guiding ideas behind comparative philosophy.

In order to see, therefore, whether his thinking has any resonance in Daoism or could engender different readings *of* this tradition, we must first locate in the deconstructions of the metaphysical sensibilities those features which could bear importance on a positive (or at least a different-from-the-"usual") appreciation of non-Western cultures, as opposed to those which merely criticize certain structures. And for this, we need first to locate Derrida's views with regard to the future possibilities of Western thinking as well as its limitations. In second place we need to look at his ideas of alterity, or what is "other" or different, and how this otherness or difference functions or relates to the Western world. This notion of the "other" figures prominently in this chapter as it holds some importance for deconstructing the strict difference of identities that has been supposed to hold between East and West.

The project of relating Derrida to the non-Western cultural and philosophical sensibilities in Daoism can then be seen to have three aspects or parts: First there is a comparative part, where we look for resonances between Derrida and Daoism and try to explain the relevance of these relations for a better understanding of both. Second, but closely related, we must try to give a differential or Derridean reading of classics such as the *Daodejing* or the *Zhuangzi*, in order to shed a different light on these important works. This is not to be understood as imposing Derridean sensibilities onto Daoism, but more in the sense of a hermeneutical understanding, where we use Derrida to try to more fully appreciate Daoism on its own terms, which in turn can only mean that we try to provide at least a wider terminology and a wider discourse or context in which to understand Daoism. Third, there must be an explanation of the attempt, by various scholars who have compared Derrida to Daoism, to use Daoism as a critique of or supplement to Derrida's deconstructive process, or in other words I must give an explanation of the attempt to read and criticize Derrida from a Daoist perspective. This attempt has taken various forms, and again it is not meant to impose Daoist ideas on Derrida but looks for a wider understanding of both. We must then see whether this Daoist criticism is valid by exploring both Derrida and Daoism. However, this third part of relating Derrida to Daoism must wait until after Daoism has been more closely studied in the next chapter, so it is part of the final, comparative chapter.

While incorporating parts of these three aspects, this chapter however has a slightly different construction, exploring the aforementioned in three different parts. In the first part I look more closely at ideas of identity and difference, and of differance and other Derridean terms, and I focus on the deconstruction of Western ideas and on Derrida's relation to Heidegger. Of course anyone even vaguely familiar with Derrida will realize that these terms need to be deconstructed and put "under erasure," that is they are used but reinterpreted and reinscribed in a different discourse, one that hopes not so much to circumvent metaphysics, but at least to point to its inconsistencies and from there maybe to find openings to nonmetaphysical thinking and with that to some non-Western cultures. This part is mostly concerned with Derrida's deconstruction of the Western tradition and forms of metaphysics and thus provides a sort of platform from which to proceed to look more closely at his possible relations to nonmetaphysical thinking.

The second part focuses specifically on the notions of language and translation, important as these are to both Derrida and comparative philosophy. The possibilities and impossibilities of translation, the relation between signifier and signified, phono- and logocentrism in language, the idea of "writing," "context," "textuality," or "discourse" in a broad sense; all these bear strongly on any intercultural encounter or comparative philosophy from a Derridean perspective. It is argued that a different perspective on language and discourse is vital to understand Derrida as well as to locate him intelligibly in comparative philosophy.

The third part then tries to initiate a reading of Derrida and the possibilities of his work with special regard to comparative philosophy. This part then, by means of the notion of the "other" in Derrida and its usefulness for comparative philosophy, tries to "apply" Derrida and by this I mean it looks for the possibility of relations of Derridean thinking to nonmetaphysical ways of thinking. This means I look into the possibilities of an intercultural dialogue "on Derridean terms," thus to see how comparative philosophy might benefit and strengthen its ideas of openness to difference if we look at it through Derrida's thinking. Here I also do the initial exploration of the possibility of different and differential readings of East Asian thinking by pointing to the inevitable metaphysics inserted in various readings from metaphysical[6] perspectives and by pointing to the fact that if we wish to do comparative thinking through Derrida, other-than-metaphysical readings are necessary. As I pointed out before, I also give an interpretation of readings and criticisms of Derrida from a Daoist perspective, but in a later chapter.

This chapter as a whole needs of course to address the inevitable question of relativism or nihilism, of which Derrida has often been accused, but against which he has vehemently tried to defend himself. The refutation of relativism and nihilism by Derrida is important as well for intercultural encounters, where it is also one of the most common criticisms comparative philosophy has to defend itself against. I hope to show, however, that a serious and thorough reading of Derrida will provide a certain idea of relations, perspectives, and language or discourse that will itself take away much, if not all, of the force of the criticisms of relativism and nihilism leveled against Derrida. I try to do this by suggesting that although Derrida might at first glance come across as a relativist who questions all the long-standing notions of philosophy without offering a "way out," his questioning should be seen more as a way of complicating the oversimplifications that absolutists take for granted.

DECONSTRUCTING THE IDEAS BEHIND METAPHYSICS

> [Writing] inaugurates the destruction, not the demolition but the desedimentation, the de-construction, of all the significations that have their source in that of the logos. [. . .] All the metaphysical determinations of truth, and even the one beyond metaphysical onto-theology that Heidegger reminds us of, are more or less immediately inseparable from the instance of the logos, or of a reason thought within the lineage of the logos, in whatever sense it is understood.[7]

Misreading Derrida

Before we begin the exploration of Derrida's thought about Western metaphysics, it might be appropriate to provide a short aside dealing with popular misreadings of Derrida's work in general, or of some of his (non) concepts, as well as his replies and elaborations on these readings. A better understanding of these misreadings and Derrida's explanations will function to deflect certain unwarranted and hasty criticisms of his work, and will thereby enable us to depopularize the supposed relativism or nihilism of Derrida, and to better focus on Derrida's own ideas, and on more warranted criticisms and Derrida's replies to them. I realize however that this undertaking of looking at misreadings might in itself be questionable. Derrida has frequently questioned the notions of authorial intent, univocal meaning, the proper, and property, and he has also argued for the important place of the reader in understanding any text. The criticism goes that since reading is interpretation, there can be no ground from which to judge between a good and a bad reading. We are left with the question of whether there is a possibility of distinguishing misreadings from proper readings, which has Jonathan Culler claiming that "understanding is a special case of misunderstanding."[8] This has led some people, both critics and followers of Derrida, to assume a certain philosophical "anything goes" attitude in his work.[9] Notwithstanding this, Derrida has made certain claims to what is at stake in his works and words, and he has argued against at least some of the interpretations that have been given of his work. So perhaps there are better misunderstandings and worse ones. Alternatively and in my opinion more Derridean, we could see understanding as something provisional, something which always gets fragmented (and, as we shall see, right from the beginning), or at least never reaches the fullness that is its ideal. This is also the meaning of the putting "under erasure" of concepts as I understand it. I think this latter position is what Derrida has in mind in most of his texts, and it is in this light that I offer some of the misreadings and Derrida's responses to them.

First of all there is the by-now (in)famous notion of "deconstruction." This notion has arguably become one of today's most used concepts, terms, or slogans, thereby losing much of its original force and direction. It could be seen on par nowadays with terms such as "culture" and "postmodern," or "*dao*" for that matter in having started a life of its own. Of course Derrida is really in no position to lament this development, since he has always argued for the inherent openness of terms and words, and for their insertion or iterability[10] in (any) historical discourse right from the moment they are conceived.[11] Derrida realizes this, but does however want to clarify that this inevitable *Wirkungsgeschichte* or history of the term is not *his* invention, and that he is not to be held responsible for the development of the word as such. On several occasions, for example in *The Ear of the Other*, he has explicitly denounced the purely negative side of deconstruction, where he says some critics think it is "a technical operation used to dismantle systems"[12] or structures and nothing else. Derrida tries to explain that the function of the dismantling of deconstruction "is accompanied, or can be accompanied (in any case, I would hope to accompany it), by an affirmation. It is not negative, it is not destructive."[13]

Originally taken from Heidegger, Derrida had intended the word "deconstruction" much more as Heidegger took it, in the sense of *Destruktion* and *Ab-bau,* and maybe even related to Heidegger's *Wiederholung*, signaling indeed a dismantling of a structure, but for the purpose of seeing "how it is constituted or deconstituted."[14] So deconstruction is not just destruction, it is more of a dissecting, and also a certain reconstruction, and its function is more to make us realize that certain structures are more complicated, less simple, and less univocal than they seem to be presented at first. Elsewhere Derrida has argued similarly that the moment of affirmation in deconstruction lies in the realization that supposedly complete identities, or closed structures, ideas, or systems are always open-ended (and from both ends) and can therefore never attain the perfect self-presence on which so much of metaphysical philosophy is founded. This realization does not therefore denounce what is deconstructed, it merely reinscribes it, makes it more provisional. As Derrida himself explains it:

> Deconstruction certainly entails a moment of affirmation. Indeed, I cannot conceive of a radical critique which would not be ultimately motivated by some sort of affirmation, acknowledged or not. Deconstruction always presupposes affirmation, as I have frequently attempted to point out, sometimes employing a Nietzschean terminology. I do not mean that the deconstructing *subject* or *self* affirms. I mean that deconstruction is, in itself, a positive response to an alterity which necessarily calls, summons or motivates it. [. . .] It is in this rapport with the other that affirmation expresses itself.[15]

In a wording remarkably similar to Heidegger which is further explored in the next section of this chapter, Derrida thus denounces the wrongful interpretations of deconstruction that have flourished, mostly, as he says, in the interpretations of his work in the United States.[16] Derrida is much more interested in limiting the overly optimistic interpretations and ideas of metaphysics and resituating them accordingly, than he is in destroying them altogether. More important for comparative philosophy, he suggests that the affirmation lies to a large extent in the "rapport with the other." We will see what this means later. And again, Derrida does not share in the optimism regarding the possibilities of the concept of deconstruction; it is just a provisional word to be replaced and "determined by such other words as 'ecriture,' 'trace,' 'differance,' 'supplement,' 'hymen,' 'pharmakon,' 'marge,' 'entame,' 'parergon,' etc. By definition, the list can never be closed. . . ."[17] That is to say that by definition there can be no one formula or definition of "deconstruction" as this would reduce "it" to "an available set of rule-governed procedures, methods, accessible approaches."[18] And more recently Derrida has said there can only be deconstructions, in the plural, since it is not one definable thing.[19] This is something of importance for comparative philosophy as I see it, in that in a similar way, comparative philosophy also cannot have a fixed theory or methodology, which can then just be applied. Any theory of comparative philosophy can only be found in the practice of comparative philosophy.

The same defense is used with regard to the idea of "the death of the subject," a common Derridean expression that has also taken on a life of its own. In reply to a question about the critics who accuse him of nihilistically getting rid of the notion of human subjectivity, Derrida explains that:

> [they] need not worry. [. . .] To deconstruct the subject does not mean to deny its existence. There are subjects, "operations" or "effects" (*effets*) of subjectivity. This is an incontrovertible fact. To acknowledge this does not mean, however, that the subject is what is *says* it is. The subject is not some meta-linguistic substance or identity, some pure *cogito* of self-presence; it is always inscribed in language. My work does not, therefore, destroy the subject; it simply tries to resituate it.[20]

Again, Derrida makes an effort to show that he is arguing against the oversimplifications that seem to occur necessarily or inevitably in the idealizations and abstractions of metaphysical philosophy and its dualistic approach, and that his work is directed at reinterpreting these ideas.

In close connection to the previous two is the last example I shall give of misreadings of Derrida's work, and this concerns the idea that there is nothing beyond language. One of the most frequently used quotations of Derrida must surely be: "*There is nothing outside of the text*,"[21] and this is at the same time easily one of the most misunderstood sentences in Derrida's work. It is *not* a statement to the effect that we are trapped in language, that we are bound by it. Again, since this aside is a defense of Derrida's intentions, if we can properly speak of his intentions, I shall let him do the talking:

> I never cease to be surprised by critics who see my work as a declaration that there is nothing beyond language, that we are imprisoned in language; it is, in fact, saying the exact opposite. The critique of logocentrism is above all else the search for the "other" and the "other of language." Every week I receive critical commentaries and studies on deconstruction which operate on the assumption that what they call "post-structuralism" amounts to saying that there is nothing beyond language, that we are submerged in words—and other stupidities of that sort. Certainly, deconstruction tries to show that the question of reference is much more complex and problematic than traditional theories supposed. [. . .] But to distance oneself thus from the habitual structure of reference, to challenge or complicate our common assumptions about it, does not amount to saying that there is *nothing* beyond language.[22]

Again Derrida seems to be suggesting that he has been misunderstood on this part of his thinking. His is exactly the search for that moment where language fails to achieve its idealistic fullness, where rendering an object present as such through language becomes impossible, and where language returns to itself and makes reference to something outside of language, something not contaminated by language, something *on its own (terms)*, problematic. Many of Derrida's opponents have taken to this idea of "nothing outside the text," criticizing what they think to be some "all or nothing" attitude, a nihilistic or relativistic position which argues that we are imprisoned in language.[23] Derrida's explanation of what the terms "writing" or "text" stand for gives us a different story, as he explains that "text" is "limited neither to the graphic, nor to the book, nor even to discourse, and even less to the semantic, representational, symbolic, ideal, or ideological sphere. What I call 'text' implies all the structures called 'real,' 'economic,' 'historical,' socio-institutional, in short: all possible referents. [. . .] every referent, all reality has the structure of a differential trace."[24] Elsewhere in the same work, *Limited Inc.*, he also affirms the idea of reference. If taken as regarding difference that is always there already, there is reference, yet it is never pure.[25] We are therefore always embedded in referential situations, where clear and distinct presence of something unto itself is immediately challenged and where language always stumbles onto that which is other to it. Language is thus more a stumbling block if seen from the subjective point of view, but what Derrida shows is that this stumbling block is all we have, it is unavoidable to work with(in) it. He is looking for a kind of nondualist approach to reference, understood as our inevitable embeddedness in situations, which would place us *inside* the world rather than outside of it or struggling to get outside. To think of ourselves as transcendental subjects who could somehow step outside of these circles and obtain an objective look at them, is itself a fallacy that others besides Derrida have also criticized, and it is in this very tradition that Derrida moves.[26] Thus the statement that "there is nothing outside the text" means rather that there is always context, and this context is both constitutive for our being, as well as structurally open-ended.

In all fairness to his critics, there is a lot of room for these misunderstandings to arise, and Derrida has to some extent been instrumental in their appearance and persistence. For example, the complexity of his texts, their inherent ambiguity and play with words are not exactly conducive to any clear-cut understanding. But of course we should remind ourselves that one of Derrida's main objectives seems to be exactly to ambiguate the notion of such a *unitary* understanding of *full* presence, but that this does not mean "*no* meaning at all." Besides this, the parts that function as his explanations are (usually) of a much later date than the original quotations which have offended or provoked so many. But, in order to save him from his readers, we need to understand that the things he writes and says are in the end *not* those of his interpreters, whether they are followers or critics. This will hopefully become clearer through the comparison of Derrida and Daoism. We also need to appreciate the fact that Derrida's approach stresses the negative against the positive of metaphysics, not to stay in this inversion, but precisely in order to overcome or undo this duality or dichotomy inherent in metaphysical philosophy. This is important for now, as are two other aspects of this aside. First of all is that I have already hinted at Derrida's close relation to Heidegger, which is explored in the next section, with special attention to those similarities or conflicts which could be of use in comparative philosophy. Second, or more in particular, many if not all of these criticisms and refutations stem from an interpretation of the notions of "identity" and "difference," which are crucial to Derrida's thinking, as well as to Heidegger's. It is therefore these notions, together with corresponding notions of subjectivity, presence, and alterity, or otherness, which we need to address.

Beyond Heidegger?

This section focuses on the rather complex relations between Heidegger and Derrida. One of Derrida's main criticisms of Heidegger has to do with the latter's notion of the Ontological Difference. This thought of Being as opposed to beings is supposedly overtaken by Derrida's notion of differance (*différance*). In order to appreciate what differance could mean, it is best to look at the notions of identity and difference first. To start with the notion of "identity," various parts of Derrida's work seek to undermine the traditional notion of any lasting identity, also and especially in the case of any enduring, transcendental subjectivity. Identity itself is not so much denied, but Derrida sees it as ever shifting in moves which remind one of Heidegger's *Identity and Difference*. This means that all forms of identity and all forming of identity or subjectivity rely on the always already implicit reference to "the other." Derrida mentions in *Monolingualism of the Other* that identity is only formed at "a site always referring elsewhere, to something other, to another language, to the other in general."[27] Something is never fully sufficient on its own; it always and ever anew needs to deal with its other, and as such is also defined by its other. This is also the idea of the opening quotation of this chapter. And as we have seen in Chapter 1, Heidegger's work is exactly about this relation with the other, and about seeing this relationality (and thus difference) as fundamental to, and not as something derivative from, the idea of identity. I deal more explicitly with this notion of the "other" in a later section of this chapter.

It is therefore important to show in this section how, by using the notion of differance, Derrida goes or at least thinks he goes beyond Heidegger. The main contribution or addition of Derrida seems to be the awareness that Heidegger was still looking for "authentic" words that would somehow speak directly from the matter of thinking, and he thought he could locate these words in ancient Greek, German, or the classical Chinese language of the *Daodejing* and the *Zhuangzi*. Against this Derrida wants to show that *all* such supposedly authentic words eventually fall short of what they aim for and only function within arbitrary webs of signification. This applies also, of course, to Derrida's own words, and he is extremely aware of this; if there is a common thread in Derrida's work, it is the intention to show this relatedness which functions everywhere and makes it impossible in principle to divide the world into strict identities.

Taking a closer look at the notion of differance we find that it is in itself problematic. Derrida's insistence that it is "neither a word nor a concept"[28] should make us realize that we are definitely not talking about something which would simply replace notions as Geist, God, or Reason, if these can be taken as representatives of the metaphysical tradition, functioning as transcendental principles. But this in itself does not mean Heidegger is surpassed in any way. For the same things that have been said about differance up to now apply to Heidegger's notion of Being. Heidegger equally considers the fact that Being is not a word in the proper sense, for then it would be a being. He also resorts to crossing out the word itself, and is most definitely opposed to any ontotheological or metaphysical interpretation of Being, realizing very much that Being is *in* beings and nowhere else. But Derrida may be right in suggesting that Heidegger was always looking for authentic words and hoped to find these words in poetic thinking and in other cultures, as well as locating them in the ancient Greek way of thinking and of course in his own words. However, Heidegger also warned against any such metaphysically optimistic interpretation of these words, since it was only in a quite radical reinterpretation of these words that Heidegger could show something of his take on them, and then immediately warned that even if they were to be considered in some way as authentic or disclosing, this only ever happens together with inauthenticity and closure. As we have seen, every unconcealing of necessity entails concealing. Thus every effort at making the ontological difference appear is useless, because *as such*, as difference, (it) can never appear (itself).[29] This should prevent the reader and thus also Derrida from focusing too much on the supposed nostalgia or metaphysical inclinations of Heidegger. In fact, Derrida is aware of this when he says that "one can find several passages in which Heidegger is self-critical and renounces his nostalgia: his practice of cancelling and erasing the term [Being] in his later texts is an example of such a critique. Heidegger's texts are still before us. . . ."[30] Derrida is deeply aware of Heidegger's importance to his own works, and even admits that "in a certain aspect of itself, *différance* is certainly but the historical and epochal *unfolding* of Being or of the ontological difference."[31] But the fact that he uses the words "in a certain aspect" already suggests that Derrida is not willing to stop there. He goes on to show that there is indeed a difference between the two. This difference is that Heidegger was still looking for a meaning or truth of Being, however he conceived of these. Differance does not succumb to this inclination. Instead differance is called:

> The play of a trace which no longer belongs to the horizon of Being, but whose play transports and encloses the meaning of Being: the play of the trace, or the *différance*, which has no meaning and is not. Which does not belong. There is no maintaining, and no depth to, this bottomless chessboard on which Being is put into play.[32]

Derrida acknowledges that it is only by thoroughly thinking *through* the ontological difference that anything like differance can be thought. But whereas Heidegger in *Der Spruch des Anaximander* still hopes for "the unique word"[33] which could somehow speak of the "root unfolding" (*Wesen*) of Being, or out of "the matter of thinking" (*die Sache des Denkens*), Derrida aims to show that there is no such word, that language always and necessarily falls short of the expectations of providing such presence, and that we must affirm this without nostalgia, indeed in a Nietzschean way. And it is therefore appropriate here to recall Nietzsche's words:

> There are no durable ultimate units, no atoms, no monads; here, too, beings are only introduced by us [. . .]. Linguistic means of expression are useless for expressing 'becoming'; it accords with our inevitable need to preserve ourselves to posit a crude world of stability, of 'things,' etc."[34]

Differance as trace does not point toward some origin of presence, or to stability. Trace (is) the play of what is "other" *inside* the structures of signification. It is therefore that differance is neither a word nor a concept, and most certainly not *the* word. This is the most important difference between Heidegger and Derrida. We should now leave this particular question of the relation between Heidegger and Derrida and return to our exploration of differance.

If differance is not a concept, then what (is it)? Derrida explains by saying that although differance is not a concept in the traditional sense, it is more to be seen as "an aconceptual concept or another kind of concept, heterogeneous to the philosophical concept of the concept, a 'concept' that marks both the possibility and the limit of all idealization and hence of all conceptualization."[35] Does that help? At least we are beginning to understand that Derrida wishes to question the whole notion of conceptuality, as he questions notions of identity, subjectivity, and language in general, again, remember, not so much to destroy them, but to reinscribe them in a less totalitarian, less idealistic web he calls "writing." All his key words thus also and immediately become questionable themselves, and this is why he never lingers around one concept for long, as Heidegger may have done by lingering around "Being" his entire career. We can also note the shift from the nouns to gerunds within Derrida's thinking. "Writing" is an example of this, and it is part of a larger effort on his side to overcome substance-based metaphysical philosophy and work toward a more processual, nondualist understanding. In this line we can think of the "a" in differance, implying the notion of temporality, deference, and think of the "texture" of the text, implying context.

The next important factor to note in Derrida's relation to Heidegger is that Heidegger offers a very different interpretation of *logos,* one of his key terms. But we need to find out to what extent Derrida still reads *logos* in the way it has traditionally come down to us, that is as discourse guided by a thread of reason and logic. Derrida takes *logos*, and indeed the derivative of *logos* that is logocentrism, to be the main feature of Western metaphysics.[36] Read in this way the metaphysical tradition is indeed logocentric, but it remains to be seen whether this can be used as an argument against Heidegger. As we have seen in the previous chapter Heidegger relates *logos* to other terms such as "clearing" and *polemos* and through this reading offers a possibility for seeing *logos* in a new way that is really not the same as it is understood in metaphysics. The question then is: Has Derrida taken this new reading for all it is worth? In several writings Derrida has expounded on the notion of *logos*, but as we will see he uses the term mostly to describe the most important traits of metaphysical thinking, as according to the *logos* understood as thinking and speech. This is exactly what the idea of logocentrism means, that there is a standard, the *logos*, toward which Western metaphysical philosophy has aspired. And it has done so by seeing speech as prior to writing and as closer to the standard than writing. The fullness of the spoken word was the guarantee for any real meaning in thinking; writing was just derivative. Derrida's whole "philosophy" is about challenging this idea by showing the interrelatedness of signs and of all signification, by complicating ideas of identity and difference, reference and presence, and so forth. Heidegger can definitely be accused of (to some extent) favoring the spoken language over the written, and of looking for authentic words; examples abound where he goes in this direction, and examples abound where Derrida points this out. Yet to me this valid criticism does not seem to warrant suggesting that Heidegger had the same interpretation of *logos* as the one which is at the basis of the metaphysical tradition. In fact, it is most obvious that he did not. And then the question arises whether Derrida is fully appreciative of this different reading. When Derrida speaks at length about the relation between *logos* and *polemos* in *Heidegger's Ear: Philopolemology (Geschlecht IV)*,[37] it seems obvious that he sees *polemos* almost solely in the negative way, as "struggle," or "war." This is partly so because this particular piece of writing is as much about *logos* and *polemos* as it is about Heidegger's engagement with Nazism in the early 1930s. The much more positive allusions which Heidegger hints at with *polemos, logos,* and with the translation of the latter as *Auseinandersetzung* to which I have tried to direct the reader in Chapter 1 are not taken at full value by Derrida when he suggests that even Heidegger is logocentric in that he focuses on the *logos*. Heidegger does focus on *logos*, but his is a very different and much broader concept of *logos* altogether. In other words, Derrida has chosen but one part of Heidegger's *logos* to focus on and thus does injustice to the full picture. In my opinion Derrida is well aware of this, and his attempts at deconstructing Heidegger consequently focus more on the idea behind logocentrism, which he calls phono-centrism, and by linking the two together.[38] But as we shall see later, phono-centrism need not develop into logocentrism,[39] and maybe Derrida should have taken more notice of the profoundly different meanings that *logos* has for Heidegger.

Then, as we have seen before, Derrida emphasizes his shifting between different terminologies as a necessary movement. But Heidegger, while his lifelong work on Being was indeed the focal point, also shifts attention between different concepts; there is a clear development to be seen in his work from Dasein to Being, to *aletheia*, to *logos*, to *Ereignis,* to Way, to Fourfold, to *Welt*, and so on. Is Derrida doing anything different? Is he not also trying to say the same thing again and again, but in always shifting terms and perspectives? As I have tried to show, these questions can be answered either affirmatively or negatively. Yes, it would seem Derrida employs the same "methodology" as Heidegger, although both would object to this word. The better word to use would be "strategy," as both Heidegger and Derrida are concerned with showing the inadequacy of language in general and of metaphysical language in particular. Yet, to come to the negative answer, we have seen that in the end Heidegger believed that language itself could provide its own critique, and that a reinterpretation of certain words could lead the way to an (although not unambivalent) understanding of Being, or of the ontological difference. Derrida points out that *all* language inevitably suffers from inadequacy, including his own.

It is obvious that Derrida thinks Heidegger's texts "harbour a future of meaning which will ensure that they are read and reread for centuries."[40] It also seems unmistakably true that Derrida has to some extent expounded on Heidegger's works, mostly so in the field of discourse and language, but also in expressing what might have been some underlying assumptions of Heidegger that would warrant placing him (at least partly) in the tradition of metaphysics. Of course neither Heidegger nor Derrida claims to be totally outside this tradition, yet both hope that somehow, in interrogating this tradition, they can partly overcome it. Yet I feel that Derrida is right in claiming in various works that deal with Heidegger that the latter was to some extent still within metaphysics, more so than Derrida himself. For Heidegger did look for a way out of metaphysical thinking that would somehow disclose the "secret" of Being to us mortals, and Heidegger obviously thought that his thinking would bring us closer to a more real understanding of what "really is as it is," and this sort of eschatological goal of thinking, whereby he foresees the end of metaphysics and a new beginning for the world and philosophy, mostly through his own thinking, locates him much more securely inside the tradition of philosophy, whereas Derrida on more than one occasion challenges exactly this eschatological structure of thinking.[41] The fact that by doing so Derrida is inevitably showing us to a certain extent "how things really are" and thus that his thinking is immediately appropriated into a certain metaphysical position is part of the double bind which suggests that we must always be drawn back into what we are trying to undo.

The importance of all this for comparative philosophy lies in the fact that we can now see that although Derrida mostly lacks the actual encounters of or active search for other ways of thinking that Heidegger displayed in his later years, his thinking seems to be even more open toward difference than Heidegger's. Where Heidegger may be read to suggest that the other is a necessary step for the development of the self,[42] Derrida goes further in suggesting that the other or difference is always already inserted into any form of cultural or other identity. This play of differance suggests that there are no pure identities; there is, rather, pure relationality of which identities are at best useful heuristic functions. There is an interesting passage in *Limited Inc.* that could make us fully understand and appreciate this profound relationality in Derrida's thinking. Expounding on the infamous "There is no outside of the text," Derrida says that what he was really saying with this is "that nothing exists outside context . . ., but also that the limit of the frame or the border of the context always entails a clause of non-closure. The outside penetrates and thus determines the inside."[43] The context itself is constitutive of any identity, and as context it can never be closed off, it is structurally and inherently open, since it is nothing more or less than "the entire 'real-history-of-the-world.'"[44]

It is doubtful whether Heidegger would go this far, so I would suggest that in the work of Derrida there lies much that is important for comparative philosophy, especially the extreme openness toward alterity and the importance of alterity, otherness, and difference, concepts which are being unmistakably elevated to the same level as identity and which thereby seek to undo the harsh distinctions with which Heidegger was still struggling in his *Auseinandersetzung* with different cultures. In the end, Heidegger kept some very clear demarcations between cultures and between different ways of thinking. Strange to say, but it looks like Heidegger was more of a differential thinker than Derrida, in his insistent keeping to difference. Derrida would, to be true to his work and in the event of any real encounter with different cultures, have to go further in explaining how these distinctions can be problematized, without thereby undoing them or denying the differences in cultures. But in doing this, Derrida is very aware of the necessity of an *Auseinandersetzung* with Heidegger's work and of the debt of his own work to Heidegger's. Especially in the field of language and its importance both for comparative philosophy and for philosophy as a whole, Derrida has had a tremendous influence on the way we think. So it is imperative that we should look into these aspects of Derrida's thinking before locating him in the comparative field.

LANGUAGE, TEXT, AND TRANSLATION IN DERRIDA

> The secondarity that it seemed possible to ascribe to writing alone affects all signifieds in general, affects them always already, the moment they *enter the game.* There is not a single signified that escapes, even if recaptured, the play of signifying references that constitutes language.[45]

This section focuses more specifically on Derrida's ideas of language and its functions, in relation to comparative philosophy. We will see whether Derrida's attacks on familiar concepts, and with that on the metaphysical ideas of conceptuality and conceptions of language, can provide an opening toward other ways of thinking. I also try to explain the invalidity or ineffectiveness of the criticism that to a certain important extent Derrida's own work might still be based on or parasitic to some idea of metaphysics.

Derrida has done almost all of his work on language by concentrating on Western, logocentric languages and on their metaphysical assumptions. We should ask whether his findings could also apply to significantly other languages, as for example (classical) Chinese. This is a question for the next section of this chapter. Suffice it here to remember that Derrida is usually speaking about, or deconstructing, Western languages and with that a very specific idea of language enters the picture. The history of Western philosophy has assumed that language has its priority in speech, where there is direct transference of meaning, and that writing is but a mere incomplete derivation of the phonic and semantic fullness of speech. This is the background of the conception of language that Derrida wants to interrogate.

One of the most straightforward ideas Derrida has on language is that words can only function by what they are not themselves. This is made obvious in the statement which is taken from Ferdinand de Saussure: "In a language, in the *system* of language, there are only differences."[46] In itself this might not seem so problematic, as anyone would agree that for example the word "lamp" only functions by being different from the words "lamb" and "ramp." But Derrida goes further and extends this idea to every signification structure, which he together then calls "writing." Words, sentences, in fact any and every form of signification, any mark can only function in relation to other signs, marks, and so on. This should make it clear that Derrida holds that nothing in (any) language, or again in any system of signification or reference, has any other than an arbitrary relation to something outside itself, or to reality. Or, as Robert Magliola puts it: "By applying to all signs the term 'writing,' [Derrida] coerces us into the 'recognition' that all signs are artificial."[47] With this recognition that speech is also a sign structure and thus suffers from the same artificiality as writing, Derrida denies the priority normally given to the spoken word. But by doing this Derrida is not arguing for the inversion of importance or priority, which would mean that writing should come to be seen as prior to speech. This inversion is just strategic and provocative; it is not the goal itself, which is to show the interconnectedness or relationality of both writing and speech, and their sameness as artificial structures, and as such to undo or transform the oppositional structure itself. This is also why differance is "*between* speech and writing,"[48] and it is exactly this betweenness that is the focus of Derrida. Because it is not just so that signs can function only because of other signs; they also only function because of the interval, spacing, or nothingness that is between them, and this is so in both speech and in writing.

Derrida wants to change the notion of language as something describing things outside of it, although he retains the idea of reference. But while he retains this, he challenges the idea of *fixed* reference. This might lead us to think that he is arguing for a certain openness of words themselves in that they can have different meanings, but in reality Derrida does not think that such a notion of polysemy goes far enough. Words do not just have different meanings according to different times or circumstances; the notion of polysemy has to be replaced by what Derrida calls "dissemination." The notion of polysemy does not suffice since it

> always puts out its multiplicities and variations within the *horizon*, at least, of some integral reading which contains no absolute rift, no senseless deviation—the horizon of the final parousia of a meaning at last deciphered, revealed, made present in the rich collection of its determinations. [. . .] All moments of polysemy are, as the word implies, moments of meaning.[49]

As such, even though polysemy admits of different meanings, it does not question the *structure* of meaning or signification as reference to or representation of something outside, and it is exactly this structure that Derrida does question because it is arbitrary and problematic. This is why instead of poly-semy "dis-semination" provides a better alternative. For dissemination evades arbitrariness because it can not be referred back to any origin or truth, or as Derrida puts it: "the quasi-'meaning' of dissemination is the impossible return to the rejoined, readjusted unity of meaning, the impeded march of any such *reflection*"[50] and as such represents the affirmation of the "nonorigin." One could cite the film *Rashomon*[51] as an example here, since it describes four different and contradictory interpretations of one event, in such a way that nobody seems to be able to give one single account of or meaning to it. Not that the event itself is thereby denied, but since the meaning of it is fragmented or unclear, we could say in the words of Steve Odin that "what gradually emerges is a total displacement of the event into a bewildering multiplicity of perspectival interpretations, an irreducible plurality of meanings."[52] Meaning of any event only arises out of interpretation, and interpretations differ, are plural. In that sense any pure experience loses much of its force, since it can only gather meaning by losing its purity in interpretation. What Derrida is telling us seems to be that the idea of polysemy still presupposes some sort of original meaning within a finite horizon, whereas dissemination challenges that idea by saying that meaning is always already divided, fragmented, relational, and so forth. Signs only function within history, and as such are structurally open to unlimited differing meanings. As Barry Allen puts it: "Each occasional sign has a historically conditioned, circumstantial effect but not a durable, self-identical content."[53] This can also be tied to the idea of iterability, which Derrida has put forward in *Limited Inc.* Iterability means that every word or sign only functions by being able to be cited or repeated. No sign can function *as a sign* if not for this iterability, which does not just mean that signs need repetition in order to be recognized as signs, but more importantly that every repetition, every citation is in fact different from what it repeats or cites. Signs then are only traces without any origin. There is no original sign to which reproduction, repetition, citation, refer back. All these do not just recall what they reproduce, repeat, or cite, but there is always difference or alterity[54] in them, from the very start. "Iteration alters, something new takes place."[55] Since signs thus have no enduring stability, but only a certain relative, historically contingent value, our ideas of them should be reinterpreted.

This interpretation of Derrida surfaces again when we take a closer look at the problem of translation. Admitting *and* denying the possibility of translation, Derrida negates the traditional understanding of translation, precisely because he questions the absolute privilege of any original to be translated by some text derivative of it, in a similar way as he challenges the priority of speech over writing and the priority of identity over difference. Since all words, text, and signification are immediately incorporated into and only function because of context or webs of significance, Derrida can say that he does "not believe that translation is a secondary and derived event in relation to an original language or text."[56]

The traditional project of philosophy has always presupposed and looked for a meaning or truth behind or beyond words, and thus it also has had to presuppose translatability, because if there is such a meaning apart from language, any language should in principle be equally able (or unable) to describe it. Traditionally seen, translation thus has to do with the transfer of meaning. But the impact of Derrida's thinking is exactly the realization that such a meaning is never pure, it is influenced or contaminated by language. Neither the "original" language nor the "translation" language can escape this predicament.

As we have seen, language functions out of difference, and as such the truth *behind* language is denied access *through* language.[57] This means that what is called the "original" is never original in the first place, since it never refers to its outside (meaning) any more or any better than the translation. So the notion of translation as the simple transfer of a univocal meaning from one language to another becomes problematic and needs to be rethought:

> [. . .] a notion of *transformation* must be substituted for the notion of translation: a regulated transformation of one language by another, of one text by another. We shall not have and never have had to deal with some "transfer" of pure signifieds that the signifying instrument—or "vehicle"—would leave virgin and intact, from one language to another, or within one and the same language.[58]

Why would the term "transformation" function better as a word for the process Derrida is describing? Because, according to Derrida, it captures two aspects of his ideas which "translation" fails to capture. First of all transformation implies that, as we said, there is no original and derivative; both texts can be eternally transformed by reading; there is an open-endedness to both. Secondly, transformation captures the fact of the radical "violence" of every translation, in that it always is something different from what is translated; as a matter of necessity it transforms instead of merely transfers the original. Now with this denial of the status of what is traditionally seen as the original text, Derrida is not so much denying that there is one text which is translated or transformed into another, but he is questioning the way the relationality between these texts is traditionally perceived. This means he questions the idea that the original would mean anything *outside* of or *without* its (ever-expanding) context, which consists precisely of its interpretations and translations. He thus argues that

> [. . .] the so-called original is in a position of demand with regard to the translation. The original is not a plenitude which would come to be translated by accident. The original is in the situation of demand, that is, of a lack or exile. The original is indebted a priori to the translation. Its survival is a demand and a desire for translation. . . .[59]

Again we see that Derrida challenges the idea of a fullness or completeness of any identity (the text to be translated) and insists on this identity being relative to difference and iterability (the text translated and as such, living).

With regard to Daoism the impact of following Derrida here would be that every so-called direct experience of *dao* can only become meaningful by placing it in context—in fact, it is always already immediately incorporated into contextuality—and that there is really no one meaning to the original classics, but that meaning only arises out of interpretations, something which the actual history of the commentaries and interpretations seems to endorse. What this means will become more obvious in the following chapters.

Now the real problem is not that since no translation is innocent, every translation means an interpretation. The real problem is that this interpretation however "does not *begin* [. . .] with what is commonly called translation. It *begins* as soon as *a certain type of reading* of the 'original' text is *instituted*."[60] How we read is what causes certain interpretations to flourish and others to wither. Taking this problem to comparative philosophy it would seem to be that our ideas of communication and of the function of language are not neutral, but might nevertheless appear or be presented as such. There is no neutral or meta-language, since "philosophy finds its element in so-called natural language. It has never been able to formalize itself integrally in an artificial language despite several fascinating attempts to do so in the history of philosophy."[61] In comparative philosophy one set or kind of these natural languages, being the Western metaphysical one, has always presented itself as the one that would be the most suited or best option, thus indirectly setting itself up as a model to which other languages have to concur. Speaking of public communication, Derrida has thus warned us that

> [. . . s]uch a discourse tends to impose a model of language that is supposedly favourable to this communication. Claiming to speak in the name of intelligibility, good sense, common sense, or the democratic ethic, this discourse tends, by means of these very things, and as if naturally, to discredit anything that complicates this model.[62]

What is profoundly "other" might then be excluded on the basis of lacking certain criteria, and we should be aware that it is our Western languages and way of thinking that impose those criteria, since they are full of metaphysical sensibilities. Yet the challenge for comparative philosophy is given by the very fact that "philosophy does not take place outside of a natural language,"[63] which causes Derrida to be extremely aware of the difficulties of translation, and of the seemingly impossible "necessity in fact of making cohabit in a same text or of grafting codes, motifs, registers, voices that are heterogeneous,"[64] which we can read as coming from different cultural and linguistic backgrounds.

How exactly do these views of language bear on the project of comparative philosophy? They are important since it is in language that intercultural encounters take place,[65] and Derrida seems to be suggesting that Western conceptuality is not suitable for such encounters:

> What then, is this encounter with the absolutely-other? Neither representation, nor limitation, nor conceptual relation to the same. The ego and the other do not permit themselves to be dominated or made into totalities by a concept of relationship. And first of all because the concept (material of language), which is always *given to the other*, cannot encompass the other, cannot include the other. [. . .] Language, therefore, cannot make its own possibility a totality and *include* within itself its own origin or its own end.[66]

Thus we need to get rid of the idea of our own supposed totality and work toward an understanding of ourselves that is more based on provisionality.

There has been criticism on Derrida's choice of words and his philosophy if you can still call it such, and much of this criticism amounts to saying he has retained a certain metaphysical perspective. He has been frequently accused himself of using a form of transcendental language which is then taken to inevitably point to some metaphysical position, especially since his work bears some resemblance to negative theology.[67] In *Différance*, for example, while stressing the fact that differance "is" not, he nevertheless speaks about "it" as "what makes possible the presentation of the being-present."[68] Reading this, one might get the idea of something which makes something else possible, and that looks like a transcendental or metaphysical principle. Similar criticisms have attacked Derrida's notions of spacing, the openness *between,* without which nothing functions, but which is implicit in thinking differance. And Derrida has spoken about differance as that which "produces"[69] differences and is "older"[70] than Heidegger's Being. Now as much as this is indeed the *use* of metaphysical language, it should by now be obvious that Derrida does not subscribe to its underlying ideas. He is well aware of the fact that he *has* to use this language, and that there is no other way, so that although it is a neo-logism, "*différance* remains a metaphysical name, and all the names that it receives in our language are still, as names, metaphysical."[71] But the fact that this name remains metaphysical is not because it points to some ineffable being beyond naming. The play of differance is not beyond anything, but as soon as we name it, it takes on metaphysical form. With this realization of what Derrida is about we turn to the relation of his thinking to other nonmetaphysical ways of thinking.

DERRIDA IN COMPARATIVE PHILOSOPHY

> We stand opposed to whatever would prohibit philosophy from [. . .] opening itself up to new objects in a way that knows no limit of principle,

> from recalling that it was already present there where no one wanted to acknowledge it.[72]

Having so far positioned Derrida only in regard to his critics or followers, in his relation to Heidegger, and in his thinking on language structures, his ideas have become only relatively clear. I now focus the final part of this chapter on Derrida himself. I am of course fully aware that relativity and relationality are to be given more attention and are in a way prior to and inherent in Derrida's thinking, much more so than seeing Derrida's thinking itself as a sort of identifiable entity, apart from these relations. This is so especially since much of this book focuses on these ideas of relationality. Presenting Derrida himself can then only mean taking a closer look at the way of thinking that he suggests and in this case especially with regard to its relevance for comparative philosophy, before moving more specifically to the nonmetaphysical thinking in some non-Western cultures. In this part I merely wish to give my view on what I think to be the most important features of his work and how they compare with the ideas of openness and difference that are so prominent in comparative philosophy, so as to have a background to work with.

Identity and Openness

To start again with differance, the clue to understanding (it) lies in its duplicity as differing and deferring. For the term differance, like other Derridean terms and no matter how many times we go back to it (and I certainly have), is forever erasing itself, which is to say that Derrida always considers differance and every word in general provisional, temporary, and inscribed in a web of signifiers that immediately take it up. It is for this reason that he has insisted, as we have seen, on not lingering too long with the term (or any term) itself, and has tried to use as many different terminologies as possible to underline this fact of provisionality and historicality of language and words in particular. Thus he says about "deconstruction" that "the word has interest only within a certain context."[73] These words then do not depict something outside of the text, but signal the play within writing in the broad sense which always situates us. This provisionality which does not give in to relativism is conducive to comparative thinking.

Another place where we could gain some insight into how Derrida sees his relation to other ways of thinking outside of the logocentric metaphysical tradition is to see what he has to say about "culture." The word "culture" is, according to Derrida, a "very obscure word,"[74] but this could be interpreted both in a negative and a positive way. If culture had not been "obscure" to start with, it would have suffered the same deconstruction as other words which appear "clear and distinct." But like identity, "a culture never has a single origin,"[75] and thus if we speak of any single culture as a unity, complete unto itself, we would have to say that "it would gather this center, relating it to itself, only in the extent that it would open it up to [. . .] divergence."[76] The completeness that is longed for is thus never achieved; relationality is always already inserted. This is so for language, identity, culture, and so on. Again Heidegger, as we have seen, does something similar in noting that the self and the other are always mutually involved, and it is only in becoming *unheimlich* (uncanny, not-at-home) that the self becomes it-self, which is only achieved and then has to be ever anew re-achieved (since it is only a relatively stable identity) by constantly and incessantly dealing with and going through what is "other." Derrida does the same when he suggests that we should stay in the *Unheimlichkeit* of the tension between self and other, in the sense that we admit affirmatively the impossibility of any closure, any strict identity. This is why traces of otherness continuously upset pure presence.

Combining the previous notions, Derrida, speaking of cultural identity, proclaims for Europe the task of actively living up to the ideas of openness and tolerance, in a recognition of the "always already there" of the other. This recognition entails what Derrida calls a double bind, in the following way:

> [. . . I]t is necessary to make ourselves the guardians of an idea of Europe, of a difference of Europe, *but* of a Europe that consists precisely in not closing itself off in its own identity and in advancing itself in an exemplary way toward what it is not, toward the other heading or the heading of the other, indeed—and this is perhaps something else altogether—toward the other *of* the heading, which would be the beyond of this modern tradition, another border structure, another shore.[77]

The double bind thus consists in affirming certain "European" values and ideas, insisting on their universality, however problematic this universality seems, while *at the same time* opening up toward and embracing difference and pluralism. This can only be done if we conceive of ourselves as provisionally right. Derrida thus makes a similar move here as in his other works, in describing a situation where values are not so much denied, but affirmed in a renewed and more complex situation or context.

Derrida frequently argues for exactly the kind of openness that is needed in comparative philosophy. In moves which challenge the conventional Western notions of philosophy as metaphysics, he argues for a different kind of thinking. The difference with Heidegger is in my opinion that Heidegger (actively) sought out different ways of thinking, as we have seen, mainly in the ancient Greek thinkers, poetic thinking, and Daoism. Derrida does not seem to make this move, but he does, as we have just seen, argue for openness toward that which is other. Similar to Heidegger, Derrida is interested in freeing thinking from what has become the too strictly metaphysical and scientistic, logic-based version of philosophy. As he says, he cares "about . . . a 'thinking,' let's say, that is not confined within the particular way of thinking that is philosophy or science. There are forms [. . .], there are perhaps 'pensées' that are more thinking than this kind of thinking called philosophy."[78] This move reminds us of Heidegger's statement that there might be "greater thinkers"[79] outside of metaphysical philosophy. Derrida also seems to think that his way of doing philosophy is that kind of thinking which is no longer purely philosophical, or it is differently philosophical, in that it questions the traditionally philosophical from various standpoints not necessarily philosophical in the traditional sense. Deconstruction is one name for this thinking, which "is perhaps no longer scientific or philosophical, in the sense in which these words can be determined today. It is in fact this indetermination and this very opening that we designate [. . .] by the word 'thinking.'"[80]

I would suggest that one of the functions of comparative philosophy is a similar thinking, in that in and through its comparisons it questions the standard conceptions, interpretations and explanations that traditional philosophy offers, from a differently philosophical or thoughtful standpoint, meaning from a culturally different paradigm of thinking. Derrida says that systems of thought which are different from those in the West are first of all "not necessarily limited" to the philosophical form of the West, neither are they "reducible to what, from a philosophical standpoint, we name with categories like 'culture,' 'worldview.'"[81]

The necessity for our limited way of thinking to seek discourse with other ways of thinking can be read from such statements, even though Derrida himself does not really use any other traditions in a serious way, neither for the purpose of showing the limitations of Western-style metaphysics (although there is some hinting at this aspect which I discuss later), nor for a development of what this other thinking might be. Yet the whole of Derrida's work is precisely concerned with boundaries, limits, limitations, and with their artificiality, and he argues persistently for the traversal and disruption of these limits. There are two points to this traversal. First of all there is the sense of traversal or disruption which we see in the fact that nothing is ever so full and complete as it might present itself. This is meant to show that everything only functions by constantly traversing through, and by being traversed through by, what it is not. Secondly, Derrida takes this idea of traversal as an imperative, as we have seen in the case of opening up toward difference or otherness. So what is important is that Derrida is not only suggesting the inevitability of the first kind of traversal, but closely connected to this is arguing for the *necessity* of philosophy to go beyond its own limits, "toward the encounter with other types of knowledge, discourse, writing."[82] Thus, reminiscent of Heidegger, Derrida argues that it is only by going *through* what is other that thinking works. The characteristics of philosophy as metaphysics could then be seen as having denied or belittled the necessity of this encounter.

The crucial thought in Derrida is that identity and difference are very much functions of each other. Only in asserting some fundamental openness and incompleteness *inside* the idea of identity, and thus problematizing its self-reliance, self-sufficiency, and wholeness can it be retained as a useful heuristic notion, meaning that identity is more an effect than it is an origin. This is, as we have seen briefly, also the idea behind the deconstruction of the Subject. The same then necessarily goes for difference or for the workings of differance, in that we have seen that we cannot think difference or differance without as much as a moment of affirmation or identity. In my opinion it is this idea which is fundamental to understanding Derrida: He argues for the provisionality of understanding, the constant deconstruction of fixed identities, the inadequacy of language, and the impossibility of assigning any lasting univocal meaning to "writing" or the context of our experience, because the play of differance and the notion of trace constantly challenge such univocality. And as such, Derrida's work is important for comparative philosophy, as it challenges preconceived notions of truth, reference, identity, and wholeness or completeness, thus opening the way for a new understanding of relationality and difference. It thus forms an interesting background from which we can explore the thinking in other cultures. We must now proceed to look at some places where Derrida flirts or plays with this possibility before we can acknowledge his possible place in comparative philosophy.

Derrida's Hints at Different Cultures

As we have seen in Chapter 1, Heidegger's position in comparative philosophy remained ambivalent. While he seemed to recognize important similarities between his own thinking and certain Eastern traditions, especially Daoism and to some extent Chan/Zen Buddhism, he also held quite strongly to his own interpretations and to his own originality as a thinker. In this light it might seem even more inappropriate to speak of Derrida in intercultural perspective. Apart from some places where he includes his own background and the Middle East in his writings, there are very few mentions of East Asia or other non-Western places or ways of thinking in his extensive oeuvre.[83] In *Glas* for example, there are lengthy discussions of Judaism and Christianity, but as we have seen these can easily be placed in the metaphysical way of thinking. Even in his recent papers on religion, gathered in the book *Acts of Religion,* it is again just the Abrahamic religions (Jewish, Christian, Muslim) that are interrogated. It seems Gayatri Spivak was right when she said in the preface to *Of Grammatology*:

> The relationship between logocentrism and ethnocentrism is indirectly invoked in the very first sentence of the "Exergue." Yet, paradoxically, and almost by a reverse ethnocentrism, Derrida insists that logocentrism is a property of the *West.* He does this so frequently that a quotation would be superfluous. Although something of the Chinese prejudice of the West is discussed in Part I, the *East* is never seriously studied or deconstructed in the Derridean text.[84]

It is indeed true that Derrida never offers any alternative or other reading of any Chinese philosophical tradition; he does not deconstruct China or any other non-Western thinking. He does however criticize the idea that Chinese as writing was seen in the earlier Western interpretations as being in an inferior position with regard to Western writing, which, as phonetic, was supposedly closer to the phoneme and thus to real meaning than the largely ideographic Chinese. Derrida challenges this outdated idea by pointing to the fact that "we have known for a long time that largely nonphonetic scripts like Chinese or Japanese included phonetic elements very early."[85] But the interesting thing about Chinese seems to be that these phonetic elements never overtook the ideogrammatic structure of Chinese, and as such Chinese never developed into the kind of phonetic or alphabetic language we find in the West. This made Derrida say that we have in the classical Chinese language "the testimony of a powerful movement of civilization developing outside of all logocentrism."[86] As we shall see shortly, Derrida seems to hold that logocentrism does not apply to the Chinese tradition since the move toward phonetic or alphabetic writing was never made, or was made only to a minor extent. However, Derrida seems content to stop just there; nothing is done with this observation, and it seems as though Derrida treats Chinese as just another way of writing, with the same ideas applying to it. This can be seen from the fact that he says that just as any other signs or sign structure, the Chinese signs can also never function without iterability and without being different to other signs in the system. At this stage Derrida does not subscribe to the idea that since the Chinese language is to some extent nonphonetic, it would therefore have some privileged access to reality, or that its signs would somehow be structurally different from "Western" signs.[87]

Later in his career Derrida seems to be slightly more nuanced in speaking of Eastern languages. When asked in an interview whether logocentrism is a Western phenomenon, he answers that

> [. . .] logocentric philosophy is a specifically Western response to a much larger necessity which also occurs in the Far East and other cultures, that is, the phonocentric necessity: the privilege of the voice over writing. [. . .] But this phonocentric necessity did not develop into a systematic logocentric metaphysics in any non-European culture. Logocentrism is a uniquely European phenomenon.[88]

The phonocentric necessity can quite simply be read as the historical fact that in any language the spoken word seems to have preceded the written. Yet it seems this necessity need not lead to a logocentric way of thinking. It is unfortunate that Derrida does not further elaborate upon this statement in the interview or elsewhere. For it seems to be that in his earlier statements in *Of Grammatology* Derrida was suggesting that phonocentrism is not a major factor in (classical) Chinese language. The idea in *Of Grammatology* seems to be that Derrida is not denying the link between phone and writing in Chinese, but that "it is a question of dislocating, through access to another system linking speech and writing [which would be the Chinese system], the founding categories of language and the grammar of the *episteme*."[89] The ingrained categories of Western metaphysics are challenged by the Chinese language structure, not so much because Chinese writing does not have a link to speech, but because this link is structurally different and therefore does not seem to admit of the radical prioritizing of speech over writing as was done in the Western metaphysical languages. Hwa Yol Jung[90] argues that Derrida has misread the Chinese language, and that in Chinese language there is such a prioritizing of speech, a claim which I do not go into now, but take up again in the Chapter 4.

Again it is unfortunate that Derrida does not seriously expand on this finding to enhance his own ideas, or to reflect more deeply on the possibilities of nonmetaphysical thinking which could be located in non-Western languages, which he could have done by expounding on this idea of Chinese language. Derrida fails to take the opportunity and returns to his own critiques of Western metaphysics, in that these passages (both in *Of Grammatology* and in the mentioned interview) that deal with a non-Western language function only as an imperative to question the traditional Western metaphysical notions of language.

However, the idea of a nonphonetic writing, or at least of a nonphonetic moment or movement in writing, is an important and returning issue for Derrida, especially in *Of Grammatology*, because such an idea "menaces substantiality, that other metaphysical name of presence and of *ousia*. First in the form of the substantive. Nonphonetic writing breaks the noun apart. It describes relations and not appellations."[91] And this is of course reminiscent of differance and its play-structure, the criticisms of both lasting identity and permanence behind appearance. What nonphonetic writing then suggests to Derrida is the possibility of a reinterpretation and revaluation of impermanence and relationality, of the ever-shifting perspectives that he himself has tried to show underlying all notions of permanence.

There are ways to read these attempts at de-absolutizing by Derrida in or into Daoism, and the structure of the Chinese language seems to play at least a part in making this possible. Although the temptation is always there to absolutize in a logocentric manner the "ideas" and "concepts" of East Asian traditions (an example being *The Dao* in capital letters translated back toward the reifying and "noun-thinking" substance ontology connected to Western standards), and this temptation is apparent both in Western and subsequent Asian readings and interpretations of the Daoist tradition, the resistance against this kind of reading could be a match between Derrida and (some forms of) Daoism. In other words, my point would be that it is still very much possible to take a Derridean, differential or nondualistic approach to Daoism, and this is not (just) imposing Derrida's standards on the Daoist tradition (at least not more so than "normal" interpretations impose their metaphysical ideas on them), but can, as I later show, (also) be read in the texts (and in differing commentaries and interpretations) themselves, in the ambiguity or equivocality, or polysemy (dissemination) of the "concepts" that are found in Daoism. All this means that I am not so much arguing against logocentric interpretations per se, I am however, with Derrida, arguing against their monopolizing of rightness and for the possibility of radically or very different readings.

The question then arises in how far Derrida has done justice to Chinese thinking and especially to Chinese language. It is obvious that Derrida's knowledge of Chinese language and philosophy was not very great, and maybe this can be one of the reasons for his reluctance to venture deeper into this area. Yet, as we have seen, Derrida does not simply reiterate the most common mistakes in interpreting Chinese, like the one that says that classical Chinese would be nonphonetic. In finding major nonphonetic elements in the Chinese language, though, Derrida saw himself justified in claiming a nonlogocentric movement present in Chinese thinking, to which I of course wholeheartedly agree. The point here is not to judge Derrida on his lack of knowledge of Chinese language and philosophy, but to understand that his hints at things "Eastern" are exactly that, hints at some way of thinking which might not be logocentric in nature. We must also understand that this hinting is done as part of and in support of the deconstruction of Western metaphysics, and that Derrida was therefore not what we would consider a comparative thinker. I have argued at the beginning of this chapter that it is in the way of thinking that Derrida advocates that there lies great value for comparative philosophy, but not in Derrida's personal efforts, at least very much less so than in the case of Heidegger.

There are, however, more occasions where Derrida hints at the East through wordplay, for example when he is arguing for the openness or the opening up of Europe toward that which is other, which comes from another shore. The quotation where Derrida propounds this kind of double bind, which we have encountered earlier, is immediately followed by a sentence in which Derrida says he wants to "orient"[92] himself, a play on words not to be taken too lightly in Derrida's work, for it is usually only in such playful hinting that he refers to the "East" and by that to any thinking other than Western metaphysical philosophy. Such hints we can also see in the wordplay on the French "est" (the "is" of which Western metaphysical thinking on Being speaks) versus "Est" (the East, which is "other") which Derrida develops in *Dissemination*. *Dissemination* seems to be by far the most intercultural book by Derrida, if only in the sense of this play on "Est," the relevance of the Chinese characters in Philippe Sollers' book *Numbers*, about which Derrida talks in a large part of *Dissemination*, and in the fact that some Chinese classics are mentioned. So let us take a closer look at these examples.

To start with Sollers' *Numbers*, Derrida approaches this text as something which absorbs its reader, in that it forces the reader to interpret and rewrite the text from the start. Any text requires this, but *Numbers*

> [. . .] is remarkable in that the reader [. . .] can never choose his own place in it. [. . .] There is at any rate no tenable place for him opposite the text, outside the text, no spot where he might get away with *not* writing what, in the reading, would seem to him to be *given, past*; no spot, in other words, where he would stand before an already *written* text."[93]

As was the case with translation, the text forces interpretation, but what is to be interpreted is not something simply given, but divided and fragmented. Because the text is "[n]umerous and plural in every strand [. . .]

it breaks up the complicity of belonging that ties us to our habitat, our culture, our simple roots."[94] These considerations already bear witness to a different approach to textuality, but the interesting thing for comparative thinking is that Derrida suggests that this idea of "a displacement and a rift, [. . .] the open system consisting of the repetition of rifts"[95] is at work in (among others) non-Western thinking, or what he calls the "enormous, condemned margins of our domestic library."[96] These margins contain such diverse works as to make it impossible to assign them a common place besides referring to them as nonmetaphysical in the traditional Western sense, and Derrida specifically mentions the *Daodejing* among these works.

The section on *Numbers* is complicated and difficult to read, and we need not go into details about Derrida's interpretation of Sollers' book itself, but we can grasp from the preceding fragments that a certain displacement of the metaphysical sensibilities usually found in Western philosophy is practiced in nonmetaphysical thinking, and that Derrida locates some non-Western thinkers and works in this nonmetaphysical thinking. This is a promising approach for comparative philosophy, but the question arises why Derrida locates non-Western thinking in the margins of *our domestic* library, which again seems to suggest that he has not looked at Eastern thinking from beyond the perspective of it being the West's "Other."

The next example has to do with the insertion of Chinese characters into the text of *Numbers*. Derrida suggests that this kind of gesture has been performed frequently (he thinks of Ezra Pound in particular), and that until now this kind of insertion has always been ornamental, or had to do with the fascination for what is illegible and thus incomprehensible. But in *Numbers*, the characters become seriously disruptive of the phonetic sequence, and as such they are "(under)mining the organism and the history of your domestic text,"[97] signaling an invasion of differences in the domestic text that "becomes more and more massive and inescapable, coming from the other side of the mirror—from the *est*."[98] I read this to mean that Derrida, in his own evasive and suggestive ways, argues that we (in the West) can no longer avoid an *Auseinandersetzung* with the East, since we are more and more aware of the East as our "other," and this means at the same time an awareness of our identity depending on such an *Auseinandersetzung*. The incompleteness, which nevertheless presents itself as a completeness, of the "est" or "being" of metaphysical philosophy should be solicited, interrupted, displaced, and supplemented by the "Est" or the thinking propounded in the East (if the East is seen as part of a nonmetaphysical tradition).[99] Even if we think not of Chinese characters, or any other non-Western script, but think instead of the Romanization of these scripts, we could still hold to the position that "foreign" words such as, for example, *dao* 道, *tian* 天, *ziran* 自然, *xin* 心, and so on do and should increasingly invade and thus interrogate our domestic texts. What I am trying to say is that our Western interpretations, in being metaphysical, can no longer come up with complete or satisfactory translations of these words, since these have no real equivalent in Western languages. Thus these "foreign words" do not so much disrupt the phonetic sequence, but they do disrupt our "metaphysical sequence," in that we can no longer assign them a place inside our traditional discourse. They therefore pose a challenge to our system.

The last example, which I shall mention only briefly, is the play of the numbers 3 and 4 in this section of *Dissemination*. Because it is too much to expound on all the instances where this play of numbers in *Numbers* functions in *Dissemination*, let us just take note of the idea behind it, which for Derrida means that the "three" symbolically stands for Western metaphysics (the trinity, dialectics), while the "four," which is found in Heidegger's *Geviert* (fourfold) and more general in Eastern thinking, challenges again this idea of completion (*Aufhebung*) of dialectics.[100]

In conclusion, these examples seem to point to a positive revaluation of the possibility of nonmetaphysical thinking as a critique of metaphysical philosophy. Even if in indirect terms (but does he ever speak in direct terms?), Derrida suggests the necessity of opening up toward other ways of thinking if the metaphysical West is not to smother itself in its closedness. Yet there is also what could be seen as a problematic aspect of these examples, which lies in the danger of which Heidegger has already warned us, and which consists in treating the East as "the other of the West," thus not so much in itself, but always as the mirror which is held before the Western eyes. And in saying "the East" we thus unjustifiably lump together many different traditions solely in their supposed otherness from Western philosophy. But we should be careful of reading Derrida in this way. Although on one hand it would seem that he does take the nonmetaphysical East merely as the metaphysical West's supplement, on the other hand the Derridean notion of "supplement" does not mean a derivative from or an unnecessary addition to what is being supplemented. As we have seen, the notion of supplement, which functions as another name in the line of differance, trace, and so forth, directly argues against such a traditional reading of supplementarity. In the same way as writing is not a supplement in the traditional sense to speech, so the "East" is not seen as a "mere" supplement to the "West." It is more the nonmetaphysical thinking found in some Eastern traditions which supplements the metaphysics found to be dominant in the history of Western philosophy. The supplement complements the lack or one-sidedness of Western metaphysics.[101]

It might be that Derrida is taking this strategy because of his conviction that it is hard—almost impossible—to get away from our metaphysical perspective (meaning we can only point to inconsistencies etc. in *our own* tradition). We are so to say "stuck" in the West, it is what we have to start with, and because of this he considers the (nonmetaphysical) East to be something which is "radically other" and thus always beyond our Western grasp. This would essentially mean that our metaphysical ideas are so ingrained as to not permit the opening toward this nonmetaphysical East under current metaphysical assumptions. Seen this way, it would make sense to call Derrida a relativist, as he points to the inability of metaphysics to go beyond its own categories. But this relativism would not mean that East and West can never meet. This criticism of relativism leveled against Derrida amounts to saying that East and West cannot meet because the East is seen by him as radically other, but to this I think we must add the crucial *supplement*: other to the Western *metaphysical* sensibilities. In short, when seen as two distinct identities with their own set of contradictory, mutually excluding, or incomparable assumptions and worldviews, East and West might indeed find it very hard to meet. But Derrida's efforts are located in trying to overcome these sensibilities (while realizing he is still at least somewhat in them), and he constantly tries to point to the relationality and provisionality of these so-called identities and the priority (or at least and in the end the equality) of this provisionality and relationality over any strict identities. If relationality thus comes "before" any clear-cut understandings, if, as we shall see shortly, the "other" is "always already there," if otherness thus always distorts the pure notion of identity and reinscribes it, then much of the criticism of relativism loses force. Things are not complete and full unto themselves, but as we have seen, the fact that Derrida criticizes this fullness or completeness does not mean we are left with meaninglessness per se. The complication to which Derridean thinking points is not a rejection of value or meaning, it is just a restriction on its possibilities; its self-understanding is widened instead of narrowed in that it is shown that the dualistic presuppositions of metaphysical philosophy only function relative to nondualistic sensibilities found in some nonmetaphysical ways of thinking. It is now time to take a closer look at the notion of "other" or "otherness" as it is used in Derrida's work.

"The Other Is Already There, Irreducibly."[102]

The notion of (the) "other" or alterity in Derrida's work is a difficult one. We have already seen that deconstruction "is always deeply concerned with the 'other' of language" and that "[t]he critique of logocentrism is above all else the search for the 'other' and the 'other of language.'"[103] So the nonconcept of "otherness" is an important one in Derrida's work, and a persistent theme.[104] The problem with this other or alterity then seems to be how it can possibly have any effect on the self, since if it is considered as the other of language, then it is also the other of all our reference structures, thus inaccessible. Elsewhere Derrida has said: "Every other is completely other."[105] In a similar way to what is called "different," what is "other" always escapes our efforts at appropriation, yet in a strange way it seems constitutive of our being while remaining ever singular and evasive. It is thus exemplary of the double bind we find in so much of Derrida's work, the combination of possibility and impossibility.

With regard to this supposedly total and radical alterity of what is considered "other," it is my opinion that Derrida would not want to be held to this relativist position. We can again take a look at a work where Derrida takes on Heidegger: *Aporias*.[106] Here Derrida argues that Dasein cannot be understood totally from its capacity for dying, its possibility of not being there. For if this death is what is completely other to Dasein, death can never become constitutive to Dasein. Therefore, Derrida argues that death is never totally other from the living Dasein; there is always dying in living. For comparative thinking this is a useful idea since it tells us that what is other is never really so radically other as not to allow some sort of communication or encounter. Other and self are mutually inserted in each other.

We must now take a closer look at the possibility or even necessity of this encounter. What is "other" is not something we can summon with our language, it is something which has to come of its own, but as Derrida says: "Yet it is necessary to prepare for it; for to allow the coming of the entirely other, passivity, a certain kind of resigned passivity for which everything comes down to the same, is not suitable. Letting the other come is not inertia opening to anything whatever."[107] This reminds us immediately of Heidegger's *Gelassenheit*. *Gelassenheit* is also not anything like a passive attitude; it is an active opening up of your own thought structures which is necessary for other ways of thinking to find an entrance. As we see now, Derrida is arguing for a similar attitude, a responsible opening. But the difference with Heidegger could be that it is actually deconstruction(s) which provide the possible opening "by bending [the] rules with respect for the rules themselves in order to allow the other to come or to announce its coming in the opening of this dehiscence. That is perhaps what we call deconstruction."[108] This notion of "dehiscence" also features in *Limited Inc.*, where it is similarly used as opening toward what is other. The Oxford English dictionary lists "dehiscence" as: "gaping, opening by divergence of parts"[109] and states that the term is mostly used in plant life. It signals the opening toward what is other in the opening of the flower or seed, and that opening up what is closed is therefore constitutive for life. Thus the space created by opening up our thought structures, by deconstructing what is supposedly an identity, is what makes any intercultural encounter between the self and the other possible.

The status of the other is therefore not something which can be subsumed in Hegelian fashion under the category of the same. It is the other that is equally active, and this can be read in the closing lines of *Psyche: Inventions of The Other,* where Derrida says that "[t]he call of the other is a call to come, and that happens only in multiple voices."[110] This can be read in a couple of ways, and the English translation makes this only slightly apparent. In French, the sentence runs as follows: "L'autre appelle à venir et cela n'arrive qu'à plusieurs voix." First of all, that 'the other calls to come' can be read as the other coming to us or inviting us to come. Then, since the future (*avenir*) is always uncertain and to a certain extent undecidable, any arriving of the other (*arrive*), if it happens at all, invariably involves multiple voices, and thus not an unequivocal one. The point Derrida seems to be making is that the Western idea of a subject–object encounter is an idealistic and therefore unrealistic abstraction of any real encounter. Especially in the comparative field, any encounter with what is other can never beforehand be appropriated, it is an encounter with multiple active voices and thus is structurally open-ended. Yet it is always there. Of interest for comparative philosophy is what Geoffrey Bennington summed up well by saying that in Derrida's work "[t]he point [. . .] is not to reintegrate remains into philosophy, but [. . .] to introduce a radical nondialectizable alterity into the heart of the same"[111] and therefore to remain with the tension this implies in the *Auseinandersetzung* that deconstruction is.

In this way Derrida has always seen himself as both on the inside and on the outside of philosophy. He remains inside because he often asks the same or similar questions as philosophy, and because he wants to expand the notion of philosophy to encompass more ways of thinking. He is outside as he has, like Heidegger, identified philosophy with Western metaphysics and ontotheology, and he tries to overcome this one-sided way of thinking in a certain way, as Heidegger had done before him. He is also outside of philosophy as this relentless questioning and thinking that is often given the generic name of deconstruction takes on many forms that are not easily identifiable within the stricter versions of philosophy, and he has thus often been ostracized from the community of "real" philosophers.

Derrida's point is that alterity and outside are not to be subsumed under traditional philosophical categories, or comfortably integrated into our system; they are to remain outside so as to upset the comfort of the inside. They are however part of the larger thinking discourse.

One other interesting aspect for comparative philosophy of the idea of the "other" or alterity in Derrida is that he seems to link these notions closely to those of duty and responsibility, in ways which are reminiscent of Emmanuel Levinas.[112] The singularity of every other that has already been hinted at makes every other irreplaceable, and as such we are responsible for it. Derrida establishes this by extending the notion of responsiveness to the other (which is the sort of Heideggerian *Gelassenheit* which we have already encountered) toward that of responsibility.

In all this openness toward the East or what is other we must not forget that this is much more an interpretation of the possibilities of Derrida's work, and not so much that Derrida has actively pursued this *Auseinandersetzung* himself, although his later works do focus a lot on international problematics. We should therefore look closely at some of his (non)concepts and see how they can provide a basis for a Derridean, and that means a nonmetaphysical, reading of Daoism. To again start with differance, Derrida says that "'There is no name for it': a proposition to be read in its *platitude*. This unnameable is not an ineffable Being which no name could approach: God, for example. This unnameable is the play which makes possible nominal effects, the relatively unitary and atomic structures that are called names. . . ."[113] Derrida's insistence that his work is *not* negative theology should prohibit us from taking the direction of the Christian-Buddhist dialogue which is evident in, for example, the works of the Kyoto school. In my opinion Derrida is not talking in terms of transcendence and immanence, the play of differance/trace is wholly immanent, and there is no outside. The "other" of language is not another or superior being. As Derrida insists, and I shall have to quote at length:

> Already we have had to delineate *that différance is not*, does not exist, is not a present-being (*on*) in any form; and we will be led to delineate also everything *that* it *is not*, that is, *everything*; and consequently that is has neither existence nor essence. It derives from no category of being, **whether present or absent**. And yet those aspects of *différance* which are thereby delineated are not theological, not even in the order of the most negative of negative theologies, which are always concerned with disengaging a superessentiality beyond the finite categories of essence and existence, that is, of presence, and always hastening to recall that God is refused the predicate of existence, only in order to

> acknowledge his superior, inconceivable, and ineffable mode of being. Such a development is not in question here, and this will be confirmed progressively.[114]

Exactly because the notion of differance is beyond or not of the order of anything "present or absent," it cannot be reduced to negative theology. Derrida's play of differance is nothing outside of the play of differences; the master narrative, however negatively stated, is totally denied. There literally is nothing ineffable. The "nothing" of negative theology is not the object of Derrida's efforts: "Deconstruction is not an enclosure in nothingness, but an openness towards the other."[115]

Related to this is the idea of the blank, the empty space between words, the spacing, whether in speech or writing, which Derrida takes to function as the condition of possibility for words to function as relative identities. Derrida says of the empty space, the blank: "since it has no meaning, it is not *The* blank proper, the transcendental origin of the series."[116] Again there is a reading that tries to undo any metaphysical notions of transcendentality, or of first principles, in favor of an idea of the play of the world itself.

The same could be said for the notions of supplement, trace, and all those other words Derrida has used. They do not denote a transcendental presence of any sort; they are carefully designed exactly to denounce this metaphysical way of thinking. A supplement is not accidental to a fullness; a trace is not a trace of something absent which by language or thinking can be brought to presence. What Derrida is about is just the way of the world where the metaphysical need for identities, closure, neat demarcations, and an idea of the Other as a metaphysical ineffable presence beyond our means, ideas which are never really possible, is exposed *as* this metaphysical need, and through this exposure deconstruction gives us back at the same time these ideas in a different possible setting, since they are the only structures we have.

CONCLUDING DERRIDA

To come to a conclusion of this chapter, I think we could say the following things about Derrida and his interest in comparative philosophy. First, it is obvious that it is in his work, and in the way he thinks and writes, his strategies of deconstruction, and not so much in any actual intercultural encounter between himself as a thinker and another cultural sphere, that we have to locate Derrida with regard to comparative philosophy. And this requires very close reading and a constant awareness of the difficulties and implications of what comparative philosophers try to achieve, as well as an awareness that we are almost always reading "out of context."

Second, we can use his (non)concepts for an intercultural understanding by comparing them with the function of some (non)concepts of other cultures, if we stay aware of the fact that, for Derrida, these concepts are not the names of "transcendental signifieds" in any way, and that as such they ultimately have no value and are therefore used "under erasure." As long as we keep that in mind, we can use words like differance, supplement, spacing, trace, and so on safely to further our understanding of thinking in other cultures.

Third, much of his work revolves around the possibility of the impossible, or the impossibility of the possible, and that, as such, any relation between self and other will always remain ambiguous. The other is never radically other, but also never fully to be appropriated. There is always a rest, a trace left by the other in the self. Dealing with these aporias, which are inevitable, is what Derrida does in his work. But he does not deal with them in the sense that Western philosophy has always done, by denying them their place and pushing them to the margins of philosophy, but by showing how we continuously *have* to deal with them, with the contamination and infusion of what is other into what is considered the self. Ambiguity, as we saw in Heidegger's equivocality (*Mehrdeutigkeit*), is not a bad thing; it is the possibility for not closing off our understanding to things different, and it is always there. Both Heidegger and Derrida then try to think relationality, the in-between. Not avoiding this ultimate relationality, but giving full justice to it, is also what comparative philosophy is about, and it is thus that a close reading of Derrida can help comparative thinking in how to approach thinking in other cultures.

CHAPTER THREE

Rereading Daoism; The Other Way

> For the Daoist, there is an intoxicating bottomlessness to any particular event in our experience.[1]

In the previous chapters I have provided an interpretation of Heidegger and Derrida that puts them in a new light with regard to comparative philosophy. In this chapter I offer a different-from-standard reading of some of the classical texts of Daoism, mostly of the *Daodejing* and the *Zhuangzi*. In following up on the conclusions of the first two chapters on Heidegger and Derrida, I explore the possibility of an interpretation of Daoism that is not logocentric, not ontotheological or metaphysical in its nature—in other words, a deconstructionist reading. With this intention also comes the realization that we should probably not speak of Daoism as a single entity or tradition with an identifiable core metaphysical teaching, but rather see 'it' more as a loosely connected variety of texts with overlapping but also different intentions and purposes. Traditional interpretations of Daoism have been at pain to explain the underlying unity of the Daoist textual corpus, whereas this unity is now supposed to be at least not so strict.[2] I should therefore explain what I mean by the notion of Daoism that I put forward here. Initially, in line with Derrida's findings, we should say that it is in principle impossible to separate the foundational texts of Daoism from their philosophical, political, or religious interpretations and developments in any strict sense. In the case of religious Daoism, which developed not too long after the tentative historical dates of appearance of the classical Daoist texts, and which as a whole has had more influence on the Chinese way of life, including intellectual life, it might seem impertinent not to take this development into account. Nevertheless, many scholars have pointed to the differences between philosophical Daoism (*Daojia* 道家) and religious Daoism (*Daojiao* 道教).[3] Maybe I could explain and justify my choice for looking mainly at the *Daodejing* and the *Zhuangzi* as philosophical works by looking at Heidegger's notion of *Seinsvergessenheit*. The fact, Heidegger would say, that there has been a whole history (both in the West and in China) of more than two thousand years of a certain dominant interpretation (if there can be such a thing) does not make this interpretation in any way justified as the only one. More or less beginning with Plato, the (wrongly named) Presocratics were interpreted according to the Platonic ideas that helped shape the metaphysical history of Western Being, in itself in fact a one-sided approach to Being which focused on beings and the highest being of them, instead of on the Being of beings. We could argue then, that so too have the Daoist classics been predominantly interpreted in "a certain way" that has been instrumental in their dissemination and understanding in the wider world. In practice this means that I think there are other, equally if not even more plausible, interpretations of the classical texts of Daoism possible.

I focus on philosophical Daoism instead of religious Daoism. For the most part, those works that belong to the philosophical tradition, meaning the *Daodejing*, the *Zhuangzi*, but also the *Liezi* and parts of the *Huainanzi*, argue against the idea of immortality, as well as against the arising cults related to immortality, whereas religious Daoism seems mainly focused on just that same immortality. The distinction is only of importance here because in focusing on philosophical Daoism I would like to explore the possibility of a reading of the Daoist classics that does not presuppose any transcendent quality.

In looking at the history of Daoism, we have to be aware that even the name Daoism did not appear until much later than the classical texts themselves, and was coined in the belief that both the *Daodejing* and the *Zhuangzi*, together with other texts, somehow shared some core philosophy through their sometimes similar, but often different teachings. I agree with A. C. Graham when he says that the *Daodejing* and the *Zhuangzi* "do share one basic insight, that while other things move spontaneously on the course proper to them, man has separated himself from the Way by reflecting, posing alternatives, and formulating principles of action."[4] But in a way this is not to be seen as a definition of Daoism, because, as the title of Graham's well-known book suggests, all or most of the early Chinese thinkers were in some way 'disputers' of the *dao*. All major classical Chinese thinkers were 'Dao-ists' in that they were involved in second-order thinking about specific *daos* and which one among them humankind should follow. Only those who were subsequently named the Daoists were involved in questioning the whole idea and notion of *dao* itself. I think it is therefore right to use the name Daoism to denote that strand of Chinese philosophy that particularly addresses the question of what *dao* (is), or rather how *dao* functions. This should not however blind us to the fact that Daoism as a name is a retrospective invention that brings together diverse texts. But in the interest of clarity I propose to stick by the name of philosophical Daoism and to write it with a capital letter, since it is admittedly a fluid, but still identifiable and heuristically viable, description of the way of thinking that is propounded in the *Daodejing* and the *Zhuangzi*.

On the Romanization of the character *dao* I am of a different opinion. For reasons that are becoming more and more obvious, I think that writing *Dao* with a capital letter perpetuates the idea of reading it solely as a noun denoting a substance or a something, and thereby facilitating the idea of seeing 'it' as a transcendent or metaphysical entity beyond the 'ten thousand things.' Other words, such as *tian* 天, *you* 有 and *wu* 無, *ziran* 自然, and so forth, have suffered a similar fate, and I am not alone in my intention to argue against this kind of metaphysical interpretation. Chad Hansen, for example, has argued extensively against imposing such Western background assumptions on classical Chinese language and thinking.[5] In unison with recent post-modern scholarship on, and the consequently non-metaphysical reading of, the Daoist classics, I therefore propose to write the Romanization of *dao* in lower case letters, not capitalized, except when it is capitalized in quotations.

In my opinion, most traditional Western readings have presupposed either of two hypotheses in trying to understand Daoism. One is that Daoism has to some degree the same sort of principles functioning behind it as Western philosophy, and thus interpretations of this kind have almost invariably focused on reading Daoism according to the standards of the interpreters. In other words, they have thought of Daoism in Western categories, even while acknowledging profound differences in the way these categories are employed. Imposing these categories on the Chinese classics was defended by stating that the Chinese people were supposed to at least share our (Western) ideas about intelligibility, or put rather simply, whatever the differences between Western and Chinese philosophy, we were eventually all talking about the same things, we were all thinking in the same categories, because those are the categories of thinking per se. For example, Fung Yu-lan says that "[e]very philosophy has that which is permanent, and all philosophies have something in common. This is why philosophies, though different, can yet be compared with one another and translated one in terms of the other."[6] This way of thinking seems to rely too much on the sameness of what is considered permanent; it seems to imply that what different traditions consider permanent has to be the same, as it can then be translated.

The other hypothesis is that Daoism is so different from Western thinking that any form of access to it using philosophical means is denied, and Daoism is then usually taken as a form of mysticism that is beyond any philosophical or rational approach. This hypothesis is common as well, and it works from the similar mindset that if we cannot explain Daoism from our Western philosophical perspectives, in line with our own presuppositions and categories, then it has to be beyond explanation per se and therefore can be dismissed as mystical, mythological, or obscure, and with that be discarded in much the same way as Western mysticism and myths were disqualified to be "real" philosophy.

Now I have to reiterate that I do not think these interpretations are either completely wrong or have no basis at all, I merely wish to convey the possibility of different readings that are also and at least equally possible, and thus point to the extraordinary richness of the Daoist classics. I would like, however, with the help of some divergent readings that have already been offered and with textual evidence, to challenge some of the standards of reading and thereby take a different approach to the *Daodejing* and the *Zhuangzi*. I also focus on other texts of what is called the Daoist tradition, such as the *Liezi* and the *Huainanzi*, and some of the neo-Daoists, for support of this different reading. My argument is that such a non-metaphysical reading is not only possible, but that this possibility of a different reading is actually a better reflection of Daoist sensibilities on the whole than the traditional interpretations. But to establish this, we must first take a closer look at these traditional interpretations.

METAPHYSICAL READINGS OF DAOIST PHILOSOPHY

> *tao* meant "the way the universe works"; and ultimately, something very like God, in the more abstract and philosophical sense of that term.[7]

To me this is an instance of metaphysical readings of Daoism, but I should first give an explanation of what I mean by metaphysical readings or interpretations. This tradition as I use it has not so much to do with the way Daoism itself has evolved throughout history. The tradition of metaphysical readings I am referring to is mostly that of the early Western scholars of sinology, translation, and philosophy, who have tended to take an approach to Daoism that is coherent with Western metaphysics in many of its features. For several reasons this approach has also caught on in China itself and elsewhere in the non-Western academic world, and many early and contemporary Asian scholars, having been educated in the same principles in Western(-ized) establishments of scholarship, work from the same perspectives.[8] By this tradition I then understand the approach to Daoism that is metaphysical or transcendental in nature, and thus works from a dualist perspective, an approach which in other words shows the inheritance of the ideas found and valued in mainstream Western philosophy.[9] I have to agree with Chad Hansen that there are two main features of this established tradition of scholarship in classical Chinese philosophy. These are an overemphasis on the importance of Confucianism and the import of Western conceptual structures to understand the Chinese classics.[10] I try to explain these features by focusing on certain translations and interpretations by scholars from the last two centuries.

To these main features can be added a third one, whereby some commentators interpret the early classical texts by standards of later times. Thomas Cleary, for example, speaks extensively about later developments of religious Daoism and meditation in his introduction to the translation of the *Daodejing*.[11] My point is that we have to be very cautious when looking at earlier works from a later perspective, so as not to impose features of these later developments on the classics. If we remember Heidegger's case of Plato and the "Presocratics" this should be obvious. Of course we cannot help the fact that our understanding always begins from a certain point. We must however be open to the fact that other understandings from different perspectives are equally possible. In the case of classical Chinese thinking, although historically different, this means that we should be aware of how we measure different strands of thinking against Confucius and the Confucian tradition.

On this basis again I see no objection against not taking the whole history of Daoism into account in my reading of classical Daoist texts. At the same time of course, as we shall see, this does not mean that the commentarial tradition of philosophical Daoism is irrelevant.

Among the first Western interpretations and translations of Chinese classics were those by Roman Catholic and Jesuit priests and other missionaries who went to work in China. While contemporary comparative philosophy owes a lot to these pioneers, it is quite naturally to be expected that they were biased in several ways; as missionaries they came with their fixed ideas and motives and tried to read these ideas into Chinese classics wherever they could, or otherwise to denounce the works where they could not find appropriate similarities. Their translations obviously show this bias, both in how they translated and in which works were considered for translation. Herbert Giles, in his translation of the *Zhuangzi*, translates *tian* as God and says that Zhuangzi offered an anti-materialist answer to Confucius. Inserting obviously Christian ideas, he states that those "who are dominated by a religious craving for something better than mortality, find in his [Zhuangzi's] pages much agreeable solace against the troubles of this world, with an implied promise of another and a better world to come."[12] One example to show that in his translations Giles turns *dao* into a metaphysical principle of substance will make this clear. Thus the passage in Chapter 2 of the *Zhuangzi* which Graham translates as "The Way has never known borders, saying has never had norms"[13], is translated by Giles as "Before conditions existed, TAO was. Before definitions existed, Speech was."[14] Those who read translations of Chinese texts like those of Giles will have no difficulty in thinking that East and West were indeed talking about the same thing.

But even in those days there was already some criticism against overly optimistic readings from a Western (religious) viewpoint. James Legge, for example, already argued against translating *dao* and *tian* along Christian Western lines in the introduction of his work on Daoism.[15] Yet in the same introduction Legge insists that Daoism was wrong in opposing knowledge, and that it was only right that "the Simplicity of the Tâo disappear before Knowledge."[16] The use of capital letters and the idea behind this sentencing is enough to show that Legge definitely saw Daoism and *dao* as some sort of transcendent and mystical principle, not fully developed though and thus to be overcome by the superior Western understandings of philosophy, science, and religion, indeed as we shall see in Hegelian fashion. Other early thinkers who had any interest in China exhibit a similar bias, whether positive or negative. Chinese classics were read from the viewpoint of Western philosophy, religion, or science. Two major philosophical examples of this type are Hegel and Leibniz. Hegel never seriously engaged Chinese thinking, but he incorporated what he knew into the grand structure of the development of the absolute *Geist* toward its culminating moment, Hegel himself. He thereby incorporated Chinese philosophy into the same history as the West, albeit at a lower level of development, and stagnated at a phase of thinking overcome by the dialectics of the superior West. Leibniz, on the other hand, was much more positive about Chinese philosophy, Confucianism in particular, and he saw Chinese religious thinking and language as a means to escape from the shortcomings of Western philosophy, a sort of salvation and reinvention of the perennial organicist philosophy he was after. He especially thought of Chinese characters as representative of a universal language, since he supposed that they expressed universal ideas directly. Consequently he was disappointed when he found out that this was not the case. Although he took an active interest in Chinese language, Leibniz was not well versed enough in classical Chinese language or history, so his interpretations of Chinese thinking were naturally colored by the available translations in more than one way.[17] Not many translations were available, and we already saw that those translations available to Leibniz were biased by the views of the translators. The missionaries took the most interest in neo-Confucianism and its focus on the principle *li*, which they found easiest to transport toward Christianity and the personal God, and consequently most translations were of neo-Confucianist works. The main sources Leibniz used were thus heavily Christian in orientation and he himself accordingly displayed that same bias, even to the extent of defending the Chinese against the accusation made by certain missionaries that they were atheists![18]

Thus in general we can say that most early translators and other scholars read and interpreted in a theological and logocentric style, thinking that the dualistic or one–many metaphysical tradition of the West with its focus on some primal source, the reality behind the appearance, be it in the form of a creative entity or of an unalterable principle, must have some sort of correlation in the Chinese history, or trying to appropriate what was known of Chinese thinking for their own projects. Today still, this kind of interpretation is favored by many. The option of translating *dao* as "The Way," a steady feature of this metaphysical reading, is still the most obvious and popular.

Enter the early days of comparative philosophy, in which some progress was made, but in which certain features of the religious, but more of the related metaphysical, background of the scholars remained largely unchallenged. And we have to add that it is not just Western, but also some Chinese scholars who operate within this metaphysical system. Wing-tsit Chan can be squarely located within this metaphysical framework when he says that Daoism "oppos[ed] Confucian conformity with non-conformity and Confucian worldliness with a transcendental spirit,"[19] seemingly lumping together philosophical Daoism (*Daojia*) with the religious Daoism (*Daojiao*) that developed later. Both the *Daodejing* and the *Zhuangzi* are said to contain mystical elements and to regard *dao* as "transcendental."[20] Although admittedly Chan mentions that both the *Daodejing's* and the *Zhuangzi's* concerns are with this world, the classification of mysticism and transcendentality for both speaks of a metaphysical prejudice. Chan also compares Zhuangzi[21] to Hegel in a couple of instances, and although again he expresses reservations as to the possibilities of such a comparison, I think he is wrong in suggesting that Zhuangzi's opposites which produce and imply each other are therefore "identical" and are thus part of a "finite series."[22] This move is meant to bring Zhuangzi in the direction of Hegel's dialectic, but I think this is problematic as the yin-yang working of opposites that Zhuangzi espouses does not suggest identity to one who is not enamoured by the metaphysical idea of oneness as a dialectic form of identity or unity or *Aufhebung* in the Western sense of these words. In short, my thesis is that the ideas of unity and identity in the West are different from those supposed equivalents of unity and identity in classical China. It is exactly the construal of certain ideas of Daoism to fit into such Western categories that has been at the forefront of comparative philosophy for too long. Herrlee Creel does something similar in the following:

> *Tao* at first meant "road" or "path." From this it developed the sense of a method, and of a course of conduct [. . .] And the Confucian *tao* was also an entity, since an individual or a state might "possess the *tao*" or "lack the *tao*." But this Confucian *tao* was still only a principle; it was never regarded as a substance, like the *tao* of the Taoists.[23]

Interpreting *the Dao* as an ontological substance is but one of many instances of reading Daoism according to Western metaphysical ideas and standards. Statements like these easily confuse the reader into believing that Daoism is really about transcendence, as opposed to Confucianism which would not be.[24] It shows that interpreters were anxious to regard *dao* as *the* metaphysical principle around which all of the Daoist classics were essentially circumnavigating. Needless to say, this was also done to impose on Daoism the sort of unity and teleology it seemed to be lacking from a Western perspective. I try to show later that other interpretations of what *dao* is or means are more viable.

There are other terms to point to, whose translation into Western languages has also asserted a metaphysical meaning of Chinese characters and grammar. For example, *xin* 心 was usually translated as "mind," suggesting first of all a mind-body dualism largely absent in Chinese thinking, and second failing to denote that *xin* primarily means the heart, which was considered the locus of thinking in classical China. *Xin* is thus, for lack of a real equivalent in Western languages, better translated as "heart-mind," since the notion of *xin* points, as Hall and Ames have made clear, "indifferently to activities we would classify as thinking, judging, and feeling, and arguably reflects all three modalities of the tripartite model in an undissected form."[25] Another famous example is *tian* 天, usually translated as "Heaven." It is really impossible to read this Western term without the immediate connotations of Christianity and the other Abrahamic religions with an identifiable afterworld of transcendent quality. Or the translation of *wuwei* 無為 by "no action" or "doing nothing," which immediately conjures up images of quietistic sage hermits who have detached themselves from this world to meditate in forests or caves or on mountaintops, whereas *wuwei* is much better translated as "non-assertive action" or something similar pointing to the fact that Daoists do not do nothing, they do things differently, that is without imposing on the natural inclinations of things. Of course these statements need to be backed up by textual evidence which will provide an understanding of why the nonmetaphysical readings and translations are a better reflection of classical Daoism. I provide this later on in this chapter.

The metaphysical prejudice is also present in the translation of *you* 有 and *wu* 無 as "Being" and "Nothing" or "Nonbeing," respectively. Graham, amongst others, has pointed out that these are misrepresentations of the classical Chinese characters and language, in which *you* and *wu* respectively denote more a presence, or having, and nonpresence, or not-having, of things.[26] There is thus at least a very different metaphysics at work if we can even speak of metaphysics here. The relation between Being and Nothing in the West is different from that of *you* and *wu* in Daoism. This means that categories like Being and Nothing, when used as translation of *you* and *wu* respectively, import a way of thinking that is foreign to classical China. I explain this in more detail later in this chapter; for now it is important to remember that Western categories, concepts, and ways of thinking are easily transported into different cultures. In general we can say that importing Western notions, which were then supposed to delineate their Chinese equivalents, was for a long time the (almost) unquestioned standard, especially in early sinology, as the following quote from Arthur Waley makes abundantly clear:

> *tao* meant "the way the universe works"; and ultimately, something very like God, in the more abstract and philosophical sense of that term. Now it so happens that all the meaning-extensions of this word *tao* (even including the last: "I am the Way") also exist in European languages, so that Western scholars have had no difficulty in understanding it.[27]

To say that *dao* meant "the way the universe works" is not that false, but then to go on to say that it *ultimately* means "God," and then to state that since this is so Western scholars have no problem understanding it, is indeed a perfect example of importing Western ways of thinking into a foreign culture, a failure at the very least to notice the many different meanings of *dao* which are not so easily transferable.

Burton Watson can be said to be guilty of that other form of scholarship on philosophical Daoism that has been predominant, which consists in seeing it as an essentially mystical tradition, beyond the realm of rational explanation. In his introduction to the complete translation of the *Zhuangzi* of 1968, he makes it clear that to him this is the work of a mystic, who has found freedom from the normal world in clinging to the "inexpressible Absolute."[28] Although his introduction to the revised version of the *Zhuangzi, Basic Writings* is much more refined, he evidently still considers it a work of mystical thinking, of freeing yourself from the world.[29] I later argue that Daoism is not about freeing oneself *from* the world, but about inserting oneself *into* the world in a different way.

Fung Yu-lan argues that "the craving for something beyond the present actual world is one of the innate desires of mankind, and the Chinese people are no exception to this rule."[30] Although he takes caution not to thereby say that Chinese are religious in the same way as Western people are, he nevertheless compares the Daoist sage-king to the Platonic philosopher-king[31] and says that "the spiritual achievement of the Chinese sage corresponds to the saint's achievement in Buddhism, and in Western religion."[32] I might seem a bit unfair here to Fung Yu-lan, in that overall he is quite careful not to conflate the Chinese and Western traditions, and in the introduction to his translation of the *Zhuangzi* he keeps repeating that *dao* is not about transcendence. But he did see the *Zhuangzi* as proposing a similar religiousness as Spinoza, where God is everywhere in the world, but not something outside of it.[33] Thus I think expressions such as the preceding give us an insight into how normal it was to use Western assumptions, terminology, and so on in trying to make Chinese philosophy understandable for a Western audience, a process in itself to be applauded, but which came with certain presuppositions that can be read in most of the early Sinologists, and which consequently made it very easy for later interpreters to start off on the wrong foot. Notions of religiousness and mysticism were essentially superimposed on Daoism. Even if we grant that working from our own languages and backgrounds is inevitable, we still need to stay aware that there are many forms of mysticism, or of mystical states and approaches. I try to explain later that if we insist on understanding Daoism as a form of mysticism, it must be made clear that Daoism would then function as an atypical sort in being a this-worldly mysticism, and is then not similar to the Western form of mysticism that seeks a unification of humanity with a transcendent God or Heaven.

Another instance of such imported reasoning is found in D. C. Lau's translation of the *Daodejing.* As he says in the introduction, "the entity called the *tao* existed before the universe came into being. [. . .] It has an essence which is genuine, and this genuineness is vouched for by the existence of the universe which it has produced and continues to sustain."[34] This passage sounds similar to that of Fung Yu-lan mentioned earlier, in that it reminds us of Spinoza. Although Lau is quick to add that to say that the *dao* "produced" the universe is really "misleading" and only works "in a figurative sense,"[35] he nevertheless denotes *dao* as an "essence" and calls "it" an "entity," which seems to be the same mistake made in the history of Western philosophy again and again, to which Heidegger drew our attention when he tried to point to the ontological difference of Being and beings. The same idea of essentiality is expressed by Isabelle Robinet, when she says that the *dao* is often understood as a first cause, yet this cause is not to be understood in the normal cause-and-effect relation: "That the *Dao* was 'cause' does not imply that the world is its 'effect,' because here it means nothing more than that the world is its unfolding, its manner of appearance. The *Dao* is 'cause' in the sense of motion, not of creation *ex nihilo*."[36] I find it unclear how something can be both a first cause and at the same time be seen as just the mere unfolding of events. In trying to explain, Robinet perpetuates the metaphysical interpretation of Daoism by stating that there are "two notions of the *Dao:* one that is indeterminate, and the other which is at the same time the source of all things and its production."[37] She speaks of the essence of the *Dao* and suggests that this essence is something beyond the visible world, thereby creating a metaphysical principle. Arguably, her interpretation comes from looking at many different interpretations, so she is not just presenting her own view. Yet this is precisely the fact I wish to argue against: Just because *dao* has more often than not been interpreted as a metaphysical source does not mean that this interpretation is the only true or necessary one. Again it is making the same substance-ontology mistake in seeing a being simultaneously just as an entity and also as the highest transcendental being.

Another scholar who seems happy to perpetuate the idea that Daoism is about some metaphysical entity wrongfully or inadequately named *dao* is Benjamin Schwartz, who speaks of Daoism as "a kind of speculative meditation [. . .] on the nature of *Tao* that seems to parallel later Neoplatonic meditations in the West on the nature of the *Logos*."[38] Many philosophers have thankfully taken this parallel and found ways of inserting the metaphysical values associated with the traditional understanding of *logos* into Daoist philosophy. As we will see when comparing Daoism with Heidegger and Derrida, there is also a different understanding of *logos* that needs not be metaphysical in nature.

In his later work Schwartz still considers the Daoism of the *Laozi* and the *Zhuangzi* a form of mysticism. Thus *dao* is considered the ineffable, unknowable reality which itself is nonbeing, but nevertheless the source of all beings.[39] Schwartz further argues that humans, or at least some of them, can achieve a unity with this unknowable *dao*. He thus takes *dao* to be a transcendental entity, to be approached in a mystical way because common-sense knowledge runs short for knowing it, and he explicitly explores the parallels in Western and Indian religious mysticisms, especially those of negative theology.[40] He thereby, and similar to Robinet, also introduces the classical idea of dualism into his understanding of *dao*, as he speaks on one hand of the *dao* as ultimate, unnameable and ineffable reality, on the other hand of *dao(s)* of which you can speak.[41]

One last example of the metaphysical reading is Max Kaltenmark's *Lao Tzu and Taoism*, which again seeks to convey *dao* as "Heavenly Order or Way,"[42] perpetuating the imposition of Western metaphysical ideas on classical Daoism.

There are many of these examples, and the outline I have tried to give here of traditional Western scholarship and translations of the *Daodejing* and the *Zhuangzi* might have focused on the negative aspects of these interpretations a bit too much. I wish to reiterate that present and future scholarship still benefits from these interpretations, if only because they show us how easily we import our ideas, through the language we use, into understandings of other cultures. Criticism of and warnings toward reading too many Western ideas into Chinese classics have always existed among scholars of Sinology and comparative philosophy, but the fact still remains that inadvertently many foreign structures of thinking were incorporated into the interpretations of these classics, and these structures have usually reinforced the metaphysical outlook.

The outline given is especially important as it shall, in the remainder of this chapter, be used to compete with interpretations that are in some important ways nonmetaphysical in nature, such as those of A. C. Graham,[43] J. J. L. Duyvendak, Chad Hansen, Roger T. Ames, and David L. Hall, and of course my interpretation of these readings.

THE METAPHYSICAL TRADITION AND COMPARISON

> Beware of the abysses and the gorges, but also of the bridges and the barriers.[44]

In this section I focus on readings that have been offered comparing Daoism in general with specific Western philosophies, and I show that many of these comparisons inadvertently retain the metaphysical perspective, in that they try to pronounce the "ineffable" *dao* as something transcendent, some metaphysical principle of origin. This section is not meant to deny the fact that interpretation always has to have a starting point, and that it is thus quite naturally to be expected that interpreters and comparative philosophers start from their own cultural and philosophical backgrounds in trying to understand other cultures. In this way many translators and comparative philosophers have been, whether consciously or unconsciously, reading the *Daodejing* and the *Zhuangzi* through their favorite philosophers' eyes. However, what I want to show is how these interpretations might be a bit too overenthusiastic about the possibilities of such comparisons between Western philosophers and classical Chinese philosophy. Many interpretations were (and some still are) content to overlook important differences in order to create a semblance of equality or sameness where there might only be a similarity in a minor part of the thought-structures involved, and in so doing they have inadvertently recreated their own particular version of what Daoism is or can offer. Some have tried to subsume *dao* to Western sensibilities, some have tried to say it is totally different from Western thinking. Most have offered Daoism as a valuable alternative which provides a way out of the suffocating self-defeating strands of Western metaphysics. It is argued later in this chapter that such a way out might be equally self-defeating, and that to think of philosophical Daoism as providing this way out is itself an imposition of an ideal on the texts which assumes some sort of transcendental thinking.

I am of course aware that this book in a way suffers from the same flaws, yet I defend my approach of using Heidegger and Derrida since I think that the similarities in thinking between certain parts of Heidegger, Derrida, and Daoism are in fact conducive to an awareness of these flaws, meaning that the comparison makes us more aware of the inevitability of having a perspective, and cautions us against being overly optimistic about the possibilities of such intercultural encounters, while not denying their value for furthering understanding among different cultures. This realization of difference is exactly one of the features of Heidegger and Derrida, and it leads them to both an appreciation of and openness to difference.

As we shall see later, the metaphysical language of transcendence, as well as the language of (transcendence in) immanence, is not suitable for translating the works of Daoism. Absence and Nothing are not to be seen as a place of unchanging principles. As we have seen for example with Schwartz, there is a tendency to subsume Daoism under the idea of negative theology, which would mean that all we can say about the hyperessential *dao* is what it is not. The point I wish to make is that there is no transcendence necessary to understand Daoism; *dao* can be seen as wholly self-transformation of the ten thousand processes.

The mere volume of books with the title "*The Tao of* . . ." should already be enough of a warning against two possible approaches. The first would be a search for *the ultimate* meaning of the *Daodejing* or the *Zhuangzi*. Since obviously these anthologies are open to many diverse interpretations, and because their historical origins are so diffuse, it would be both futile and denying of their diversity to look for one and only one true meaning. However, the second approach, which claims that therefore the books are open to whatever we want them to mean, is equally at fault, and I think that many comparative philosophers have taken the opportunity provided by the vagueness and inherent openness of the texts to conflate them with their own interests.

In general then we can say that most interpretations of the Daoist classics have proceeded, or continue to proceed, to read into these works the quest for a foundational principle, a permanent moment of rest beyond the turmoil of ever-changing things, and that the Daoist sages are those who have for all time found this metaphysical ground of all things, being "The Way," and who try (in vain, though, since language cannot convey this ultimate ground) to find ways of expressing this to their readers. Against this dominant interpretation of Daoism, a different reading is possible.

THE POSSIBILITY OF DIFFERENCE

> Within the rhythms of life, the swinging gateway opens and novelty emerges spontaneously to revitalize the world, tempering whatever has moved to an extreme, and reclaiming whatever has strayed from the path. Whatever is most enduring is ultimately overtaken in the ceaseless transformation of things.[45]

As we have seen, reading Daoism as one coherent school of thought is in itself a prejudice which tries to undo the diversity of the classics which have been subsumed under this name.[46] This tendency might be compared superficially with the tendency to subsume under the umbrella of postmodernism everything which challenges and questions the ideas that are usually associated with "modernity." And both in China and in the West, these challenges have usually been understood as derailing, nihilistic, and relativistic.

So while we have to acknowledge the fact that there is some commonality in what we usually call Daoism, we must also be aware of the differences between the classical Daoist works. There are important differences between the *Laozi* or *Daodejing* and the *Zhuangzi,* and to read the *Zhuangzi* only as the inner chapters suggest is also to try to undo the importance of the commentarial tradition in favor of a single original. We know that almost none of the Chinese classics are such original, one-author works as we are more familiar with in the history of the West, but that their form developed through commentaries and editing from various sources over a considerable length of time. This is not to say that with the commentarial tradition evolving, we are necessarily getting closer to the "real" meaning of the Chinese classics. It is merely to point out that the identity of the Chinese classics is fluid to say the least. We must see this fluidity as something inherent in these works and thus as something which influences how we read them.

In what follows, I explore the possibility of a differential reading, one that incorporates the postmodern critique of metaphysics and thus tries to read Daoism in a nonmetaphysical way. Graham notices that while many translators and interpreters have tried to read some metaphysical reality behind the appearances of the everyday world into the ineffability of *dao*, the fact is rather that "[D]aoists are not thinking of the Way as ultimate Truth or Reality. They merely have the good sense to remind us of the limitations of the language which they use to guide us towards that altered perspective on the world and that knack of living."[47] In order to understand the different way of thinking of the Daoist classics, it is most important first to explain how classical Chinese language and thinking have influenced each other and how interpretations of classical Chinese language have influenced interpretations of the supposed way of thinking behind the Chinese classics in general and the Daoist classics in particular.

Interpretations of Classical Chinese Language

It is not my intention to provide here a theory of the classical Chinese language, but more to provide an overview of some theories of classical Chinese language, and with that an overview only of what I take to be the most interesting and conflicting points of view that bear immediate importance on my project. From this largely incomplete overview I hope only to distract a feasible idea of the impact of the perceived function, structure, grammar, and semantics of classical Chinese on the thinking or philosophy of classical China, and especially the impact on the *Daodejing* and the *Zhuangzi*. This idea will aid me when I present my reading of Daoism.

Benjamin Whorf, in his influential work *Language, Thought, and Reality*, argues that language is constitutive of reality in the sense that it is understood that language presents the world in a certain way and is not a neutral medium, and it is my opinion that a similar view is held by the earliest thinkers in China, who consequently looked upon language in a different way than their Western contemporaries did, or later Western philosophers for that matter. The Sapir–Whorf hypothesis suggests the following:

> The possibilities open to thinking are the possibilities of recognizing relationships and the discovery of techniques of operating with relationships on the mental or intellectual plane, such as will in turn lead to ever wider and more penetratingly significant systems of relationships. These possibilities are inescapably bound up with systems of linguistic expression.[48]

In other words, language is not just the medium through which otherwise nonlinguistic ideas are reproduced or represented, but language itself shapes and is thus constitutive of these ideas, and these ideas are relational because language is relational. Whereas in the West this has been a relatively recent discovery and one that is still contested, the thinkers in classical China were aware of this important factor of language from an early time onward, and used language accordingly. From the "rectification of names" to the "ineffable *dao*" to thc "white horses and nonhorses," examples abound to show that philosophers in early China took this phenomenon of language as a serious issue. But the Sapir–Whorf thesis does not necessarily lead to an extreme linguistic relativism. Graham has argued that although certain arguments or concepts can not be translated from classical Chinese to Western languages or vice versa, the fact that we seem to inhabit profoundly different conceptual schemes does still not necessitate extreme relativism. We can cross over to different conceptual schemes and still maintain that they are different from our own schemes, so we can learn from the differences in our respective ways of reasoning.[49]

Although there are different theories about the existence of grammar, or about the function and structure of language in general and the largely pictographic and ideographic character of classical Chinese in particular, all these theories agree on the fact that the language was an important influence on thinking and its development in classical China. And most agree that because of the different structure of classical Chinese in comparison to Indo-European languages, thinking largely developed in directions different from the Western metaphysical approach.

Some of these theories work from the view that has become standard or orthodox in the West and thus try to accommodate classical Chinese language into this framework. Others challenge this standard and its applicability to classical Chinese and argue that we cannot impose Indo-European standards on classical Chinese. The latter ones are obviously closer to the views of Heidegger and Derrida.

Many authors have focused on the supposed vagueness of classical Chinese, but more recent scholarship has established that there is much more structure than was previously supposed. Graham, for example, admits to the "syntactic mobility"[50] of classical Chinese characters but argues that as scholarship is evolving, this mobility or vagueness is becoming more and more restricted. Yet Graham retains the idea that classical Chinese is special because of this inherent openness.[51] Again, some authors have seen this as a disadvantage in relation to Indo-European languages, while others have argued for a more positive approach, meaning that this openness and vagueness is a productive rather than a negative feature, a claim which I explain later.

Hansen argues against the orthodox bias that phonetic writing, or rather the writing based on phonemes, is "better than" non-phonetic writing. First of all, this bias perpetuates the idea of Western superiority, and then it usually further debases classical Chinese in trying to make it conform to the Western standard. Hansen suggests we just deny the bias and see language in its totality (that is as both speech and writing) as:

> [. . .] an abstract symbolic system. Sounds are *one familiar example* of linguistic symbols, not their essence. Pictures, gestures, electromagnetic modulations, graphs, map conventions, eyebrow movements, ideographs, logical notation and so forth are other possible symbol systems that can token words of a language.[52]

Hansen introduces the type–token distinction, which suggests that a language, consisting of words, has different word-types in it, which are abstract theoretical objects. These types can be represented by different tokens, sound-tokens or written tokens being examples. With this distinction Hansen points to the fact that it is not necessary for a written language to be derived from the spoken variant. He suggests that classical Chinese writing is an instance of a symbol system which arose not from speech, but from "a ritual practice connected to divination."[53] With this interpretation Hansen undermines the universal claim that all writing must be a transcription of spoken language.

Having argued against the traditional interpretations of classical Chinese language and philosophy, Hansen then introduces his own ideas of the language and how it affected thinking. He also notices that Chinese ideas about language never fail to "note explicitly the conventional nature of language and the crucial role of acceptability of use. Chinese theorists emphasize the relation of language and society, perhaps even more than they emphasize the relation of language and the world."[54] Language depends on social convention, not on a metaphysical theory of meaning that would place ideas in a special, Platonic realm, as is usually done in the West.

Hansen thinks it is better to treat classical Chinese characters as consisting of, or rather functioning as, mass nouns.[55] This would make us better understand the difference between the ontology in the West and what he calls the mereology of the classical Chinese worldview. The former is concerned with individuality as a permanent structure of things, their so-called essence, while the latter is "an ontology of non-contiguous stuffs with a part-whole structure."[56]

Ames, together with others like Rosemont and Hall, has also argued for a separation of the writing and speech of classical Chinese. Rosemont and Ames argue that

> [. . .] classical Chinese is not now and may never have been understood aloud as a primarily spoken language; therefore spoken and literary Chinese are now and may always have been two distinct linguistic media, and if so, the latter should clearly not be seen as simply a transcription of speech.[57]

Classical Chinese thus differs significantly from the linguistic ideal of Indo-European languages, in that it cannot be understood (solely) by seeing it as a transcription of the spoken language, whereby the pure presence denoted by the spoken word is transported (in a deficient way) into the written word. According to Ames and Hall this means that classical "Chinese language is not logocentric. Words do not name essences. Rather, they indicate always-transitory processes and events. It is important, therefore, to stress the gerundative character of the language."[58] Both Hansen and Ames and Hall thus see classical Chinese more in line with a process thinking than with a substance ontology. Because of this character, and because of the inherent vagueness of classical Chinese which Ames and Hall attest to and see as a positive feature rather than as something negative, they suggest to try to understand the language "paronomastically—that is, in terms of the semantic and phonic web of allusive relationships that obtain among [clusters of philosophical expressions]."[59] The vagueness of the language carries a certain unpredictability with it. Notions have more than one meaning, often opposite or at least very divergent meanings at that. To give a pertinent example, one passage in the second chapter of the *Zhuangzi* is translated by Watson as "The torch of chaos and doubt—this is what the sage steers by."[60] The same passage is translated by Graham as: "the glitter of glib implausibilities is despised by the sage."[61]

This is an example of the vagueness of classical Chinese, and it shows how scholars competent in classical Chinese can by a different translation make the same sage do something completely opposite.

Yet, as said, Hall and Ames suggest that this inherent vagueness in the language should not be seen as a hindrance to understanding, but as a source of richness that enhances the relational context in which real understanding comes about. Understanding a term is not taking it *from* its context and providing it with a fixed definition, as one would in a world shaped largely by essentialist or substance thinking; it is rather putting something *in* its context and acknowledging that it can only be understood from there, as one would in a world that is more process-oriented. This calls for a further explanation of the term "paronomasia," which Ames presents as a guide to understanding the language and thus the thinking of classical China. In a recent article Ames tries to show the importance of relationality for the classical Chinese worldview, and he extends this importance in the direction of understanding the classics and the classical Chinese language they were composed in. According to Ames, understanding characters paronomastically entails that meaning is only found by "a redefining of our terms of understanding, explanation, and performance through semantic and phonetic associations."[62] The stress on relationality excludes the normal Western assumptions about how to define terms. In the traditional Western metaphysical sense, terms are mostly defined *per genus et differentiam*, that is, by putting them simultaneously in a class with similar characteristics and by drawing boundaries that delineate and differentiate one term from another. In this sense a definition is an abstraction, through classification and differentiation, from the context in which the term is found, in order to find the essence or true meaning of a term which would always be the same, even in and despite very different contextual circumstances. In the Platonic tradition it is this essence which is then defined as the real meaning of a term, whereas the individual instances of things and terms are mere derivations. This is basically the Platonic position that distinguishes between a world of forms and one of matter, with the former having a definitely higher status. The basic source of meaning then comes to be seen as a transcendental principle, the "One Reality" from which the many instances or particular things are derived.

Compared to this, the classical Chinese worldview does not acknowledge such a top-down order but works from the premise of starting from the perspective of the particular and defining it in terms of its surroundings. This also means that things are not static; they are not defined once and for all. Because of situational developments and the ongoing transformation of things, they are more parts of processes than strict identities.

We can find this way of thinking in the *Zhuangzi*, where Zhuangzi, upon realizing he is himself entangled in a web of creatures preying upon each other, says that "[i]t is inherent in things that they are ties to each other, that one kind calls up another."[63] Zhuangzi (although uneasily)[64] assents to the fact that he is a situational being. Graham's translation here might at first seem odd, as he translates not that things *have* ties with other things, but that things *are* these ties. This translation, however, makes it even clearer that relationality is prior to identity and individuality. A subject is not first a subject which then has relations with other subjects or objects; it is the relations which first make the subject what it is, and in that sense, when the relations change, the subject changes with them.

From this particularly Chinese worldview of relationality, Ames seeks to find the implications of understanding the language of the Chinese classics. For example, there is the understanding in Daoism that *dao* can not be named. But this is not because, as so many (Western and Chinese) interpreters have assumed, it is a transcendental principle above the rest of the world, but because the complete process of transformation is, as its nature implies, not something we can pin down or relate to anything else or behind it. As Ames puts it:

> With no assumed "One-behind-the-many" as the ultimate source of meaning, there is no single-ordered world, no "*uni*-verse," only the ongoing evolving harmony expressed as the quality of life achieved by the insistent, co-creating particulars.[65]

Daoist thinking implies an understanding that this relationality is ever changing, an ongoing process of transformation, and this implies that any "rectification of names" or use of language is therefore provisional and in need of constant renewal. Not only *dao* is beyond naming, but *all* naming is only a provisional, temporary fixation of what is essentially always in flux.

What reading texts in a paronomastic way means can also be clarified when we look at the often-found parallelism in the prose and verse of the Chinese classics. Not only are words paired with similar words (phonetic or semantic), but sentences with the same structure and close to each other are paired as well. Both this parallelism and the switching between prose and verse that often occurs in Chinese classics, function similarly as a means to further understanding and clarity: the poetry is connected to meaning. Parallel sentences have definite connections. I will come back to this when looking at the first chapter of the *Daodejing* later. Meaning is generated as a result of all these connections.

One major implication of Ames' ideas is that the strict distinction between metaphorical and literal meaning that is so often held in high esteem in the West does not apply to the worldview of the Chinese classics. There is no literal meaning of a term; all terms, concepts, notions, and so on rely on other terms, concepts, and notions to be explained.

The question of reference then becomes complicated. In the traditional Western sense nouns refer to objects and such, and in general we can say that language is seen as a representation of reality; it refers to something outside itself.[66] Hall and Ames, building on the mass-noun hypothesis of Hansen, deny that this is so for classical Chinese, and argue that "no ontological referencing serves to discipline the acts of naming. That is, there is no object language in the strict sense. Language is, in this sense, nonreferential."[67] As another way of saying the same thing, Hall and Ames argue that "names 'reference' functions or roles which are themselves other names."[68] The metaphorical explanation of paronomasia is in the end the only one by which we get insight into the provisional meaning of terms. The reason why there is no strict distinction between literal and metaphorical meaning lies in the nondualistic worldview of the Chinese classics. Since there is no enduring reality behind the transient appearances, all is relative to all else, and that means that the meaning of words is relative to the language around them. The way to define something is not by appeal to some transcendent principle of permanence, as we will see later, but by locating it within its immediate surroundings, and that includes words with similar phonetic elements and close in metaphoric meaning.

Meaning thus only arises out of the web of signification that language is. In this way, language is also not seen primarily as a description of reality, but as a presentation of reality in a certain way. In Chinese philosophy, the focus is on the prescriptive instead of the descriptive. In fact, the strict distinction made between descriptive and prescriptive language might itself be artificial and a feature of the imposition of Western ideas on Chinese classics. In the traditional worldview of which classical Chinese language is an exponent, *ming* 名 (to name) is associated with *ming* 命 (to command). *Dao* as a term is associated with the term for "leading, guiding" and can also mean "speaking." It thus has an obvious prescriptive component. Hansen has pointed out that the usual sense of *dao* was understood to be something like "guiding discourse," which also suggests a prescriptive element. Hansen, as we have seen, argues extensively for an understanding of classical Chinese that would not subsume it under the supposedly universal standards of Western, Indo-European languages. He likens classical Chinese to a computer program, where the program functions as a guide to action. This means that the descriptive function of language, or the mere communication of information about objects, is only one function of language in the whole system, and not the most important one. As a whole, and more importantly, language is prescriptive according to conventional standards, but these standards are not permanent, hence the discussion about which *dao* to follow is indeed the discussion about how to see language:

> The distinctive claim of the Taoist is that [. . .] our conventional ways of doing things with prescriptive language are always changing—there is no constant, absolute, guide to behaviour in all circumstances. [. . .] And, as the *Lao-tzu* points out, the reason no such discourse is constant is that language (names) is inconstant—artificial, conventional, changeable. No Tao is constant because no name is constant.[69]

The early Daoists understood the relativity of a guide that has no permanent standard to refer to. Hansen's reinterpretation of the first lines of the first chapter of the *Daodejing* shows us that names, or rather language, does not point to anything metaphysical and unchanging. It is a conventional tool that is dependent on situation. As Ames and Hall put it:

> Daoist naming [. . .] is presentational rather than just representational, normative rather than just descriptive, perlocutionary rather than just locutionary, a doing and a knowing rather than just a saying. [. . .] Such knowing is dependent upon an awareness of the indeterminate aspects of things. The ongoing shaping of experience requires a degree of imagination and creative projection that does not reference the world as it is, but anticipates what it might become. [. . .] And having access to the "name" of something is not only a claim to knowing it in a cognitive sense, but more importantly, to knowing how to deal with it. [. . .] Hence such knowing is a feeling and a doing: it is value-added. It is naming without the kind of fixed reference that allows one to "master" something, a naming that does not arrest or control.[70]

In the *Zhuangzi,* Chapter 27, there is mention of three kinds of words used in the *Zhuangzi*, or of three ways of using language which are important to understand this provisionality. Graham has explained how the first two kinds seem to follow normal conventions. The first one, "saying from a lodging place," which means arguing from a particular standpoint, is discredited throughout the *Zhuangzi* because for every "this," every standpoint, there is a "that," or another standpoint. The second one, "weighted saying," is based on authority of experience. It thus suffers from the same shortcomings, although less. But the third one is the most important, "spillover saying," which Graham characterizes as "the speech proper to the intelligent spontaneity of Taoist behavior in general, a fluid language which keeps its equilibrium through changing meanings and viewpoints."[71] So it is not so much that there is nothing to be said, it is more that we must always realize that what is said is provisional, prone to shifts in meaning, and open to different interpretations from different standpoints. Words can be used in a variety of ways, none of which is permanent and none of which will overcome this impermanence.

It is often argued that Daoists in general and Zhuangzi in particular propose to do away with language because of this impermanence, but I think this is a misunderstanding. Let us look at one of the passages often invoked in this argument:

> The fish trap exists because of the fish; once you've gotten the fish, you can forget about the trap. The rabbit snare exists because of the rabbit; once you've gotten the rabbit, you can forget the snare. Words exist because of meaning; once you've gotten the meaning, you can forget the words. Where can I find a man who has forgotten words so I can have a word with him?[72]

It is important to understand this passage not as saying that we can do without language once we have the meaning of life, but as saying we must always return to language, even when we think we no longer need it. You can only forget the fish trap for a short moment, while you have fish. Once the fish runs out, is exhausted, you need the fish trap again, and you might have to do some repairs as well. The same goes for the rabbit snare. On the level of language this means that the metaphysical idea that there is some ultimate and unchanging reality conveyed by words but essentially in a different realm, is undone by pointing to the provisionality of words, not with respect to this ultimate truth, but with respect to the description of the world. You need first to forget about words as having a fixed reference, but not to leave them behind permanently. After forgetting them, the realization that you will still need them sets in, and then you need to reinvent or reintroduce, or reinscribe them. Dealing with this fluidity of language is like the goblet of the "goblet words," which is another translation of the "spillover saying" that Graham mentions, in that the goblet does not get rid of itself, but of what it has too much of, as it rights itself after emptying itself. Zhuangzi does not suggest overcoming language in some mystical state; he argues for the equality and provisionality of *all* language and thus of all views, which means that any mystical state is not better or worse than another state, but also suffers from the same provisionality. As the second chapter of the *Zhuangzi* shows, there is not one language which can proclaim to be representative of the "piping of heaven," nor can any man claim to have a special access to this "piping of heaven." In a typical move Zhuangzi first seems to assent to the idea that the "piping of heaven" is more valuable or more real than the "piping of man," but he then goes on to show that there really is no way of distinguishing between these two, which on the level of language means that all language is permissible and not permissible in the same way.

A similar idea is also found in the *Daodejing*, where it is not argued that we should *stop* using language, but that we should know where its *limits* are. Chapter 78, for example, does not say that all language is bad per se, but that "appropriate language seems contradictory."[73] That means that appropriate language is not to be understood in the same category as normal language. Appropriate language is language aware of its own provisionality. I would thus also argue against the interpretation of the *Daodejing* that suggests that we should get rid of language altogether. Both the *Zhuangzi* and the *Daodejing* are written as realizations of the need for language, although not as in the common language, but in a different way. They do not argue for a total dismissal of language. Chapter 23 of the *Daodejing* has it that "It is natural to speak only rarely,"[74] and not that it is natural to not speak at all. And further on in Chapter 32 it is said that:

> When we start to regulate the world we introduce names.
> But once names have been assigned,
> We must also know when to stop.
> Knowing when to stop is how to avoid danger.[75]

Even the sages have to speak—there is no sense in avoiding it—but there is great sense in knowing how to speak, when to speak and when not to, and when to stop depending on fixed meanings. The caution taken when speaking or using language in general is a common feature of much of classical Chinese philosophy. Graham has said that "in Chinese philosophy argumentation is conceived solely in terms of whether the name fits the object."[76] The specifically Daoist contribution seems to be an increased awareness of the provisionality of this fitting. So what Graham has called the most distinguishable trait of the Daoist, that "knack of living,"[77] has a lot to do with language. The examples of cook Ding and other skilful craftsmen can be seen as illustrations or metaphors of the Daoist sages, who have this knack in everything they do, and most certainly in their use of language. They are the ones who by default have to be very aware of the possibilities and impossibilities of language, and that is why they are said to be extremely cautious and sparing in their use of language. And it is also how they can attune their language to the changing circumstances, thus playing along with the process of transformation and not hindering it with false fixations. To the sages, this has become a so-called second nature. Like cook Ding, whom we can only assume to have achieved his "knack" by a lot of practice, the Daoist sages must remain on constant guard against the reassertion of propositional and representational language and thinking. It is only by such constant awareness that the sages develop this second nature. To become *ziran* 自然, one must practice *wei wuwei* 為無為. And one must practice it constantly. Even cook Ding, when he comes to a difficult part, pauses and has to tell himself "to watch out and be careful, keep my eyes on what I'm doing, work very slowly. . . ."[78]

In a larger setting I take this to mean that if we unwittingly stick to one interpretation, we become dogmatic. But we cannot assume that once we have left this dogmatism behind, we can then rest on our laurels, since that would just mean shifting the dogmatism one step further. In asserting things, we must see that what we assert is never the "truth" as such; it is always an interpretation and a point of view which cannot be neutral or objective in the Western ideal sense of these words. "The Way has never known boundaries; speech has no constancy."[79] Once this is realized, we can no longer assume to be beyond the boundaries, and with that comes the realization that we can and must use language "under erasure."

As a corroboration to my interpretation of language in Daoism, we can look at recent writings about language in Chan/Zen Buddhism, not just because Chan Buddhism is in some way a descendant of Daoist thinking, but also because interpretations, especially Western ones, of Chan Buddhism have suggested that the experience of enlightenment sought in Chan Buddhism also transcends language, in a similar way as Daoism would do by seeing *dao* as an ineffable reality. However, recently there has been criticism toward this standard view of Chan Buddhism by scholars such as Youru Wang and Dale S. Wright.[80] Both Wang and Wright argue that Chan experience is not about transcending language, but about opening it up, about showing the traditional limitations that were imposed on language by understanding it in a metaphysical way. In arguing for this opening up and for the idea that the sought-for Chan experience of *satori* is not a pure experience that transcends language, but one that is located within the particular language community of Chan Buddhists, and thereby locating experience inside a language web or in seeing language as essential to meaningful experience, I concur with their findings and wish to repeat that what I think Daoism tries to do is similar, in that *through* language it disrupts the standard view and use of language, without thereby denying its necessity. In Wright's words, the "awakening" in Chan/Zen Buddhism is "an awakening *to* rather than *from* language."[81] And of course I argue that this is also what Heidegger and Derrida do.

With regard to the social and prescriptive function of language, the Daoist sage must thus stand somewhere "in the middle," or, as we shall see later, in the gateway that opens to both sides of the yin-yang dichotomies, of the *shi-fei* 是非 assertions, or of the *you-wu* 有無 distinctions. The sage must not adhere to the artificial distinctions made by fixed references, and thus Chapter 2 of the *Zhuangzi* says that this sage:

> [. . .] illuminates all in the light of *tian*. He too recognizes a "this," but a "this" which is also a "that," a "that" which is also a "this." His "that" has both a right and a wrong in it; his "this" too has both a right and a wrong in it. So, in fact, does he still have a "this" and a "that"? Or does he in fact no longer have a "this" and "that"? A state in which "this" and "that" no longer find their opposites is called the hinge of the Way. When the hinge is fitted in the socket, it can respond endlessly.[82]

This provisionality seems to me to be one of the key ideas behind the Daoist approach to language. My interpretation goes against the common idea that Daoists, and especially Zhuangzi, are arguing for an escape from the world into some eternal realm of freedom. In my opinion, and I have shown how their ideas and use of language support this opinion, they are arguing, in their own way, against these superficial escapist theories in favor of a reinterpretation of our way of being *in* the world that would be less interfering.

To conclude this section, it seems that most theories of classical Chinese language focus on a couple of basic ideas. Social convention, entailing prescription and relationality rather than description of an underlying unchanging reality, is the major function of language. The fact that there seems to be a different ontology backing the classical Chinese language means we cannot assume too much similarity with thinking in Western languages. My point would be to claim that the often mentioned denial of the value of language should be understood differently. Language per se is not to be discarded, but used with ultimate caution and awareness of its provisionality, because it could otherwise lead to dangerous dogmatisms and an unrealistic narrowness of focus. I can now take this rather lengthy excursion into certain interpretations of classical Chinese language to function as a background for the next section, which to some extent rests on the particularities of classical Chinese to explain a certain philosophical attitude that I ascribe to Daoism.

INCONSTANCY OF *DAO* 道: NO TRANSCENDENCE NECESSARY

The focus of this whole chapter so far has really been a matter of "a certain way of reading" that is increasingly under fire. It is not that other ways of reading the Daoist classics are neutral or objective, but the one that has been dominant in the discourse of comparative philosophy needs reconsideration, and this reconsideration is found in some contemporary, but also in some earlier, sinologists and philosophers. We have seen that even minor prejudices and habits of our own languages can easily distort the ideas of other cultures. Even using the definite article "the" instead of the indefinite "a" or opting for the singular instead of the plural in translations makes a difference. If we look at the first chapter of the *Daodejing*, translating the character *chang* 常 from the first line as "eternal"[83] is different from translating it as "constant." "Eternal" could easily suggest a platonic realm of reality behind the appearance of the worldly things and thus reinforces the idea of a duality and hierarchy between reality and appearance, whereas "constant" suffers less from such an interpretation. Relative constancy can still be accommodated within a thinking based on process and transformation.

Hall and Ames have argued against translations of Chinese classics which take Western notions and their apparently literal application toward Chinese characters for granted. They argue that because the Chinese tradition has no concept of strict transcendence, translations must anticipate their audience to the extent that "in the Chinese worldview, the act of translation is not complete until readers have read the text. This simply means that the coherence of the Chinese order must take full account of context."[84] This puts a duty on translators not to impose their own standards of thinking on the works in translation, and to anticipate the fact that for readers raised and schooled in the Western metaphysical traditions, translating a term such as *tian* with "Heaven" will engender definite connotations which should be avoided as they do not do justice to the worldview of the Chinese classics. In translation we are to keep any text in its own context as far as possible, and not insert it into *our* context.

If we are to provide a different reading of Daoist thinking that is not metaphysical, we must stay aware of the danger of reappropriating *dao*, understood as the ongoing process of impermanence and change of everything in the world, back into the metaphysical tradition, in which case we would be seeing it as the principle of impermanence which stays permanent as a guiding principle itself. The proposals of Hall and Ames on the idea of the absence of transcendence in Chinese thought in general, and Daoism in particular, are very promising, and something more should be said about them. Hall and Ames understand and define transcendence in the following way: "A is transcendent with respect to B if the existence, meaning, or import of B cannot be fully accounted for without recourse to A, but the reverse is not true."[85] This notion of transcendence is then taken to task with regard to the notions of *tian* and *dao*, where Hall and Ames find that since *tian* and *dao* are both *ziran* (self-so), they require no further postulation of transcendence. In other words, there is no God, Heaven, or eternal Way out there for us to follow, and *tian* and *dao* are nothing more than the ongoing processes of the world in its countless transformations, nothing more than the *wanwu* 萬物 or myriad events, things, and processes that together constitute the world. Reading Daoism in this way might seem to be imposing some pragmatist or postmodern ideas on it, yet throughout history there have been some Chinese commentators who shared this view, for example Guo Xiang, Chen Jingyuan, Du Guanting, and also Li Daochun.[86] So while we may say that the position we are looking for has not been dominant throughout history, whether in the Western interpretations or in the Chinese commentaries, it would be a mistake to assume that this particular understanding of Daoism did not exist in both the early and more recent history of Chinese thinking.

Further, this absence of transcendence is not a case for negative theology, which is to say that Chinese thought is not to be regarded in terms of the usual opposite of transcendence and immanence. Hall and Ames have argued in *Thinking Through Confucius* and again in *Thinking From the Han* that it is the language of *both* transcendence *and* immanence that confuses Western notions for Chinese sensibilities.[87] The contrast between transcendence and immanence has its root, as they argue, in the theological tradition, and thus both terms are part of a framework that has arisen in the Western religious worldview. This means that whenever scholars deny the existence of transcendence, plausible in itself, but then go on to explain Chinese thinking in terms of immanence, they are perpetuating the framework itself that is to blame for the whole Western infusion of ideas. Since negative theology works within the same conceptual structure it is thus inappropriate for understanding the different ideas of classical China, in the same way as it is inappropriate for understanding Derrida.

However, Hall and Ames also object to the idea of a secular transcendence, one whereby *dao* would be translated and seen as some sort of essential "Reason" or "Absoluteness."[88] Both forms of transcendence, the positing of a transcendent principle outside the world as well as the essentialist version, are absent. One can read this absence of transcendence in a similar way in the commentary of the neo-Daoist thinker Guo Xiang on the *Zhuangzi,* quoted by Graham:

> I should like to ask whether the maker of things is something (*yu*) or nothing (*wu*). If he is nothing, how is he able to make things? If he is something, he is unequal to making things in their multitudinous shapes. Therefore it is quite pointless to discuss the making of things with someone until he understands that the multitudinous shapes become things of themselves.[89]

The importance of Guo Xiang for a reading of Daoism that is not metaphysical is not to be underestimated. Although his only surviving work is a commentary on the *Zhuangzi,* Guo Xiang's ideas show that there was an understanding of Daoism which in most definite terms did not subscribe to the metaphysical reading. Guo Xiang's commentary is full of both implicit and explicit denials of the idea that *tian, dao, ziran,* or other concepts would have anything to do with transcendence, or with anything remotely resembling a God, or otherwise with any idea of transcendent quality or metaphysical reality, and as such Guo Xiang forms a strong antidote to the metaphysical inclinations of certain interpreters. Elsewhere in the same commentary he states his case in the following way:

> Who, then, produces things? They spontaneously produce themselves. . . . That everything spontaneously becomes what it is, is called natural. Everything is as it is by nature, not made to be so. Therefore, when Chuang Tzŭ spoke of heaven (*t'ien*), he meant the natural, not the blue sky. . . . *T'ien* is the general name of all things. There is nothing that can be specifically called *t'ien*. Who can be the Lord that commands things? Everything produces itself and is not created by others. This is the way of nature.[90]

This is exactly why the language and ideas of negative theology will not do, as negative theology still assumes something outside of all immanence and thus an ineffable and hyperessential reality, indescribable but in negative terms.

Scholars have naturally focused on the first chapter of the *Daodejing* to provide readings of a negative theological nature. Does it not say that the *dao* which is real is ineffable and cannot be described by any of the impermanent things of this world? Not necessarily, for in the words of Brook

Ziporyn, the first lines could easily also be translated as: "Guiding ways can be taken as guides, but they are then [no longer] constant [or reliable] guides."[91] So there are different ways to read this first chapter, and even if we insist on reading these lines in some more traditional translation, it still does not mean that transcendence is necessarily meant. If we look at a standard translation like "The Way that can be spoken of is not the constant Way, names that can be named are not constant names," we must not fail to notice that these lines do not say that there *is* something like a constant way or constant words. In fact, the second line is usually taken to mean that names are *never* constant, yet the first line, which has the same parallel structure, is usually interpreted as hinting at a constant way that is just ineffable. There is an inconsistency in these traditional translations that inherently favors metaphysical readings. Now if we deny the idea of transcendence the first line can be taken to mean that *dao* is just the process of change, the ongoing process of all things happening, and as such, as the whole process (it) does not change, because "it" "is" change, open-ended. It can then also mean that when we speak of *dao*, we are already creating a rupture in thc processuality of the process, or in other words we are seeking to take one part of the process and see that particular part as the totality or as something beyond the totality. As Chapter 42 of the *Daodejing* reminds us, one and many, or continuity and difference, have their same source in *dao* understood as process. Or as Zhuangzi said: "We have already become one, so how can I say anything? But I have just *said* that we are one, so how can I not be saying something? The one and what I said about it make two, and two and the original one make three."[92] The ineffability of *dao* need not mean anything else than the fact that the totality cannot be represented by any one of its parts. Or, in other words, the recognition of a provisional pattern or continuity within change does not have to lead to positing such a pattern as a guiding principle outside of change. Even speaking of parts and totality would already introduce some sort of closure that is resisted by the processual understanding of *dao*, which, as said, is structurally open-ended.

Denying transcendence for Hall and Ames, however, does not mean that they deny a religiousness or spirituality to the people of the classical Chinese culture. It is more a question of a mystical attitude, if we are fully clear about understanding mysticism in a nontranscendent way, thus as a way of thinking that is profoundly this-worldly. It might be that because of the historical background of the concept of mysticism we should discard the notion altogether, since it has usually been associated with other-worldly experiences, or expressions of unity with some metaphysical reality. Yet it need not be understood that way. We could understand mysticism or at least the Daoist mystical approach as propounding a unity, or continuity, or relativity in the form of relationality, found solely in *this* world, with no need for anything external.

A similar approach is taken by François Jullien, who argues that although there is a way in which we can understand Daoism as mystical, it is definitely not the same mysticism as for example the Neo-Platonists. Although sometimes Jullien seems to employ the language of metaphysics, and although his reading of Daoism comes about through an *Auseinandersetzung* with the Neo-Platonists, he is careful to set them apart. For example, speaking about the "invisible" *dao*, Jullien argues that

> [. . .] the invisible is indeed beyond the visible but as an extension of it; [. . .] it transcends the sensible through its infinite capacity for transformation [. . .], but it does not *hypostatize*. This invisible is rather the *diffuse basis* of the visible from which the latter ceaselessly actualizes itself. In short, this invisible lacks metaphysical consistency.[93]

From this we can see that although Jullien uses the metaphysical language of transcendence, he does not endorse the metaphysical way of thinking. It might then be better to refrain from using the metaphysical language, as Ames and Hall urge us to do, yet the point is the same: We might be able to speak of mysticism with regards to Daoism, but it is not the same mysticism as in the Western tradition.[94]

Despite these attacks on the idea of transcendence in Daoism, many scholars today still think it feasible to speak of *dao* explicitly as a transcendent reality. Although my own position is that the nonmetaphysical reading is closer to the Daoist sensibilities as we can know them, to be consistent in my belief that the Daoist classics are inherently open to multiple interpretations I must admit the possibility of these metaphysical interpretations. Yet my criticism of seeing *dao* as a metaphysical reality lies with the exclusive claim to rightness that these interpretations often put forward. The entire volume 29 of the *Journal of Chinese Philosophy* (2002) is devoted to the topic "Tao and God." In the preface, Chung-Ying Cheng says that "Dao and God are two names that represent two forms of ultimate reality,"[95] implying a profound similarity between these two notions. In the same volume, Robert Cummings Neville argues for a metaphysical interpretation of Daoism that would put it closer to negative theology, basing his arguments on the unnameable "*Dao*" of the first chapter of the *Daodejing*. In his vocabulary, metaphysics is about the "development of hypotheses about the broadest characteristics of reality and their conditions," where the "subject matter of metaphysics [is] anything real."[96] The perpetuation of transcendence thinking lies in the fact that in Neville's approach, the "broadest characteristics" of "the Dao" include the familiar splitting of *dao* in "the eternal unnameable and the temporal, mothering, nameable Dao,"[97] an arbitrary splitting that we have encountered before and that only functions to facilitate the idea that the first *dao* is an ultimate reality.

Another scholar who defends the transcendence approach is Eske Møllgaard, who in a recent article has defended the view that Zhuangzi distinctly holds to transcendence views. Møllgaard's idea of transcendence, however, is not the usual one Hall and Ames argue against, but more an immanent transcendence. Comparable to Heidegger's *Sein*, Møllgaard argues that the "essential form of transcendence in Zhuangzi is the pure appearance of things, which transcends things without being some-thing beyond the realm of things."[98] This means that appearance, or the "being-so" of things cannot be reduced to those things themselves as purely individual things. This is Platonic in the sense that there is an insistence that the idea or the "pure appearance" of the thing has to be informed by some principle. The way Møllgaard states his idea of transcendence seems relatively innocent, yet he goes on to insist that Zhuangzi also has a notion of transcendence that is more strict, even going so far as to take the metaphorical statements of Zhuangzi about a creator literally and calling the "pure appearance" of the world "an act of pure grace."[99] He thereby conflates the softer version of transcendence with the stricter. As Hall and Ames have argued, this insertion of metaphysical vocabulary is unnecessary and only leads to confusion. Møllgaard, for example, argues that when Zhuangzi speaks of *dao* as the "realm before there are things," he is speaking of a metaphysical realm beyond and other than the myriad things, an idea many interpreters also read into for example Chapter 25 of the *Daodejing*. But as we shall see shortly, we can also see the realm of "things" as the realm of human distinction-making, and then we can see the realm of *dao* as the natural self-so (*ziran*) world before man turned to the arbitrary subject-object distinctions. In my view Møllgaard's reading of the *Zhuangzi* is unjustifiably selective. When he argues that Zhuangzi sees human life as "misery"[100] and that therefore man needs to hear and attune himself solely to the "pipings of heaven," he seems to be forgetting that, as we have seen already, Zhuangzi introduces this distinction between heaven and man in his second chapter only to question this kind of dubious distinction-making, something Møllgaard obviously does not question, and this displays his (Western) tendency to view Daoism as "otherworldly." Yet a different way of living, something which Zhuangzi definitely promotes, does not need to lead to a notion of transcendence, and when Møllgaard notices a "tendency for transcendence as the pure emergence and being-*so* of the thing to slip into transcendence as an agency and cause beyond the thing,"[101] he seems more than willing to promote this tendency.[102] The pure appearance of things is not something that can happen without the things, or rather processes, and seeing things as processes solves much of Møllgaard's dilemma. He still works with the idea of a strict identity of things, and in order for him to explain how these things develop, he needs the "pure appearance" to guarantee their unity over time. There is however no necessity to see "pure appearance," if we insist on this term, in transcendent ways.

We have already seen that identity or unity as Western concepts cannot (and should not) be transposed as easily into classical Chinese philosophy as some would like. The same also holds for other terms. Neither term of the Western metaphysical pair of Being and Nothing has any strict equivalents in classical Chinese thinking. Nor is the idea of Being as *opposed* to Nothing prominent, and thus the *relation* between Being and Nothing in the West is also different from that of the supposed equivalents, *you* 有 and *wu* 無, or *shi* 是 (this) and *fei* 非 (that). Graham, as we have seen briefly before, has argued extensively that to conflate these terms with the Western ontological notions Being and Nothing is to make mistakes at two levels.[103] First of all, the terms to be translated from the classical Chinese, although they have certain overlaps with Being and Nothing, do not precisely fit these Western notions, and neither is there a copulative verb "to be," on which much of Western philosophy as metaphysics or ontology depends, to be found in classical Chinese. *You* does not mean Being as an ontological category, it means more "to have" or "to be present," and thus should not be conflated with defining existence pure and simple. The same goes for *wu*. It means "not have" or "not present," again not signaling a pure denial of ontological existence, but rather a pragmatic approach to things and events. We can see that different categories are at work. When the *Daodejing* says that "being comes from non-being," this can be read as meaning that something was nonexistent before it became existent, and in due time it will return to its state of nonexistence again. All things, then, when present, come from and return to being not-present. There is no need to read in this *wu* anything transcendent with ontological implications.

The second reason why the Chinese terms used in Daoism differ from the Western structures is in their mutual relations. Whereas in the Western tradition there has been a focus on Being, which implied a hierarchy that says Being is better or more valuable than nonbeing, in the Chinese tradition we do not find such a hierarchy. The yin-yang cosmology of the Daoist worldview sees both *you* and *wu* as mutually defining structures that are interdependent and can never be disconnected. The same goes for *shi* and *fei*. Ideally, in the Daoist way of thinking, to see things as "this" means also to realize that from a different standpoint, they are "that." So both "this" and "that" are always relative to each other, everything is always both "this" and "that."

Of course, as I have mentioned briefly earlier in this chapter, it is insufficient to merely state different views from different scholars of Chinese thinking about transcendence and metaphysics and choose the one we like best. That would amount to underwriting the sometimes highly selective reading of certain scholars. We must therefore look for more textual evidence in both the *Daodejing* and the *Zhuangzi* that notions of transcendence, metaphysical reality, and negative theology do not fit philosophical Daoism, or at the very least are not required for an understanding of these classics.

Chapter 2 of the *Daodejing* has the following line: "Determinacy (*you*) and indeterminacy (*wu*) give rise to each other."[104] This shows that there is a mutual dependency between the two terms that does not readily admit of favoring one over the other, however much that may be our Western inclination. Chapter 11 is also about the relation between something (*you*) and nothing (*wu*):

> The thirty spokes converge at one hub,
> But the utility of the cart is a function of the nothingness (*wu*) inside
> the hub.
> We throw clay to shape a pot,
> But the utility of the clay pot is a function of the nothingness inside it.
> We bore out doors and windows to make a dwelling,
> But the utility of the dwelling is a function of the nothingness inside it.
> Thus, it might be something (*you*) that provides the value,
> But it is nothing that provides the utility.[105]

This chapter has often been read as suggesting that Being is inferior to Nothing, since nothing (*wu*) provides the utility of the being in question. Yet something (*you*) also provides the value; without the something there would be no utility of the nothing. It is only in the working together of *you* and *wu* that utility arises. The nothingness inside the clay pot is as much a function of the clay shape surrounding it as the other way around. Another chapter worth looking at is Chapter 40:

> "Returning" is how way-making (*dao*) moves,
> And "weakening" is how it functions.

> The events of the world arise from the determinate (*you*),
> And the determinate arises from the indeterminate (*wu*).[106]

Again it might be suggested that *wu* is what produces *you*, and that therefore *wu* is logically or metaphysically prior to *you*. Yet looking at the whole chapter, we see that it says that *dao* works by returning. This returning is however not a one-way stream, which we can read in Chapter 34, where it is said that "Way-making (*dao*) is an easy-flowing stream, [w]hich can run in any direction."[107] This suggests that both *wu* returns to *you* and *you* returns to *wu* within the yin-yang cosmological worldview that is present in the *Daodejing*. The process is reversible, or maybe cyclical, something which can also be read in Chapter 42. *Dao*, taken as impermanence of conventionality, of language, of things, does not admit of a permanent hierarchy between things. There are different events, different *daos*, not just one guiding principle. As Hall and Ames have put it, "*dao* constitutes the noncoherent sum of all names and forms," and *dao* is "the process of the world itself."[108] If this is so, there is no justification in taking *wu* more serious than *you*, or in taking them to differ on any ontological level, since they are both part of, and together constantly forming, the whole.

Yet with all this impermanence and provisionality the question of reference arises, and we must ask: Is there anything to which the word *dao* refers? The answer to this question can only be: nothing but different *daos* and the constant, open-ended play of these provisional structures of signification. Hansen explains how "[t]he belief in a single, absolute tao/way . . ."[109] has blurred alternative readings. In his own reading of the *Zhuangzi* he says this:

> Chuang-tzu neither presupposes nor does his doctrine entail that a single ineffable Tao exists, nor that there is such a thing as knowledge of a single, ultimate Tao, nor that we ought to follow such a Tao, and so on. In short, Chuang-tzu's theory is *not about The Tao*. Another way to put this point is this: "The Tao" or "The Way," as used by most English speakers who choose to speak of such things, is not the correct translation of the Chinese character tao/way as found in this text.[110]

The question of reference is not so much denied, but rather blurred, as *dao* refers to numerous *daos*, not just one. We can also read this in Graham's assertion that "even the Way is interdependent with man."[111] This means that different people can also differ in their interpretation of "the way," or as Zhuangzi said: "The Way comes about as we walk it."[112] Reference is thus also relational or situational; it is not something permanent. As has been noted, meaning in the classical Chinese worldview comes about by placing things *in* their context, and not by abstracting them from it.

Ames and Hall translate *dao* as "way-making," and this also shows their focus on the structural impermanence of *dao*. Any *dao* is a new particular field opened, and there is thus no one permanent field which we have to discover. Since this is so, all language and thus all reference is situational. Or as Zhuangzi says in the story of the happy fish: "I knew it from up above the Hao [river]."[113] The language of focus and field, which Ames and Hall employ, or of particularity and its constituted order, can be helpful to explain this. Since every particular has an equal ontological status, views about almost anything can and will differ. This is also why Ames and Hall have opted to translate *dao* as "way-making," in order to point to a number of features of Daoist thinking that other translations have overlooked. First of all, as we have seen, this translation has the merit of understanding *dao* as something which does not have a separate status from active living, in this case of humans (but who says that animals or other things do not have their "way-making"?). Humans make the way; it is not something laid out before them. Second, this feature means that ways are ever changing, evolving in different directions according to changing times and other unknown or uncontrollable forces. This does not mean there is no order, but that any order is relative. I quote Hall and Ames extensively:

> While the articulation and stabilizing regularity of any specific event anticipates the way in which it will continue to unfold, the chaotic aspect within the event itself defeats any notion of necessity or absolute predictability. The combination of pattern and uncertainty challenges the possibility of universal claims and renders precarious any globalizing generalizations. All we can depend upon is the *relative* stability of site-specific and particular expressions of order, with constant attention to stochastic variables at every level that well might amplify into large-scale changes. Order is thus both *local* and *focal*.[114]

Related to this, "way-making" also brings out the verbal or gerundative qualities of *dao*, thus strongly favoring a process ontology, which has more resonance in the Daoist worldview, over a substance ontology.

We must again proceed to provide some textual evidence for this reading by reinterpreting (with Ames and Hall, Hansen, Duyvendak, and others) parts of the *Daodejing* and the *Zhuangzi*. I focus on what are usually seen as pivotal chapters, but I also look at chapters that are traditionally overlooked. In the case of the *Daodejing*, I reinterpret the first chapter according to Duyvendak's interpretation which conceives of *dao* as the process of change. As he says, *dao* "is not a First Cause, it is not a Logos. It is nothing but the process of change and growth."[115] Herrlee Creel finds the difference in the translation by Duyvendak (especially of the character *chang*) with standard readings of no importance,[116] but I disagree and think it is important as it makes for a different reading. It is very different whether you say in the standard version: "the *dao* which can be spoken of is not the constant *dao*" or you take seriously Duyvendak's translation, which has: "the Way that may truly be regarded as the Way is other than a permanent Way."[117] It is the "other than permanent" aspect of this translation which brings to it a nonmetaphysical ring. The theme of constancy and especially the way in which it is interpreted can reveal a metaphysical inclination toward seeing *dao* as an unchanging guiding principle behind the myriad things, whereas seeing *dao* as the process of change proposes to undo that metaphysical idea. Hansen, whom I have used before in interpreting the first chapter of the *Daodejing*, similarly insists that this problem of change is not metaphysical in nature:

> *No* philosophical problem arises from the mere fact that change takes place in a *part-whole* ontology. Stuff changes. But that observation, by itself, raises no philosophical difficulty. The perennial *Western* problem lies in explaining how the object can remain *the very same object* while its constituent stuff flows in and out. Daoist worries about constancy and inconstancy, however, did not arise out of that familiar Western conceptual framework. [. . .] They worry about linguistic constancy, not object constancy.[118]

This suggests that the idea of constancy as an essence or unchanging reality behind appearance, a metaphysical realm, is not an issue in Daoist thinking.

Duyvendak's translation has the further merit of making good sense of the parallel structure of the first twelve characters of Chapter 1 of the *Daodejing*, and I have already alluded to the fact that the form of the classics is important in understanding meaning, in that the poetry and verse have definite functions. If names are not constant, and the whole Daoist tradition suggests that we should indeed see language as provisional, then what is the point of speaking of the "Real" name? There is no such thing. And if we follow the parallel structure, then the same thing would go for *dao*. Since *daos* are not constant, there is no reason why there should be an overarching constant *dao* other than the whole process of *wanwu*. Or, as Zhuangzi says:

> The Way is without beginning or end, but things have their life and death—you cannot rely upon their fulfilment. One moment empty, the next moment full—you cannot depend on their form. The years cannot be held off; time cannot be stopped. Decay, growth, fullness, and emptiness end and then begin again. It is thus that we must describe the plan of the Great Meaning and discuss the principles of the ten thousand things. The life of things is a gallop, a headlong dash—with every moment they alter, with every moment they shift. What should you do and what should you not do? Everything will change of itself, that is certain![119]

There is nothing other than transformation, and humans are no exception to this transformation; humans are neither somewhere outside of this process, nor is there an overarching principle behind it all. The regularity *in* the process is not something other than the process. To end this section, I present a few more passages where Zhuangzi puts this idea forward:

> Joy, anger, grief, delight, worry, regret, fickleness, inflexibility, modesty, wilfulness, candor, insolence—music from empty holes, mushrooms springing up in darkness, day and night replacing each other before us, and no one knows where they sprout from. Let it be! Let it be![120]

There really is no reason to think that we should be asking for a guiding principle which would be directed to some end. Instead we should just let the process run its natural course:

> Then the four seasons will rise one after the other, the ten thousand things will take their turn at living. Now flourishing, now decaying [. . .] At the end, no tail; at the beginning, no head; now dead, now alive [. . .] its constancy is unending, yet there is nothing that can be counted on.[121]

The Alpha-to-Omega teleology typical of Western thinking, and conducive to an invention of a "First Cause" or "origin" as a metaphysical principle that can be "counted on," is absent in Laozi and Zhuangzi, because *dao* as the process itself does not aim at anything, it is nothing more than constant change without a goal behind it. How to deal with that change is to be shifting yourself, and that is where the gateway character comes in.

Inside & Outside: The Gateway (*Men* 門)

The inconstancy both of the world and of language are things that any Daoist sage should acknowledge and try to attune to. In this section I pay special attention to the situational character of Daoism, and to how Daoists should live the relationality which Hall and Ames speak of. In its language, in its nonmetaphysical approach, Daoism focuses on the interrelatedness of all things, and thus also of humans with those things. Humans are part of the whole process of *dao*, so they are neither pure Being nor pure Nonbeing, neither this nor that, neither purely natural nor purely conventional. Be the male, but preserve the female. Or the other way around. Put another way, human beings are always a bit of both of these yin-yang opposites. Being neither this nor that, humans should understand that *dao* is always the in-between that itself is not, or in other words, is nothing else than the interplay of things and processes. Humans stand in awe and deference of this process and naturally seek some harmony. Some kind of balance between opposing dichotomies is sought after, yet the Daoist is well aware of the shifting state of this balance, since the balance itself is equally prone to the fate which always tends to upset this balance in temporary favor of one or the other of the extremes.

If we take this idea seriously, then in my opinion the point of the first chapter of the *Zhuangzi* is to show that there is difference in understanding, that conventional understanding will not get beyond itself, and that there is a need to overcome this restricted way of thinking. The bird Peng and the fish Kun have many more capabilities than their counterparts, the smaller animals. Yet Peng and Kun too are in some way restricted, as is Liezi's flying exercise. And their hugeness effectively prevents them from being able to do what the small animals do. Therefore I think the first chapter of the *Zhuangzi* is meant to show a preference for the overall view, or for the bigger picture, but this bigger picture is not something beyond all different perspectives, but rather a wider or broader view which acknowledges different views as necessities, which entails equally an awareness of the situatedness of all thinking, as the Autumn Floods chapter and numerous other instances suggest:

> A beam or a pillar can be used to batter down a city wall, but it is no good for stopping up a little hole—this refers to a difference in function. Thoroughbreds like Qiji and Hualiu could gallop a thousand li in one day, but when it came to catching rats they were no match for the wildcat or the weasel—this refers to a difference in skill. The horned owl catches fleas at night and can spot the tip of a hair, but when daylight comes, no matter how wide it opens its eyes, it cannot see a mound or a hill—this refers to a difference in nature. Now do you say that you are going to make Right your master and do away with Wrong, or make Order your master and do away with Disorder? If you do, then you have

> not understood the principle of heaven and earth or the nature of the ten thousand things. This is like saying that you are going to make Heaven your master and do away with Earth, or make Yin your master and do away with Yang. Obviously it is impossible.[122]

Although the preference thus often seems to be one side of the dichotomy or opposition, it is really both sides which are needed and the equilibrium and harmony between the different functions, skills, and natures that is sought. At first glance Jullien seems to favor the view that all this is not about harmony but about "an aspiration toward going beyond the limits,"[123] which would again mean he is very much tied up in the language of the metaphysical tradition. But again on closer inspection we find he does acknowledge both the "harmony" view I have in mind and that the "going beyond" view he seems to espouse is not a going beyond this world: "From one angle or another, the goal is to open up *points of view* to rejoin *vision*; to return from exclusive perspectives to *globality*—that of the Tao—in which all are equally possible."[124] In both cases, no metaphysical principle is invoked or needed.[125] One side is merely privileged since the other side needs to be reigned in.

All these considerations lead me to the necessity of a renewed interpretation of the gateway character (*men* 門). Is it a coincidence that the legendary Laozi was stopped by the "gatekeeper"[126] and that this gatekeeper persuaded him to write down his teachings before he definitely moved to the other side of the gate? And that the gatekeeper said to him: "As you are about to leave the world behind, could you write a book *for my sake*?"[127] I take this to mean that the Daoist gatekeeper wanted to know how to stay at his post, the gate, from where he could respond to the diverse challenges that would inevitably come to him, yet without turning this into a fixed dogmatic position.

The whole *Daodejing* is concerned with polar opposites of the yin-yang character, but the point is not so much to favor one of the opposites over the other. Western interpreters have often understood the *Daodejing* in this hierarchical manner, and have mostly argued that the Daoists favor the other side of the dichotomy more than or over the side which the West has always favored, perhaps as these interpreters were searching for an alternative, but could not break themselves loose from thinking in hierarchies. Although some of the language suggests this, as there is much more focus on the *yin* character traits that one should develop, in the end it is the equilibrium or tranquility *jing* 靜 that is sought after; it is to be skilful in staying at the threshold. As Chapter 42 of the *Daodejing* says: "Everything carries *yin* on its shoulders and *yang* in its arms [a]nd blends these vital energies (*qi*) together to make them harmonious (*he*)."[128] The harmony of this place for which I want to take the gateway as a metaphor should however not be understood as a permanently fixed place, it shifts according to situation and brings out a harmony which is itself a blending of differences "so that they come together with mutual benefit and enhancement without losing their separate and particular identities."[129] This form of harmony thus does not seek to deny or resolve the differences, but to bring them out.

According to Ames and Hall, "[t]he swinging gateway [. . .] is *where* and *when dao* spontaneously 'opens out' to provide creativity a space through which to make its 'entrance,' qualifying the processive nature of *dao* with the immediacy and specificity of the creative act."[130] To be constantly experiencing afresh means to be constantly alert to dogmatic fixations that would close off avenues to the future, and thus it means to stay at the threshold of possibility. The creativity Ames and Hall mention would be that openness and responsiveness to whatever would come to be experienced, the inclination to maximize the possibilities of what is offered without imposing on what offers itself.

The gateway is thus not to be understood as a threshold between this world and another one of transcendent quality, nor to be seen as some escapist hiding place in pure tranquility, detached from the world. Like the *yuan* 原 source, which is more like a *yuan* 源 spring, a fluid and earthly source, than a fixed principle, the gateway is that shifting place of productivity between reversing opposites. That this place is itself equally prone to changes and shifts in perspective can be read from the following quote from the *Yuandao*:

> In the innumerable different directions there are countless changes,
> Untrammeled I am in no fixed position.
> I alone am in great spirits, and leaving things behind,
> Travel along the same path as *dao*.[131]

Not to be in a fixed position is to follow along with the myriad processes as they unfold, neither escaping or keeping away, nor attaching to the specific instances. The Daoist sage, in another metaphor, keeps to the root and acknowledges his(/her) place: "The myriad things have their progenitor, yet he alone knows to abide by the root; The events of the world have a source out of which they come, yet he alone knows to abide by the gateway."[132]

Another factor to be argued for in favor of my reading of the importance of the gateway character has to do with the relation between presence and nonpresence. As I have argued, presence comes about through nonpresence, and vice-versa. That moment between existing and not yet existing can also be conceived as going through a gateway, and if we understand this moment in a nonmetaphysical way, that gateway is the final thing we can say about the whole process:

> The convergence of the myriad things
> Goes through a single aperture;
> The roots of the various happenings
> All issue forth from a single gateway.[133]

Things come into existence from the gateway. The interesting thing I find most in favor of a nonmetaphysical interpretation is that there never seems to be any significant mention of something beyond this gateway; it is the gateway itself that is the final port of call. Again we must look at the first chapter of the *Daodejing*. The standard or metaphysical interpretation of Daoism would have it that the gateway would be that place between the "real" *dao* and the artificial language used to describe it. Yet I have tried to show that both language and *dao* are constitutive of that gateway in different ways. The gateway *is* the meeting place of mankind and *dao* exactly *through* language. At least this is how I would interpret the last lines of Chapter 1 of the *Daodejing*: "These two—the nameless and what is named—emerge from the same source yet are referred to differently. Together they are called obscure. The obscurest of the obscure, [t]hey are the swinging gateway of the manifold mysteries."[134] The nameless and the named, although the most obscure, are the innerworldly gateway. Notice that these lines do not say that they come from somewhere else *through* the gateway, but that they *are* the gateway.

Yet there is a slight problem in putting so much emphasis on this gateway character. First of all, it is obviously just one of many metaphors used in describing *dao* and/or the Daoist sage. Yet I have tried to argue that it is an important one. The other problem arises when we have to explain the lines in Chapter 52 of the *Daodejing*, which are repeated in Chapter 56: "Block up the openings, [a]nd shut the gateways, [a]nd to the end of your days your energies will not be used up."[135] These lines seem to offer a somewhat negative understanding of the gateway. Yet we can explain this in the following way: to shut the gateway is to make sure one is not disturbed or influenced by external factors and by arbitrary fixations. As Ames and Hall explain, it is to "conserve one's vital energies and to avoid depletion that is caused by externally induced agitation."[136] This does not mean a retreat to "the inner circle" but an awareness of the possible consequences of attaching to various external values and things.

Standing in the gateway as I have tried to explain it is also exactly this awareness and the ability to respond to what comes your way in ever-differing appropriateness.

Now for the Daoist sage, the way to get to this ever-shifting place is by asking (*wen* 問) and hearing (*wen* 聞), characters that stress the importance of language, and I now focus on these characters and especially on the "space-between" (*jian* 間) character as characters that are paronomastically close to the gateway character. Chapter 5 of the *Daodejing* talks about the "space-between" heaven and earth as man's abode. The "space-between" character is closely related to the gateway character and should therefore be seen as that shifting place that is itself nothing, but from which all diversity issues. Chapter 10 has the lines: "With nature's [*tian*] gates swinging open and closed, Are you able to remain the female?"[137] This is usually understood as suggesting that one should keep to the *yin* side of the dichotomy, yet it can also be understood as suggesting that one should not venture beyond *tian* as the realm of heaven and earth toward some otherworldly entity or principle, something which can also be read in Chapter 73: "*Tian*'s net is cast wide, [a]nd although coarse in its mesh, nothing slips through it."[138] The mother and the female can then, in similar fashion as the *yuan* source, also be read as being metaphors for the this-worldly approach that I have been arguing for as characteristic of Daoism. This approach and the idea of the *in-between* feature prominently in the comparison with Heidegger and Derrida in the next chapter.

The character for hearing (*wen* 聞) is normally used in the *Daodejing* just for the faculty of hearing, yet in some instances it is better understood as learning or knowing, specifically against the knowing (*zhi* 知) that is common knowledge. This seems to be the case in Chapters 41 and 48, where learning (about) *dao* is specifically connected to hearing. Another character close to the gateway is *wen* 問, or asking. Although not prominent in the *Daodejing*, it does appear in the appendix that Ames and Hall added in their translation, which was part of the 1993 Guodian archaeological find. All these characters, hearing, space-between, and asking, are paronomastically related to the gateway, which means that we can further our understanding of this position by seeing it as something in which openness and willingness to hear, learn, and ask ever anew are important features. Chapter 58 has another related character, *min* 悶, often translated as "muddled." Again the text exploits the inherent vagueness of such a character as a positive point, in the same way as the gateway, and *dao*, are said to be obscure and mysterious. Wing-tsit Chan translates this character as "non-discriminative and dull."[139] The Daoist sage or government will not be enticed into making artificial and arbitrary distinctions, but are content to stay with the undifferentiated. Another place where we can read this is in Chapter 20, where another character related to the gateway is translated as "obtuse."[140] Read paronomastically, these characters that are related to the gateway character argue that the Daoist sage should be staying in the realm of the undifferentiated, in that gateway between the opposing and arbitrary ways of differentiating.

Chapter 25 of the *Daodejing* speaks about *dao* as if it was prior to the world. Yet, as I argued before, we can understand this differently, in the sense that *dao* itself is not the metaphysical entity that seems to be suggested here, because it is not the endpoint since *dao* itself is modeled on what is *ziran*, so of itself. I think therefore that this chapter speaks about *dao* before man introduced the distinction between heaven and earth and placed himself in the middle. So *dao* is not earlier than what is natural or self-so of the world, it is only earlier than artificial distinctions. In my opinion this is also why some metaphysical language seems to get used under erasure in Daoism. I am thinking of the frequent occurrence of constructions in which, in translation,[141] the verb "seeming" plays an important role. In Chapter 4 of the *Daodejing* it is said of *dao* that "it" "seems" the predecessor of *wanwu*, and that "it" "seems" only to persist. Chapter 6, speaking of the gateway and root character of *dao*, also says "it" just "seems" to be there. And as Chapter 14 tells us, the reason for this seeming is that *dao* as the whole process is beyond determination, and being indeterminate "it" cannot be determined by anything determinate. Things are not what they seem to be, and this is especially so for *dao* or *tian* and similar concepts, which can too easily be misunderstood as standing for determinate entities or principles. But what Daoism tells us is that since language only works through such determinations, we must use it carefully and not lose sight of its metaphorical nature.[142] Seen in this way, the mainly Western distinction between reality and appearance seems not to feature in any significant way in Daoism.

Turning to the *Zhuangzi*, there the gateway (*men* 門) character mostly occurs in its ordinary use of door, or gateway, although there are a number of instances where the more philosophical use I am focusing on can be found. *Tianmen,* the gate of heaven, is mentioned in Chapters 14 and 23. In Chapter 14 it is said: "Only he who complies with the Great Change and allows no blockage" is able to follow *dao.* "If the mind cannot accept this fact, then the doors (*men*) of Heaven will never open."[143] Following *dao* thus does not mean seeing the world as static, but rather following the process of change. In chapter 23 we can read that *dao* has "no source, [. . .] no place where it resides, [. . .] no beginning or end,"[144] and as such it is called "the Heavenly Gate."[145] The message is similar to that of the *Daodejing*:

the artificiality of making fixed distinctions between this and that, right and wrong is attacked, and in its place comes an understanding of the world that focuses on acknowledging the open-ended process nature of *dao*. To have this understanding is to reach the "gate of heaven." The sages should therefore seek positions which allow them to see both "this" and "that." This state, as mentioned before, "is called the hinge of the Way. When the hinge is fitted into the socket, it can respond endlessly."[146] So Zhuangzi is also speaking of the gateway, or at least of the hinge, itself not anything, but still imperative as a responsiveness to the process of change. In Chapter 33 it is even said that the sage will "make Heaven his source, Virtue his root, and the Way his gate (*men*), revealing himself through change and transformation."[147] With the undecidability between "this" and "that" Zhuangzi argues for a similar "in-between" stance that sees the processes of the world as ever changing. Thus, things are never strict identities, they are always in motion and thus always becoming something other than what they are. In that sense the processes form an ever-shifting gateway between the opposite forces of yin and yang. This is what is meant by seeing things not as being, but more as becoming. Since this is *ziran*, the sage should thus identify with this becoming or transformation, so as to overcome the narrow perspective of identity as unchanging. Things as processes have no strict boundaries; there is a necessary vagueness or penumbra that Zhuangzi explores extensively,[148] and which precludes the permanence of our artificial naming of them, and thus precludes our seeing them as fixed entities. In Zhuangzi's terms, the processes of the world are always somewhere between the potter's wheel and the grindstone of nature, between emerging and vanishing. The sage's job is to see both this emerging and vanishing as equally necessary. A similar idea is expressed in the *Yuandao* chapter of the *Huainanzi*:

> Thus, where the attention of the spirit is directed toward the small, it is oblivious to the big; Where it is directed toward the internal, it is oblivious to what's going on externally; Where it is directed toward what is above, it is oblivious to what is below; Where it is directed toward the left, it is oblivious to the right. It is only when there is no place that the spirit does not fill that there is nowhere toward which the focus is not directed.[149]

The trick is thus not to escape the realm of the human into something other, it is not to go to the other side of the gate and try to stay in the "heavens," but it is to have that knack to respond to differing situations, which demands both internal and external attention. In Chapter 6 of the *Zhuangzi* there is another determination of *dao,* and here it is called "Peace-in-Strife."[150] The tranquility is to be found inside the world of strife, not somewhere outside. The idea of this is to be able to follow the ever-changing equilibrium between *yin* and *yang* forces, something which can also be read in Chapter 11, where the "dark and mysterious gate"[151] is exactly the passage from *yang* to *yin* (and of course this passage is reversible). This idea of responsiveness which the sage embodies is being sometimes a companion of Heaven, sometimes a companion of man, but more likely a bit of both, according to the shifting circumstances. This is why Zhuangzi advocates following the "torch of chaos and doubt."[152] And it is also why Zhuangzi has Kuan-yin, the keeper of the gate, saying:

> Within yourself, no fixed positions:
> Things as they take shape disclose themselves.
> Moving, be like water,
> Still, be like a mirror,
> Respond like an echo.[153]

Again, by arguing for the importance of an inner-worldly understanding of this gateway character, I am in fact arguing that not only are nonmetaphysical readings of Daoism coherent and supported by textual evidence, they are closer to the Daoist sensibilities than the metaphysical readings.

CONCLUDING DAOISM

To conclude this chapter I suggest the following: by offering at least the possibility of a different reading of the Daoist classics and way of thinking, I hope to have shown that traditional metaphysical interpretations are in many ways biased. The language, worldview, and philosophical background that have often been employed in translating and explaining the Chinese classics to a Western audience are not necessarily those of the Chinese themselves. In fact, we have found that their ideas of the world and their place in it can be explained in a profoundly different way, a thing which we can only fully appreciate if we are both aware of, and willing to a large extent to let go of, our own prejudices. If these metaphysical prejudices are not needed for a coherent explanation of classical Daoism, which is what my reading suggests, then we should not employ the concepts and thought structures that are characteristic of the metaphysical tradition, or when we cannot avoid them, be aware of their provisionality and use them "under erasure."

As the Daoists argued against what they considered the artificial Confucian strictness of public life, in similar ways did Heidegger and Derrida struggle against the prevailing opinions in the societies of their respective times. Heidegger and Derrida specifically argued against the metaphysical tradition of Western philosophy. The Daoists had no such need, since they were not taking aim at a metaphysical tradition to start with. So, although in different circumstances, these struggles in all cases resulted in a nonmetaphysical interpretation of the world and mankind's place in it. There are numerous places in the classical texts where we can find this nonmetaphysical approach, but it is up to us to stay open to such a different approach, and not to demand or expect that Daoism shares much of our Western metaphysical concerns.

In Chapter 4 my focus is on the interaction of Derrida, Heidegger, and Daoism, to get a better understanding of their respective approaches and see the similarities that arise from understanding Daoism in a nonmetaphysical way.

CHAPTER FOUR

Thinking, Philosophy, and Language

Comparing Heidegger, Derrida, and Classical Daoism

> Then everything would hinge on reaching a corresponding saying of language. Only a dialogue could be such a saying correspondence. But, patently, a dialogue with its own particular character. [. . .] And it would remain of minor importance whether the dialogue is before us in writing, or whether it was spoken at some time and has now faded. [. . .] Because the one thing that matters is whether this dialogue, be it written or spoken or neither, remains constantly coming.[1]

> What then, is this encounter with the absolutely-other? Neither representation, nor limitation, nor conceptual relation to the same.[2]

> Where can I find a man who has forgotten words so I can have a word with him.[3]

In this chapter I focus on how the previous interpretations of Heidegger, Derrida, and Daoism can yield an interesting comparison which might shed some more light on the underlying ideas of comparative philosophy. I anticipate that the ideas behind comparative philosophy will be subjected to some rethinking, but that this rethinking should be understood as a strengthening of these ideas through a better understanding both of their functioning and of the dangers implicit in comparative philosophy. The areas of comparison between Heidegger, Derrida, and Daoism that are the most promising are those that bear upon the thoughts on what philosophy and thinking are or should be, and those connected to thoughts on language. These two areas are first explored and then used as a ground for further comparisons opened up by the readings of Heidegger, Derrida, and Daoism that I have proposed, eventually looking at the possible ethical and political implications of these ways of thinking.

In the previous chapters I have argued how a different understanding of language is needed to fully explore the possible relations between Heidegger, Derrida, and Daoism. One of the points I make in this chapter is that none of the protagonists of this book deny the value of language; instead they are acutely aware of the importance of language in shaping thought. Yet Heidegger, Derrida, and the Daoists do wish to point to the limitations of "everyday" language and its reference structure, and thereby to the limitations of metaphysical language. In doing so they argue for the possibilities that arise from a thorough thinking through of, and thereby a different view and use of, language.

My comparison then necessarily has to return to the notion of *Auseinandersetzung.* Derrida would likely say that using the Heideggerian notion of *Auseinandersetzung* is tantamount to working within the metaphysical structures of identities, as the notion seems to imply two different cultural identities. Yet in the first chapter I have shown how, through a clearer understanding of what Heidegger meant by *Auseinandersetzung*, we can deny or amend such an incomplete reading of *Auseinandersetzung.* An *Auseinandersetzung* does not presuppose two different identities; it is more that the identities are side-effects of the more primordial or more originary[4] *Auseinandersetzung* or *Polemos. Auseinander setzen* means to set apart, to dis-sect, with the understanding that there is nothing behind the dissection. In the same way *différance* is the more originary play of the world, of which particular differences are the consequences and not the causes.

I hope to show that Heidegger is more viably compared with the *Daodejing* and that Derrida's thoughts are more in line with those of the *Zhuangzi.* This is an important point, because although not necessarily historically the same in both situations, it would seem that Derrida and the *Zhuangzi* are in some philosophical way the descendants of Heidegger and the *Daodejing*, respectively, so it could be fruitful to look for some particular similarities. By seeing the *Daodejing* and the *Zhuangzi* in this way I am not trying to impose the very complex connection between Heidegger and Derrida on Chinese history. But I do think that in a philosophical way the *Zhuangzi* is expanding and progressing on ideas found in the *Daodejing,* and that to see this development in a comparison with the development from Heidegger to Derrida can lead to a better understanding of both.

Although I have presented both Heidegger and Laozi as proposing a non-metaphysical thinking, we have to realize there is the distinct possibility to read in both Heidegger and Laozi some remnants of metaphysical thinking, or in other words there are certain passages open to a metaphysical interpretation, which later scholars have followed up, at the expense of non-metaphysical readings. As we saw earlier, Derrida, although highly appreciative of Heidegger's thinking, nevertheless sees him as to a certain extent stuck in metaphysics, and Laozi has often been interpreted as expounding a metaphysical view of *dao.* And even in the Zhuangzi there is talk of a "creator." But if my understanding of Heidegger, Derrida, Laozi, and Zhuangzi is correct, these metaphysical interpretations lose much of their plausibility.

In order to see and fully appreciate these problems in comparing Heidegger, Derrida, and Daoism, we must first take a closer look at some comparisons that have already been offered between Heidegger and/or Derrida on one hand, and Chinese philosophy in general and Daoism in particular on the other hand.

METAPHYSICS, DIFFERENCE, AND COMPARISONS

> Derrida's deconstructive grammatology [. . .] seeks an absolute interiorization of writing as an autonomous act.[5]

Does it really? Actually it does not. Of the many comparisons that have been made between Daoism and Heidegger and/or Derrida,[6] most have tried to establish, in the case of Heidegger, that *dao* is similar to Being (*Sein*) or Way (*Weg*), or, in the case of Derrida, that *dao* is similar to differance or trace. While this is naturally to be expected, the fact has been that in the process of doing so, in many cases metaphysical ideas of presence and origin have been reinstated, in direct contradiction to the Heideggerian and Derridean nondualist, nonmetaphysical ways of thinking in the West. In other instances, comparisons have sought to infer relations beyond the actual similarities in ways that are not always valid, that have overlooked important differences. In other words, it is my opinion that some of these comparisons have in important ways distorted the views of Heidegger, Derrida, and of Daoism either by reappropriating them to the metaphysical tradition, or by inferring more affinity than is called for. This section looks at specific instances where this has happened in comparisons of Heidegger and/or Derrida with Daoism.

Difference and Comparison

In comparative philosophy we must foremost not lose sight of the important differences in cultural approaches to thinking, and here that means we must actively be aware of the differences that pertain between the three participants in this particular intercultural dialogue. Differences in background assumptions need to be explored, differences in form, style, and goals, as well as historical differences. For example, the anxiety (*Angst*) that Heidegger sees as a fundamental characteristic of Dasein in his earlier work, seems to be a very Western, twentieth-century phenomenon that has to do with the sense of loss of foundation. The apprehension that classical Chinese thinkers might have had concerning living out their years or concerning their political surroundings is nowhere the same. Another difference that is obvious is the individualist approach of Heidegger, because although Dasein is always *Mitsein* (being together), there is nevertheless a profound individualization taking place in much of Heidegger's early work, where Dasein is only authentically itself as possibility in its understanding as an individualized entity which realizes its mortality.

Another difference is found in focus. Where Daoists seem to put emphasis on the continuum rather than the differences between the parts of the continuum, Heidegger and Derrida focus their efforts on the deconstruction of this sort of continuum as it has been perceived by metaphysics, in the sense of a unity and identity that is independent of actual differences. Both difference and continuity are implied though, both by Heidegger and Derrida as well as the Daoists. It is merely a matter of both the historical and philosophical background in each different case dictating the focal approach. One reason for this could be that Heidegger and Derrida were actively engaged in a struggle with metaphysics, whereas for the Chinese thinkers such a struggle did not exist in the same way.

In itself the idea that highly complicated and controversial notions such as Heidegger's *Sein*, Derrida's *différance*, and the Daoist notion of *dao* could mean the same is naïve to say the least. Yet while most thinkers who have compared Heidegger and Derrida with Daoism do not really make this mistake, they still argue for a seeming overlap between some of these notions, which needs to be taken with extreme caution, especially since the translations of these terms into English (or into any other *one* natural language) already make it easier to "find" similarities. This danger of re-appropriating different ways of thinking through translation must constantly keep us on guard. But if the similarities are merely found in the supposed vagueness and ensuing difficulty for common sense or rational understanding to come to grips with what these terms have to say to us, such comparisons merely have provisional value. And, more likely, in the process of a comparison via rational structures that is intent on finding *the* meaning of these terms, it is much easier for metaphysical notions such as transcendence to reappear. The ideas of *Sein*, *différance*, and *dao*, respectively, and other related notions as *Weg*, trace, supplement, *wuwei*, and *ziran* with them, are then in danger of being reified in the direction of a substance ontology, against the often explicit intentions of the authors behind these notions to the contrary. The idea of a comparison itself could easily suggest such reification, if we believe that although outwardly different, on a deeper level, behind the appearances, there must be similarities. So even though this book is itself a comparison of similarities between Heidegger, Derrida, and Daoism, we need to be on constant guard against implying more connections or similarities than are warranted, and be aware of how we see any similarities.

We saw that by translating *you* and *wu*, respectively, as 'Being' and 'Nothing,' understanding could inadvertently be guided to see these terms from within the metaphysical structure of the West, and therefore Heidegger's writings on 'Being' and 'Nothing' seem to offer an easy comparison. Yet at first this is only superficially so, since Heidegger started *from* the metaphysical tradition of the West, arguing against its insistence on a highest being and its philosophy of presence. We have already seen and shall again see later that the relation of *you* and *wu* in Chinese philosophy comes from a very different background, one that did not start out from this metaphysical framework. That means that comparisons are not always that easy, and similarities might have to do more with translations and the wish to find such similarities than with the actual intellectual culture and worldview of both parties.

Metaphysics and Comparison

One of the earliest comparisons of Heidegger and the *Daodejing* is a reading and translation of the latter by Chang Chung-yuan. While in his introduction Chang tries hard to avoid metaphysical ideas, he nevertheless seems content to imply a strong sense of mysticism in both Daoism and Heidegger, evident in the following quote:

> *Tao* is the highest attainment of primordial intuition. *Tao* is preontological experience, which is gained through the interfusion and identification of the subjectivity of man and the objectivity of things. This preontological, inner experience is the spontaneous reflection of one's being, which simultaneously transcends both time and space.[7]

Now while this may to a certain extent be said of Daoism (although my reading of Daoism in Chapter 3 questions this whole attitude of seeing it as mysticism, at least as far as transcendence is inserted), Heidegger has always argued vehemently against mysticism, which he saw mostly as an attempt to escape from the finite world into some realm of eternity. Mysticism, which for Heidegger consists of "the mere counterimage of metaphysics," exactly because it remains in this inversion, is for those who are "still trapped in utter servitude to a metaphysics they think they have long since suppressed, [and] seek escape routes to some arcane realm, some world beyond the sensuous."[8] As such, Heidegger argues against such a mysticism functioning in philosophy. Although Heidegger was highly interested in medieval mysticism (especially Eckhart), he nevertheless saw this mysticism as belonging to religion, and as such it belongs to the realm of faith, and not to that of philosophy. And although he did borrow freely from the language that is often employed in mysticism, Heidegger on the other hand wished to ground every philosophy and way of thinking and living on or in a thorough understanding of finite existence. In this way Heidegger's work is really not about generating "preontological experiences" which would transcend space and time, but about the way in which to see experiences in a different light, from a different thinking perspective within space and time. Chang here seems too eager to explain the ideas of Daoism along the lines of Western-style mysticism, whereby subject and object become (momentarily) interfused in the "preontological experience" which is then supposed to transcend space and time. If the conclusions of my third chapter are correct, these comparisons miss the point that Daoism is trying to bring across. If there is a form of mysticism in Daoism, it is about interfusing *with* space and time exactly *as* a spatial and temporal being, and not about transcending these categories. If seen in the first, this-worldly way, it might be compared to Heidegger,[9] but that is not what Chang does. Besides that, the idea of interfusing subject and object is itself misleading, since Heidegger's project was to find ways of thinking that were before or beyond (in the sense of more originary than) this distinction, where Chang seems to take the distinction itself as given primary to any subsequent interfusion.

Chang also frequently refers to Chan Buddhism for a clarification of his translation and interpretation. This in itself is not an illegitimate enterprise since Chan Buddhism is for a large part a direct descendant of earlier Daoism, and I have done the same in Chapter 3 and will again on occasion refer to Chan Buddhism to strengthen or clarify my own case. But one must take caution to see this as just clarification. Seeing in Chan Buddhism the ultimate meaning of the Daoist classics, which is something Chang seems to be aiming at exactly with his notions of "primordial intuition," "enlightenment" and especially when he translates *xuande* 玄德 of the final sentence of Chapter 10 of the *Daodejing* as "mystic attainment,"[10] is not justified.

There are other comparisons of Heidegger and Daoism in which, at least partially, this metaphysical scheme is perpetuated. Graham Parkes, whom I usually agree with to a large extent, in one of his earlier papers on Daoism and the early Heidegger, seems eager to translate or interpret *wu* as "absolute Nothing,"[11] thereby reinforcing a metaphysical reading of Heidegger's early work that seeks to interpret Heidegger's *Nichts* as the absolute and not relative opposite of Being. Two things need to be said about this. First of all, in his later work, Heidegger denounced these kinds of readings, and he himself recognized that the way of *Sein und Zeit* was flawed, and consequently did not speak of Being as "absolute Nothing" anymore, but as *Ereignis*. This in itself should give us pause when we compare Heidegger's earlier work alone, as standing by itself. Second, Parkes makes the point that in both Daoism and Heidegger, "the realization of a particular emptiness, lack or non-being within the world conduces to a realization of the Nothing that is the ultimate ground of everything."[12] In my view it is exactly this metaphysical extensionism in the trend of Plato and Descartes that fallaciously transfers findings in one realm to another, that (at least the later) Heidegger, Derrida, and Daoism have been seeking to avoid. In the case of Daoism, Parkes mentions Chapter 11 of the *Daodejing*, where the nothingness or emptiness functions as the provider of the use of things. But surely this, as I have tried to explain in Chapter 3, is about relationality and not about absolute Nothing. *You* and *wu* belong together, always work together, as presence and absence. As Ames and Hall have explained, there is really no need to see *you* and *wu* as ontological categories.[13] Similarly we need not understand Heidegger's *Sein-zum-Tode*, Being-unto-death, as being about this absolute idea of Nothing, as Parkes assumes. Dasein's relation to death, its own death, is not that of a being toward absolute Nothing, but of a being toward its own possible and inevitable demise, and that means essentially that the nonbeing is as relative to the being as the being is relative to the nonbeing.

Parkes further notices the similarity between the Daoist *yin-yang* dichotomy or dynamic on one hand, and the "strife" (*Streit, polemos*) of Heidegger on the other.[14] While I agree with this similarity, there is no need to further postulate something beyond the "strife" or beyond the dynamic of *yin* and *yang*, which is exactly what Parkes seems to do with this notion of absolute Nothing.

On a different level, the Kyoto school of thought as an expression of one of the later developments of classical Daoism, Chan/Zen Buddhism, also takes Heidegger back to metaphysics. Nishida and Nishitani, with their idea of 'Absolute Nothingness' as the opposite of Western thinking, seem to get stuck in this inversion and fail to go beyond it when they insist on their other-worldly understanding of Zen Buddhism. Trying to incorporate Heidegger into the mainstream Western tradition,[15] the Kyoto school thinkers failed to notice how notions such as the ontological difference, Being, and Dasein function as this-worldly concepts by their implicit design, and they thus saw Heidegger as not going far enough because he did not establish the link back to the essential religious experience, where Nishida and Nishitani insist on the religious nature of their thinking. In my view, the argument against mysticism that Heidegger makes applies to their thought. Nishitani, for example, says that the "self has its home-ground at a point disengaged from the world and things."[16] Although my point here is not necessarily an argument against Zen Buddhism and its perceived religious nature, it does point to the fact that Heidegger was often wrongly interpreted as promoting an absolutist view of Being and Nothing. Interestingly, in his contribution to *Heidegger and Asian Thought*,[17] Nishitani seeks a similar closeness between Zen Buddhism, Christianity, and Heidegger, in which he counters the idea of transcendence but advocates an absolute standpoint. Nishitani seeks to appropriate Heidegger's play on the notions of *Heimat, heimisch, unheimisch,* and *Unheimlichkeit* to the Buddhist idea of universal suffering and subsequent detachment from the transitory world,[18] where I have argued and argue again in this chapter that Heidegger's work is about dealing *with* the transitory world, but not from a detached point of view, but from a committed, inserted, and situational point of view.

Similarly, there have been many examples of comparisons of Derrida to Chinese philosophy, and most notably these seek to compare Derrida's differance to *dao.* Most of the thinkers who try to deal with Derrida's possible relations to Chinese thinking and language, however, seem very one-sided. They tend to overemphasize writing as opposed to speech, or overemphasize the negative in Derrida in general. One of the first points where many interpretations go wrong is in the failure to notice that while *dao* is arguably one of the most central notions of Chinese philosophy in general and Daoism in particular, differance is just one of the words Derrida uses to try to describe what he thinks, and that this particular word, as opposed to *dao*, is itself to be abandoned. To make a strong comparison between *dao* and differance that purely focuses on the importance and centrality of these terms is itself a neglecting of the provisionality that is espoused especially by Derrida and, if my interpretation is right, also in Daoism. I now proceed by giving a couple of examples where interpretations of Derrida are inconclusive.

One of the readings of Derrida's encounter with the Chinese language (which, as I have shown in Chapter 3, was far from comprehensive) is by

Hwa Yol Jung.[19] My main objection to Jung's article is that he adopts a very superficial understanding of Derrida's *Of Grammatology* which fails to realize that Derrida's "writing" is not the opposite of speech, nor the mere inversion of the hierarchy between speech as closer to meaning than writing, this hierarchy itself being one of the essential features of Western logocentric metaphysics.[20] With "writing," Derrida has argued for an understanding of language, including *both* speech and writing, as equally arbitrary and provisional sign structures. Oddly, Jung makes some claims similar to Derrida, but in an attack on Derrida that perceives him as stuck in the inversion of the hierarchy. First Jung agrees with Samuel Beckett, saying that "in language as gestures the spoken and the written are identical."[21] But later on in the same paper Jung propounds a version of the Chinese language that puts it squarely in the logocentric or at least phonocentric tradition, favoring speech over writing, going so far as to say that "(w)riting is an artefact, whereas speaking is not," and following this up with the claim that "speaking is an unmediated medium for human communication."[22] The point is not so much that Jung tries to relocate classical Chinese into the logocentric standard, but that in the process of doing so he misses Derrida's point totally in saying that Derrida thought that Chinese ideography is "the pure and simple act of writing purged of the phonetic."[23] Anyone with a more than a superficial understanding of Derrida knows that Derrida thinks there is nothing pure and simple, and certainly not "writing." Even in *Of Grammatology*, as I have shown before, Derrida has pointed to the fact that classical Chinese had phonetic elements in it.[24] Derrida's point of the so-called inversion or reversal of the opposites is to overcome the artificial hierarchy itself.

Edward T. Ch'ien, in an article seeking to explain *dao* in terms of an ultimate reality, perceives similarities with Derrida.[25] However, Ch'ien also does not do justice to Derrida when he says that Derrida's idea of a noncenter is merely to be understood in the field of language. Although obviously Derrida's main efforts have been concerned with language as a play of differences with no center and no ultimate meaning other than within this play, this by no account means that that is where Derrida stops. His work has much wider implications, in that the conclusions he draws about language point us to a way of thinking that underlies our most fundamental metaphysical convictions. Ch'ien argues that Daoism is about the ontology of *dao* as the ultimate reality, but if we take serious the similarities Ch'ien finds with Derrida, and admit that Derrida's work is about questioning this whole ontology, as it is an attack on this logocentric metaphysics, then seeing *dao* as an ultimate reality becomes problematic. Since Ch'ien does not want to draw this conclusion, he seems happy to confine Derrida to a philosophy of language, but as we have seen, the idea that "there is nothing outside the text" does not support such a confinement, but rather challenges it.

In an article in *Critical Inquiry*, Zhang Longxi[26] agrees with the standard reading of Daoism that explains it as metaphysical, and thus similar to the Western tradition. Zhang's article is another example that does not so much seek to find similarities between Daoism and Derrida, but seeks to reintegrate Daoism into the mainstream standard by denying that Derrida's claims have any application to Chinese thinking and language. Zhang does so by insisting that the mistrust of language, and especially writing, as a conveyor of true meaning, and by extension the logocentric approach to thinking, is common to both Western and Eastern traditions, thereby perpetuating the metaphysical claim that there must be something "beyond" language. As he says: "Logocentrism, therefore, does not inhabit just the Western ways of thinking; it constitutes the very way of thinking itself."[27] Zhang then, rightly, uses Derrida to argue for the fact that nonphonetic language suffers the same inadequacy as phonetic language, but with exactly the reverse conclusion that Derrida comes up with. Where for Derrida, according to Zhang, and rightfully so in my opinion, this "inadequacy" leads to the understanding of language as "a trace without origin,"[28] Zhang argues that "a Chinese intertext is always a trace leading back to the origin, to the fountainhead of tradition, the great thinkers of Taoism and Confucianism."[29] Writing, for Derrida, means the impossibility of any origin. In Zhang's opinion, Chinese writings have the power to "transform [. . .] the author into authoritative text."[30] If I understand correctly, Zhang then means that thinking is metaphysical, and that Chinese language is somehow capable of transforming an author whose existence is doubtful into an authority that is present, whereby language revenges itself against the claim of being a mere supplement. In my view Zhang then merely uses the ideas behind deconstruction as a tool to reinstate metaphysical beliefs about something beyond language, but unfortunately only accessible through language.

David A. Dilworth reaffirms my earlier suggestion concerning Heidegger, that the Kyoto school is intent on profiling itself as the opposite of Western logocentrism, and that it seeks to include Heidegger and Derrida in the Western tradition.[31] Dilworth's reading of Derrida fails to understand that employing the semantic form of the metaphysical tradition does not necessitate being firmly within that tradition. Dilworth says that Derrida privileges "the concept of *differance* as the final a priori structure of writing."[32] To say this is to mistake the "concept" of differance for a metaphysical form of identity, a logocentrism. The point of Derrida's critique is really that his thinking is no longer reducible to such a fixed standard, but that this at the same time does not mean Derrida admits of no standards. The polarization Dilworth speaks of as ensuing from the post-modernist's insistence on difference is another instance of a superficial reading of Derrida.[33] Derrida sees opposites at work everywhere, but as we have seen that does not mean that these opposites can never meet. Indeed, the whole point is that they must of necessity meet, all the time, since the supplement, or the trace of otherness always upsets identities and therefore also upsets strict dichotomies or oppositions. Dilworth is right in assuming that the Kyoto school profiles itself as the opposite of Western thinking, but he is wrong in suggesting that Derrida espouses the same opposition. This inversion, as we have seen and will see again later, is just a necessary phase, which, if succumbed to and not thoroughly deconstructed as well, retains one firmly in the metaphysical tradition.

This section has argued that a lot of misunderstandings and/or misapplications of Heidegger and Derrida have occurred in comparing them to Daoism or other East Asian schools of thought. Through such comparisons the dominant metaphysical tradition is usually reinforced. It is imperative to find ways of comparison which challenge such one-sided approaches. Even if there is a danger of my own interpretation being one-sided in the reverse direction, we shall see how this inversion should be seen in the end.

THINKING AND PHILOSOPHY

> Thinking is not a means to gain knowledge. Thinking cuts furrows into the soil of Being.[34]

Derrida has always maintained that his thinking is both inside and outside of philosophy. His questions are therefore no longer (solely) a part of the philosophical discourse in a strict sense. Both Heidegger and Derrida question philosophy on its grounds, its presuppositions, its most basic assumptions. This being partly outside of philosophy is of interest to comparative thinking in two ways. First of all, it is increasingly understood that the ways of thinking of Daoism (and of many non-Western cultures) do not benefit from being squeezed into the harness of philosophy as it is commonly known in the West. In other words, Western-style metaphysics or ontotheology and Daoism are not that compatible, but both Heidegger and Derrida have made it easier for us to argue that while not philosophical in the traditional, metaphysical, and logical sense, this Daoist tradition has a lot of thinking to offer. Secondly, we can use the different ideas found in Daoism to challenge and question the normality of Western philosophy by arguing that different views of the world will lead us to different conclusions which are not necessarily better or worse in any sense. Thus Daoism is very much a part of the "community of *thinking*."[35] Philosophy as metaphysics is also part of this community, but the point is to see that neither metaphysics nor other ways of thinking should be perceived as better or as more authentic. We must no longer see them in a hierarchical way but rather as complementary. Both have their respective places, and we can understand this from the interpretation of Daoism that I have given in the previous chapter, whereby not one side of an opposition is given preference, but both sides are needed for a full understanding of the whole field in which the opposition takes place.

Heidegger has similarly argued that his *Wiederholung* or *Überwindung*, or deconstruction of metaphysics should not be seen as a demolishing of metaphysical thought to be replaced with something else (presumably its opposite), but as a thinking that leaves behind the narrow confines of metaphysical thought, without thereby denying metaphysics its place. In fact, neither Heidegger nor Derrida sees himself as completely free from metaphysics. Rather, their works revolve around metaphysics and are located on its margins, its boundaries. Yet as deconstructive they aim at the heart of metaphysics, not to overcome the metaphysical tradition, but to get to its fundamental presuppositions and show how these constitute only one part of what is called thinking.

This section then argues for seeing the position of comparative thinking in a similar vein, as being both inside and outside of philosophy. The definition of philosophy and thereby the inclusion or exclusion of other types of thinking in the greater discourse of philosophy, that is to say the limits of philosophy and its delimitations, has always been a special problem for comparative philosophers, who have struggled to include many different ways of thinking while feeling obliged to keep to at least some of the rational structures of philosophy. Yet my whole point would be that to conceive of culturally different and thus often substantially different ways of thinking as situated both inside and outside of philosophy is especially suited to the whole program of comparative philosophy, as it is not a matter of thinking in a dualistic inside *or* outside, philosophy *or* thinking, but a nondualist thinking that tries to overcome these sorts of distinctions and hierarchies or, in other words, tries to think *in-between* different cultures. That *in-between* I have tried to locate in Chapter 1 in Heidegger as the *Auseinandersetzung* and the *Lichtung* and *Ereignis*, in Chapter 2 in Derrida as the trace, differance, spacing, and play, and in Chapter 3 in Daoism as *dao*, the gateway (*men*), the hinge, and the interplay of *yin* and *yang*. These notions thus stand in need of comparison, which is the aim of this chapter.

Regarding the inside and the outside, the point of Heidegger, Derrida, and Daoism seems exactly to not succumb to the temptation of going to either side, but remaining *on* or *in* the hinge, the gateway, the margin or dehiscence. Thus the protagonists consider themselves neither above the play of differences nor to be denying or overcoming this play in a dialectic third position, but in a way they are *both* inside *and* outside, in the "between," or the openness. Comparative philosophy can never be from some neutral perspective, some place above or detached from what it seeks to compare. But as *in-between* it is also always shifting, depending on what is compared. Comparative philosophy can then never have a final or purely theoretical form, applicable to different instances, but is itself a changing process that lacks strict identity. In Derridean fashion we could say that any identity that comparative thinking has is purely a function of the differences that make it up.

In Heidegger's later work the notion of *Ereignis* (appropriation, event, happening) becomes increasingly important. This idea, which receives more attention later in this chapter, could compare well with the idea of *dao* in the sense that Ames and Hall give it, as "way-making," precisely because both the notion of *Ereignis* and *dao* as "way-making" make it clear that the focus is on the relationship(s) of human beings with their world. *Er-eignen* as "appropriating" should however definitely not be read under the metaphysical assumption of a subject appropriating an object to itself, making it its own, or of possessing an object, but more in the sense of relating from a particular focus (*de*) toward the environment, the world. This particular focus, as we have seen in the *Zhuangzi*, is unavoidable and need not necessarily mean something negative. In the same way as Hall and Ames have argued for the preference of situation over strict agency and against the subject–object distinction, Heidegger argues for the *event* of *Ereignis* as the place/time where Being happens, and this *Ereignis* happens to Dasein as much as it is of its own making. In his earlier work, especially *Being and Time,* the focus is more on the Dasein and its *Jemeinigkeit*, about how Dasein actively relates to its world. Yet even there the distinctive mode of Being that puts Dasein in its place as *Sein-zum-Tode*, that is *Angst*, is not something Dasein chooses but is something that as an event happens to it beyond its control. In Heidegger's later work the attention shifts and then the event, the *Ereignis,* comes increasingly to be seen as the more originary, yet not of course without any Dasein. *Ereignis* is somewhere in-between.

When thinking along the lines of Derrida's all-pervading contextuality we come to a similar conclusion, one that privileges situation, relation, and context over identity. On this note it would be impossible to exclude the commentarial and religious traditions of Daoism. There is never a clear-cut line. This is where the notion of *in-between* becomes important, and this notion is further explored in this chapter. My approach is to first compare Heidegger and Daoism, and then later Derrida and Daoism. After that I use these comparisons for the more important section on language.

HEIDEGGER AND DAOISM

In this section we must start by placing Heidegger's particular interest for Daoism in perspective by pointing to his equal interest in ancient Greek thinkers and German poets, and in some medieval mystics. The point to see is that these interests show that Heidegger is a very profound thinker in his own right, and that he uses these other ways of thinking mostly for his own project. As we have seen, Heidegger uses poets, but is not a poet, he uses the ancient Greeks, but is not one of them. This was shown clearly in the quotation in Chapter 1 where Heidegger said that we have to become "more Greek" than the ancient Greeks themselves.[36] In the same way, Heidegger uses Daoism, but is not a Daoist. The Heideggerian imperative is to think *through* these other ways of thinking. Yet there are many similarities with Daoism which are fruitful for a better understanding of both Heidegger and Daoism, and Heidegger's interests in and rethinking of the ancient Greeks and the German poets can be used for furthering our understanding of how Heidegger sees the connection between himself and Daoism.

In returning to the ancient Greeks Heidegger has tried to provide us with unorthodox readings of their way of thinking. These readings are unorthodox exactly because they try to undermine the "traditional" metaphysical readings that have been offered to us throughout the Platonic history of Western philosophy. We could therefore look and see whether Heidegger's vocabulary is also applicable to a nonmetaphysical reading of Daoism. We must be aware, however, that any applicability of Heidegger's language does *not* mean to say that the thinking of the ancient Greeks is to a large extent the same as that of the Daoist classics. However, it *does* mean that a language and vocabulary of nontranscendence, of nonmetaphysical import could be more suitable to express the sensibilities of Daoist thinking.

Heraclitus propounded the idea that "*Physis* loves to hide," and we can now reinterpret this in Heidegger's terminology to mean that every unconcealment comes with concealment; there is always mystery involved. Profound thinking is not the rational solution of mystery but the thoughtful acknowledgment of the fact that thinking is necessarily concerned with both concealing and unconcealing. Heidegger also saw this in Daoism:

> Perhaps there lies concealed in the word "Way," *tao*, the mystery of all mysteries of thoughtful saying, as long as we let this name return to its unspokenness and are able to accomplish this letting.[37]

We must see Heidegger's new or different reading of the poets in a similar vein. Far from traditional, it is yet a very thoughtful reading that keeps in mind the profound difference between Heidegger himself and the poets. And again, it is a reading which seeks to undo the predominance of metaphysical ways of conceiving of poetry. Heidegger was very much aware of the poetic strength of the Daoist classics. He had two lines of Chapter 15 of the *Daodejing* inscribed in calligraphy in his studio, a present from Paul Shih-yi Hsiao, with whom he partially translated the *Daodejing*. On one occasion Heidegger wrote these two lines back to Hsiao in a letter. These lines are usually translated along the following lines:

> Muddy water, when stilled, slowly becomes clear;
> Something settled, when agitated, slowly comes to life.[38]

Heidegger translates, or rather interprets, these lines into his own idiom and way of thinking:

> Who can be still and out of stillness and through it move something on
> to the Way so that it comes to shine forth?
> [Who is able through making still to bring something into Being?[39]

The point of these lines, and especially of Heidegger's take on them, is that they do not show preference for stillness as such, but acknowledge the process of reversing that was mentioned earlier. Things in motion return to stillness, things in tranquillity return to life, or motion. Although Heidegger's translation shows this less clearly than the more standard ones, Hsiao explains that indeed "Heidegger thought this [the lines in question] through farther, in saying that clarifying finally brings something to light, and subtle motion in the tranquil and still can bring something into being."[40] So again it is not about valuing stillness as such, but about the interplay of stillness and motion. Through this, and through Heidegger's thoughts on the Greeks and the German poets, we return to the idea of *Auseinandersetzung*, which aims at setting two things in relation. This relation is the space between. The *Auseinandersetzung* similarly is itself nothing, yet it is what takes place in-between. This *in-between* is a constant focus of Heidegger's work, as evident from the following passage from *Unterwegs zur Sprache*:

> The intimacy of world and thing is present in the separation of the between; it is present in the dif-ference. The word dif-ference is now removed from its usual and customary usage. What it now names is not a generic concept for various kinds of differences. It exists only as this single difference. It is unique. Of itself, it holds apart the middle in and through which world and things are at one with each other. The intimacy of the dif-ference is the unifying element of the *diaphora*, the carrying out that carries through. The dif-ference carries out world in its worlding, carries out things in their thinging. Thus carrying them out, it carries them toward one another. The dif-ference does not mediate after the fact by connecting world and things through a middle added on to them. Being the middle, it first determines world and things in their presence, i.e., in their being toward one another, whose unity it carries out.[41]

It is difference that is most important, and from this difference we start looking for what is common. Yet the opposites are always already connected in an essential way. The "intimacy" or unity of the differences does not exist anywhere else but in the interplay of the differences. For example, in Heidegger's earlier work, the notions of authenticity and inauthenticity play an important role. In the *Verfallen* of *das Man*, in our modern societies, we have lost touch with what we really, existentially, authentically are. But Heidegger takes caution not to see the relation of authenticity to inauthenticity in a moral sense. Inauthenticity is a necessary part of what we are. Only when understood in that sense, as two sides of a coin, could one say that Heidegger argues for a return to authenticity, our nature as Dasein. In much the same way the *Daodejing* argues that we need to undo the artificial social structures that keep us from becoming ourselves. In Philip J. Ivanhoe's words:

> [. . .] the natural state to which the Daoists appeal is not the status quo but the *dao*, which lies beneath successive layers of socialization. For those in the fallen state of society, the *dao* is not easy to discern or to follow. The challenge is to become aware of what we—in some deep sense—are and then work and live in light of this awareness.[42]

We can see this double layer of two opposing sides working together in much of Heidegger's work, and we see it in Daoism. If we compare the notion of *physis* with *tian*, together with *ziran*, we begin to understand nature as self-emerging and self-hiding. Concealing is essential to unconcealing. Every possible unconcealing is based on concealing; we never have access to the things in themselves, except through our human perspectives and signification structures. We can further our understanding of this when we take into consideration the notion of *aletheia*. The *aletheia* of Being is based as much on unconcealing as on concealing. First of all, every unconcealing that Being grants conceals Being as itself. Second, one way of unconcealing tends to conceal other ways, in the same way as the metaphysical tradition of unconcealing concealed other possible ways of thinking. Heidegger asks himself rhetorically, does not concealing belong essentially to unconcealing:

> because self-concealing, concealment, *lethe* belongs to *a-letheia*, not just as an addition, not as shadow to light, but rather as the heart of *aletheia*? And does not even a keeping and preserving rule in this self-concealing of the opening of presence from which unconcealment can be granted to begin with, and thus what is present can appear in its presence? If this were so, then the opening (*Lichtung*) would not be the mere opening of presence, but the opening of presence concealing itself, the opening of a self-concealing sheltering (*sich verbergenden Bergens*).[43]

This is why Heidegger was much more fond of the star metaphor instead of the traditional sun/light metaphor, since the former reveals much more clearly that light, as clearing, as unconcealing, is always surrounded by and only possible through darkness, as concealing. Presence, as unconcealment, is never pure; there are always traces of otherness or concealment in it. I come back to this notion of trace in Heidegger's work later. *Tian*, or *dao*, thought of as the process of nature, works similarly. *Tian* and *dao* are obscure, dark, granting but never showing themselves.[44] *Tian* is like *dao* as Heidegger's *Zeit-Spiel-Raum* or *Zeit-Raum* (time-space). It is not a fixed source; the idea is more that of *yuandao*, not as the source of *dao* but as the fluid spring of *dao*. There is no endpoint, and in that sense it might be comparable to Heidegger's notion of "abyss." It is the framework in which everything happens, yet which itself is nothing. Heidegger explains the *Zeit-Raum* as the abyss (*Ab-grund*)[45] that is the grounding emptiness, precisely as the absence of a fixed ground (thought in a metaphysical and substantial way). There is a sense in which *yuan* can be read in accordance with this notion of abyss, since, as Lau and Ames have explained, the source (*yuan*) of which the *Yuandao* speaks should not be understood as pointing to a metaphysical principle but to a fluid this-worldly source, as a life-force like water from a spring.[46]

As I have already indicated, in Heidegger's later work the idea of *Ereignis* (event of appropriation) becomes more and more important. *Ereignis* is a notion closely related to the clearing of unconcealing and concealing. *Ereignis* should first be explained more carefully before it can be compared to any notions in Daoism. First fully explored by Heidegger in *Beiträge zur Philosophie*,[47] the notion of *Ereignis* is meant to think beyond the subject–object dichotomy, in the sense that the subject is always already included in the event. The subject belongs to the more originary event and can only be derivatively understood from *Ereignis*. Dasein abandons itself to the event, which means it seeks to understand itself as part of some ongoing process and from that process, which in turn means that we understand our Dasein not as something apart from this process. This is what Heidegger means by *Ereignis*. When Heidegger moved from thinking Being itself from Dasein to thinking Being and time together as *Ereignis*, or appropriation, he made it very clear at least that this is not to be thought in any metaphysical way: "Appropriation is not the encompassing general concept under which Being and time could be subsumed."[48] *Ereignis*, as Hans Ruin describes it, is "the free and incalculable and abyssal opening in and through which beings obtain their place and significance."[49] *Ereignis* then has to do with the always-already-there of the shifting relationality between otherness and self (or rather Dasein).

Another way to understand this is by employing the notions Ames and Hall propose: focus and field. Only within the field of process does there arise anything like a specific focus. The reading of *dao* that I have given in Chapter 3 concurs with this approach. Both *Ereignis* and *dao* are to be seen as processes, both singular processes of things and referring to the whole process nature of the world to which man belongs. Thus thinking becomes an experience both of and from this processuality, and Heidegger, Derrida, Laozi, and Zhuangzi all in their own way try to convey as well as guide us into this experience, of which I say more later. This experience is necessarily one of turning—turning from artificial structures to a more originary event of appropriation.[50] As Heidegger says: "*Be-ing essentially happens as Ereignis*. That is not a proposition but the non-conceptual, silent telling of the essential happening that opens itself only to the full, historical enactment of inceptive (*anfängliches*) thinking."[51] *Ereignis* is the more originary (in the sense of *Ursprünglich* and *Anfänglich*) event, and it is how the world comes to us, how it shows itself, how we are in the world, and the same could be said of *dao*.

Important for our comparison of Heidegger and Daoism is that he also understands *Ereignis* fundamentally as *in-between*:

> Yet this "in-between" is not a "transcendence" in relation to man, but on the contrary it is that openness to which man as founder and keeper belongs, since as Dasein he is en-owned (*er-eignet*) by Being itself, which is as nothing else than Ereignis.[52]

In other words, Being is nothing else than what happens in *Ereignis*, and this is definitely not to be understood as transcendence but as "opening in-between." In a similar vein Heidegger also says: "*Ereignis* is the self-ascertaining (*ermittelnde*) and self-effecting (*vermittelnde*) middle (*Mitte*), in which all presencing (*Wesung*) of the truth of Being has to be thought back beforehand."[53] This "middle" as the *in-between* is not a dialectic third, but the endurance of difference, since "truth happens as clearing concealing."[54] I have tried to present through the gateway (*men*) character a similar idea in Daoism which acknowledges the nothingness of the *in-between*, while not succumbing to a metaphysical reading which would see it as an overarching third position outside of the play of differences. As the process of differing, *dao is* this play of differences through this *in-between*.

Another notion comparable to *dao* in the same way would seem to be *logos*. Here what is important is how to perceive of this comparison. As we have seen, sticking to the traditional metaphysical explanation of both *logos* and *dao*, we might indeed perceive similarities. Thomas In-Sing Leung for example, seeking to understand *dao* as the underlying ultimate process or ultimate truth, and *logos* as the ultimate order of things, accordingly finds many connections.[55] But if we start reading in a nonmetaphysical way, and do so for both *dao* following Ames and Hall and others on the Chinese philosophy side, and for *logos* following Heidegger (and Derrida) on the other side, we begin to see the comparison in a different light. Heidegger understands *logos* as *polemos*, as was argued in Chapter 1. This means that difference and the interplay of differences is constitutive for any constancy, which would be relative to this more originary play. Con-frontation or *Auseinandersetzung* is the more originary "begetter" of things.

We can find a similar understanding in the *Zhuangzi* as well. As we have seen, in Chapter 6 of the *Zhuangzi* another one of the provisional names for *dao* is offered as "Peace-in-Strife."[56] Graham translates these characters as "[a]t home where it intrudes" and the following sentence as "[w]hat is 'at home where it intrudes' is that which comes about *only* where it intrudes into the place of something *else*."[57] Wing-tsit Chan translates: "tranquillity in disturbance."[58] The general idea behind all these translations in my interpretation would be that only within and through the process of change can there be found a relative stability, so that again this stability is only as a function of the more originary play of differences.

Other comparisons of *logos* and *dao* can be found using Heidegger's thinking. Already in *Being and Time*, Heidegger explained *logos* as "discourse," and the fundamental meaning of discourse as "letting something be seen."[59] Seeing how a letting-be-seen always, as unconcealment, contains concealing, we can understand *logos* as the discourse which lets things be seen as unconcealing/concealing. As such, *dao*, which is similarly translatable as "discourse," is also a letting things be seen as they are in their relationality to what they are not. In a different but related way, Heidegger explains the related concept of *physis* as *Fuge, Fügung* in the sense of Harmonia.[60] Heidegger's translation of Fragment 8 of Heraclitus is the following: "Das Gegen-fahren ein Zusammenbringen und aus dem Auseinanderbringen die eine erstrahlende Fügung."[61] Translation of this Heideggerian jargon is difficult: "The reciprocal play a bringing together, and from the distinction the one shining jointure" would be my loose translation. Heidegger understands *Gegen-fahren* as the play of differences, which is at the same time a bringing together of differences as well as a distinguishing of differences, understood from the idea of jointure, which is nothing else than the space between things filled up by their necessary interaction, in other words, *Auseinandersetzung*. Difference and jointure belong together, thought in a nonhierarchical way. This way of thinking is also found in Daoism. The title of the second chapter of the *Zhuangzi* explains how sorting out can be seen as both differentiating and equalizing (*qi* 齊), which we can then read in comparison to *Auseinandersetzung* or *Das Selbe* (the "same"). The idea of the force of *Auseinandersetzung* brings me to Heidegger's *logos* as *polemos,* something which must be addressed in the light of any translation of *dao* as *logos.* The point I have made is that this translation will only hold if *logos* is seen in a Heideggerian way, which does not admit of turning it into a guiding principle outside of the differential structures of the world, outside the great clod. Chapter 25 of the *Daodejing* seeks to portray *dao* as the unchanging whole of change.[62] Within this whole, things are always reversing, returning, growing, and degenerating, and that is the sense in which *logos* necessarily entails *polemos*, especially if we relate *logos* to the notions of concealing and unconcealing As such, *dao* is similar in that it is also the workings of these *yin-yang* forces. As Heidegger puts it in the *Beiträge zur Philosophie:* "*Strife* (*Streit*) is essential being (*Wesung*) of the »in-between.« (*Zwischen*)"[63] This in-between remains a guiding thread of my comparison. Never showing itself, *dao* works within the logic of difference, transformation, and *aletheia.* As such, the Heideggerian jargon I have employed thoughout this book, and especially in the last paragraphs, although often the subject of ridicule and misunderstanding, might actually be better suited to that changed perspective of a nonmetaphysical reading of Daoism. Those who are impervious to this change in direction will not see this value, yet I hope they will at least understand the Heideggerian jargon as a serious attempt to convey a different way of thinking.

Heidegger's later work has many instances comparable to a possible description of *dao* as the temporal flowing together of all things. For example, in *Zur Sache des Denkens* he says the following:

> Being is not a thing, thus nothing which is, and yet it is determined by time as presence. Time is not a thing, thus nothing which is, and yet it remains constant in its passing away without being something temporal like the beings in time.[64]

Thinking along these lines could lead to some sort of relativism, yet this relativism is harmless in my view in that it merely acknowledges time and temporality, and thus processuality and finiteness, as fundamental structures of everything in the world. As Heidegger says: "every thing which actually is, every being comes and goes at the right time and remains for a time during the time allotted to it."[65]

With the idea of *Ereignis*, the notion of thinking as *Erfahrung* or experience becomes important. Note again that we are not thinking here about the so-called mystical experiences, which have been unmasked as residues of metaphysical thinking by Heidegger. Experience here is the experience of thinking, which is to say that Heidegger wants us to see the process of thinking understood as an experience, this-worldly: "To experience means *eundo assequi*, to obtain something along the way, to attain something by going on a way. . . . To experience is to go along a way."[66] This experience, however, is of necessity "an experience with language."[67] So it is not unmediated as a so-called mystical experience would like to have it. *Dao* is also understood as this "going along a way," and with it an experiencing through language in the sense that when giving meaning to the experience we are of necessity within language. For any experience to get any meaning it needs immediate insertion in the iterability structure of language. And it is in this sense that both the nameless and the named were conceived of as the gateway of man's experience of *dao*.

Translating *dao* as "way" could lead one to erroneously assume some definite connotations with a stretch that connects two fixed points. Heidegger's thoughts about *Weg* have tried to undo this understanding of "way." Heidegger gave his Gesamtausgabe the subtitle: "Wege, nicht

Werke." Ways, not works. This can be compared to *Zhuangzi* Chapter 1, of which the title is "Free and Easy Wandering."[68] The meaning of this title and chapter (and indeed one of the central concerns of the *Zhuangzi*) I take to be this idea that the way is not fixed, it has no definite goal, but is structurally open-ended itself. We are always, and will always remain, underway, on the way. And this "way" is not one fixed road, but multiple in itself and open, or as Heidegger explained referring to *Sein und Zeit*, this way is "*a* way, not 'the' way, which never exists in philosophy."[69]

Being on a way as such it is inevitable that we are always leaving traces. Thinking cuts furrows, leaves traces. Thinking is acting. To end this section I refer back to these notions of trace, cutting furrows, tracing, *Spur*. In my opinion notions such as "trace," "furrow," and "*Spur*" have connections with the notion *dao*, which are conducive to a reading of *dao* that sees "it" as less determined, open-ended, and referring more to the human aspect without succumbing to subjectivism. It is man that makes the way, but it is easier to see and less anthropocentric to say that it is man that leaves traces as being part of the environment. In trying to be as nonanthropocentric as is humanly possible, the point made by the Daoists would be that the traces one leaves should not be interfering with other traces, they should be *ziran* and *wuwei*. This acknowledges man's place in the universe, yet on first sight does not seem to grant man special status. Yet I do feel that mankind in Daoism is special in that humans are the only ones who have seemingly strayed from their *dao*, and who are thus capable of thinking and relating to *dao* in a special way. Heidegger similarly gives man a special status, but not so much as subjects against objects, and on this I have to quote Heidegger at length:

> We always say *too little* of "being itself" when, in saying "being," we omit its essential presencing (*An-wesen*) *in the direction of* the human *essence* (Menschen*wesen*) and thereby fail to see that this essence itself is part of "being." We also always say *too little* of the human being when, in saying "being" (not being human) we posit the human being as independent and then first bring what we have thus posited into a relation to "being." Yet we also always say *too much* when we mean being as the all-encompassing, and in so doing represent the human being only as one particular entity among others (such as plant and animal), and place them in relation to one another. For there already lies within the human essence the relation to that which—through a relation, a relating in the sense of needful usage (*Brauchen*)—is determined as "being" and so through this relation is removed from its supposed "self-independence." ("*an und für sich*") [. . .] In truth we cannot then even continue to say

> that "being" and "the human being" "are" the Same (*das Selbe*) in the sense that *they* belong together; for when we say it in *this* way, we continue to let both subsist independently.[70]

Being does not happen without human beings, and in the same way there is no experience of *dao* as the whole of processes, without humans. Heidegger tells us that "Being requires/uses (*braucht*) man, so that it can unfold (*wese*), and man belongs to Being, on which he can fulfill his utmost destination as Da-sein."[71] The interplay of Being and Dasein is what makes both possible, or as Heidegger phrases it, "[t]his counterpoise (*Gegenschwung*) of requiring (*Brauchens*) and belonging (*Zugehörens*) makes up Being as *Ereignis*."[72] In Daoism, only (some) humans can experience *dao* as *dao*. To quote Zhuangzi on the subject: "The Way (*dao*) comes about as we walk it."[73] There is thus no pre-fixed road or way which we only need to find, the way is made by what we think and do. This suggests a similar idea of interplay with an important role for humans, which can also be seen in the *dao* 道 character itself, as it is made up of head and foot. There is (or at least there should be) a continuity between *dao* and *de* 德 as man's specific *dao*. In the *Daodejing* Chapter 23 it is said: "Way-making (*dao*) is moreover enhanced by those who express character (*de*), just as it is diminished by those who themselves have lost it."[74] Both Chapters 16 and 25 of the *Daodejing* express similar ideas in their establishment of an essential connection between the king, *tian* and *dao*. The description by Ames and Hall of way-making and its essential human component is enlightening here. By translating *dao* as "way-making" they put more emphasis on the human experience of *dao*ing, the human experience of process. This is why Ames and Hall relate *dao* to terms as "fluidity and reflexivity," and why they call the *dao* character "gerundative, processional, and dynamic."[75] This is not solely to point to the process character of *dao*, but also to denote the human factor in the experience of this process.

Humans, then, have a specific *dao*, or at least a specific relation to *dao*, and they would do well to attune this relation to more natural *daos*, in other words, not to see *dao* as fixed, but to accommodate their *dao* to change and process. It then becomes necessary to compare the interpretation of Daoist way-making by Ames and Hall to Heidegger. First of all, Heidegger's understanding of *Weg* is just as far from a fixed path and just as close to human experience as is *dao* in my interpretation.

> "To clear a way [. . .] is in the Alemannic-Schwabian dialect still called *wëgen* even today. This verb, used transitively, means: to form a way and, forming it, to keep it ready. Way-making [*Be-wëgen (Be-wëgung)*]

> understood in this sense no longer means to move something up or down a path that is already there. It means to bring the way [. . .] forth first of all, and thus to *be* the way. Appropriation [*Ereignis*] appropriates man to its own usage [*Brauch*]. Showing [*Zeigen*] as appropriating thus transpires and Appropriation is the way-making [*Be-wëgung*] for Saying [*Sage*] to come to language. This way-making puts language (the essence of language) as language (Saying) into language (into the sounded word)."[76]

Heidegger speaks of "a more originary call,"[77] indeed on more than one occasion, of the belonging together of man and Being, which seeks to undo the artificial rule of technology and metaphysics, the artificial subject–object distinctions. Similarly Laozi speaks of undoing the artificial Confucian impositions and attuning oneself to *dao* as the more natural, originary way of life.[78] As with Heidegger's *Geviert*, humans (mortals) can only be seen as acting and becoming themselves in a constellation, and not outside of their surroundings, and this includes more importantly, of which I say more later, not outside of language. The divinities of Heidegger's *Geviert* need not be understood as outside of this world, as has been shown in Chapter 1. Heidegger rather understands divinity as an essential part of the world, which means that he is trying to say that our everyday understanding of the world is superficial, whereas he thinks that all things have more meaning than we can imagine with our scientifically oriented way of knowing. The divinities thus point to the mysteriousness of the world also found in Daoism. Any way we look at it, humans are a special part of the constellation that is called *Geviert*. This is also why Heidegger is closer to the *Daodejing* than to the *Zhuangzi*, as the *Zhuangzi* is much more explicit in challenging the special position of mankind. Yet in my view even in the *Zhuangzi* man is special in that man is the only one able to mediate between *tian* and earth. Man, or at least the sage, has the ability to step outside of the purely natural world and take on a wider perspective in accordance with *tian*. But that said, Heidegger is definitely closer to Laozi here. Although there are analogies of man, mostly in the form of sages, with the non-human world in the *Daodejing*, there is to my knowledge no paradigmatic shift of perspective from human to nonhuman as there is in the *Zhuangzi*.

Another feature of the closeness of Heidegger to Laozi is in their style. Both tend to write in an obscure fashion, which is one of the reasons why mysticism has been invoked in both. Especially Heidegger's later work is shrouded in obscurity, difficult terminology, and suggestiveness. Yet it is important to see that Heidegger wrote in such a way on purpose, since as we have seen, this is part of the impact of arguing for the interdependence and relationality of unconcealing and concealing. In the case of Laozi, the obscurity in the writing is similarly a calling to attention of the retreat of things profound into darkness, an acknowledgment again of the untraceable trace-character of the world. We will see later how Derrida and Zhuangzi, although their writings are equally obscure, are also linked in a different way, in their more playful style of writing.

Yet if thinking is acting, or experience, then how do Heidegger and the Daoists see this acting/experience? Here we have to make a comparison between Heidegger's *Gelassenheit* and the Daoist notions of *wuwei* and *ziran*, but we can also think of *Entschlossenheit* and *Erschlossenheit*, openness (or actually "dis-closedness") and preparedness. If we compare *Gelassenheit* to notions as *wuwei* and *ziran*, we should note that none of these suggest a negative or passive attitude toward things, and also not toward language. *Gelassenheit* is an attitude which listens to the call of Being, to Saying. And that attitude seems to entail an abandoning of the self to the primacy of the event, the *Ereignis*. This is in line with what we have seen in Chapter 1, where Heidegger talked about the relation of Self and Other, and established that it is only *through* the other that a self arises. Similarly, *wuwei* as nonassertive action does not mean one cannot speak, but that one will naturally be extremely careful with one's words, so as not to upset the *ziran* workings of the world by artificial constructions. This, however, only happens after having unlearned the artificial, propositional use of language. Chapter 48 of the *Daodejing* conveys this idea that "in learning of way-making (*dao*), there is daily decrease: One loses and again loses [t]o the point that one does things non-coercively (*wuwei*)."[79]

Etymologically the *wu* 無 character could be compared to Heidegger's notion *Lichtung. Lichtung*, or clearing, which as we have seen is how Heidegger describes the unconcealing concealing play of differences, is an open space in the woods.[80] The *wu* character is similarly based on men cutting trees, clearing the woods, and both thus can be understood as pointing to a void within a larger whole. Again we see that this void (or nothing) is not something opposed to being or beings, but is with being just another integral part of the whole process.

Heidegger's understanding of "trace" is important in this context, as both nothing and being are not to be understood as pure identities, but there are always traces of the one in the other. They only function together. This will also help to explain how Heidegger is closer to Laozi than to Zhuangzi. In both Heidegger and the *Daodejing* there is still the possibility of a reading that assumes that there is something behind the trace, and while that need not be some transcendent entity, it does point, in both Heidegger[81] and Laozi,[82] to some originary source even if that source is this-worldly and obscure. As we will see later, both Derrida and Zhuangzi will question this whole notion of a source behind the traces.

Yet I do not want to suggest translating *dao* as "trace." Etymologically this might be possible, if stretching, but does it fit in the text? If we think about the notions of head and foot, tracking, leading forth, the experience of going through something, a middle way, of thinking cutting furrows in the soil of Being, then there might be some interest in comparing *dao* with trace. The etymology of *dao* can certainly be read as having to do with going forth and thus leaving traces, but Heidegger might not be the thinker with whom to continue this line of thought. Derrida, on the other hand, has taken up this notion of trace, and in my view succeeds in making it clear that in his case, trace does not imply some transcendent or transcendental "trace-creator."

Derrida and Daoism

I begin the comparison of Derrida and Daoism where I left off with Heidegger, with the notion of "trace." Derrida uses many terms related to this "trace" thinking, which have definite correlations to *dao*, when read as way-making. In this context "breaching" (*Bahnung* [German] or *Frayage* [French]) plays an important role in Derrida's thought. "Spacing" and "supplement" are other terms used in this connection. In the second chapter I have explained that "trace" as Derrida understands stands for the play of otherness, of differences, that which no longer belongs to presence, and has no real origin or source. Derrida refers to this play of differance as temporization,[83] which also points to the deferring part of differance, or what we could call temporal tracing. Presence is always deferred; it is always only a trace of presence, a wandering without goal, the presence of which does not exist. Traces are all we have. It is in this sense that Derrida denies that there is a Heideggerian, more originary call from somewhere. In other words, there are no fundamental words and no profound connection between humanity and being. These are ideas which he dismisses as remnants of metaphysical thinking. As such he is closer to Zhuangzi, who also challenges similar ideas in his nonanthropocentric approach.

In trying to see *dao* in this way, it would then become impossible even to refer to *dao* as a principle, since the notion of principle already implies that there is something guiding something else, before something else, a presence before the trace. To explain what I mean we could look at Chapter 62 of the *Daodejing*, which says that "Way-making (*dao*) is the flowing together of all things (*wanwu*)."[84] This passage implies a process thinking which is comparable with Derrida's trace thinking, since there is nothing behind the flowing together of things, meaning first of all that there is no guiding principle behind it, and second that all things flow together in the sense that they have traces in each other. Again, this reading proposes a denial of the presence of pure identities. Other chapters of the *Daodejing* can be read in the same way. Chapters 4, 6, and 14 all talk about *dao* as ever evading, as only seemingly there, which means there is no getting beyond the hinting traces. And in Chapter 21 it is said:

> As for the process of way-making,
> It is ever so indefinite and vague.
> Though vague and indefinite,
> There are images within it.
> Though indefinite and vague,
> There are events within it.[85]

The traditional or metaphysical reading would interpret this passage as suggesting that behind the appearances which are vague and indeterminate, there is a reality which is easier to understand, a Platonic world of ideas and principles. On my reading, I take this passage to mean a very similar thing as what Derrida suggests that within the system, only differences function and thus only traces with otherness are to be found. The system itself is nothing else than this play of differences, but within that system of course there are references. These references, however, never attain the fullness that is suggested by the metaphysical tradition. Two arguments in Chapter 2 of the *Zhuangzi* say something similar. When everything has a "this" and a "that," full identities are denied, and the way is opened for seeing things as traces in traces. And a bit further Zhuangzi says:

> There is a beginning. There is a not yet beginning to be a beginning. There is a not yet beginning to be a not yet beginning to be a beginning. There is being. There is nonbeing. There is a not yet beginning to be nonbeing. There is a not yet beginning to be a not yet beginning to be nonbeing. Suddenly there is being and nonbeing. But between this being and nonbeing, I don't really know which is being and which is nonbeing.[86]

I take this to refer to the fact that "otherness" is always inserted. *Yin* is always *yin* becoming *yang*, and vice versa. There is always a regression, which means we cannot see things otherwise than as infinite traces only identifiable within or by an ever-expanding context. Outside and inside then become categories which are no longer strictly separable. I could do no better than

Graham, who describes this thought in a compelling way, although I do not agree with his use of capital letters: "Perhaps *Lao-tzu*'s Way is how the Trace will look to us when we are no longer haunted by the ghost of that transcendent Reality the death of which Derrida proclaims."[87]

We have seen that although Derrida sometimes seems to insist on certain Western features of philosophy, like the question, the critique of culture and a certain rationality, this does not mean he subscribes to the ideas of Western philosophy. To remember this, I refer the reader back to Chapter 2 of this book, where I have explained the connection between Derrida and negative theology, which showed that although Derrida is obviously aware of the necessity of using metaphysical language, and of keeping certain ideas "under erasure," this does not mean that either Derrida or Daoism need succumb to this metaphysical inclination. What we can at the very least argue together with Derrida is that the metaphysics of being as presence has obscured different possible readings, both within the Western tradition and of readings of those texts of the Chinese tradition we are discussing here. Differance then is not (about) an overarching principle, (it) is relationality, the neverending play of differing and deferring, in which each identity is only a provisional abstraction of the more fundamental relationality, the interplay. There is a bottomlessness to this endless processuality, endless referencing, endless tracing, and this is something which is also acknowledged by Heidegger's notions *Abgrund* and *Zeit-Spiel-Raum*, and which we can see in the indefiniteness and vagueness of the process of *dao*.

While speaking of differance, Derrida says that "temporization is also temporalization and spacing, the becoming-time of space and becoming-space of time."[88] Both temporization and "spacing" have the same intention. Differance then, as this interplay of what we like to describe as space and time, is located "*between* speech and writing, and beyond the tranquil familiarity which links us to one and the other, occasionally reassuring us in our illusion that they are two."[89] Similarly, "*Différance* is the systematic play of differences, of the traces of differences, of the *spacing* by means of which elements are related to each other."[90] And we need to remember what Derrida really means when he said there was nothing beyond the text, which is that this text means context, and this context means the whole play of differences that make up the world at any time.

Toby Arvard Foshay, among others, points to the fact that many comparative studies that deal with Derrida take no account of the fact that Derrida does not deny that there is a referential structure between language and its outside, but that deconstruction is first and foremost targeted at the relation between signifier and signified, and not between sign and referent.[91] Yet this obviously valid criticism does not mean that deconstruction has no implications beyond this signifier/signified relation. By aiming at this relation, "deconstruction tries to show that the question of reference is much more complex and problematic than traditional theories supposed. [. . .] But to distance oneself thus from the habitual structure of reference, to challenge or complicate our common assumptions about it, does not amount to saying that there is *nothing* beyond language."[92] There is a whole world out there; it is just that Derrida denies that we can ever have unmediated access to it, and that the mediated access we do have is always provisional. This leads us to the question about the permanence or impermanence of *dao*. A merely relative stability means there is no possibility of generalizing beyond the situational events, in Daoism the process of change takes precedent over any local ordering. There are structures that endure for a certain time, there is some permanence to things, but there is also and more importantly the impermanence of *daos*. This is especially so for the relation of man to things, because it is exactly man who seems to forget this impermanence. As Graham notices: "It is all right to make fluid distinctions varying with circumstances, it is when we make rigid distinctions misleading us into judging that something is permanently what it is temporarily convenient to name it that thinking goes wrong."[93] Both Derrida and the Daoists thus argue for the provisionality of our thought and our language, but not against thinking and language per se.

By now it should be clear that any comparison which looks for similarities between Derrida and Daoism should not focus on those metaphysical interpretations which have tried to see *dao* as a foundational principle in the same vein as God or some sort of Platonic idea. So if we are to compare this nonconcept of differance to *dao*, we should find a way to read this kind of denial of transcendental principles in(to) the Daoist classics. Here it might be useful to look at Ames' interpretation of Pang Pu:

> Pang Pu in explaining the "birthing, life, and growth (*sheng*)" of the cosmos makes a crucial distinction between "*paisheng*" in the sense of one thing giving birth to an independent existent, like a hen producing an egg, and "*huasheng*" as one thing transforming into something else, like summer becoming autumn. [. . .] In this process of *creatio in situ*, there is no product independent of the producer. Discourse is simply the outside of an inside. Cosmologically there is no progenitor independent of the progeny, but rather a proliferating and living on of the progenitor in the progeny. Analogously, in community, there is no speaker independent of the speech, but rather a living on of the speaker in the speech.[94]

In principle, the possibility of a transcendent creator or creative principle is denied in the classical Chinese worldview. In its place, or rather as some other way of seeing things, we look for generation of meaning from the inside. The birthing metaphors abundant in Daoism are one way of seeing the emergence of meaning. These metaphors also imply that there are always traces of otherness in the self, each and every mother is also a daughter; the process is continuous. As such, the blank and the in-between, the swinging gateway that in themselves are nothing, but which make possible any signification can be read in resonance with *Daodejing*, Chapter 11, where it is suggested that emptiness is exactly what provides the possibility of signification, yet without "itself" being anything outside the process. But again, as we see, there is an interpretation needed here of the *Daodejing* which is not at all standard or obvious, because it has affinities with Derrida's nonmetaphysical thinking. Also, Chapter 1 of *Daodejing* does not only talk about *dao* as ineffable, but of the need to stay with the mystery of the interplay between the nameless and what is named:

> Together they are called obscure.
> The obscurest of the obscure,
> They are the swinging gateway of the manifold mysteries.[95]

It is precisely this gateway, this hinge that I have already taken as an important idea in the previous chapter, that I want to take again as my point of departure in the comparison. I have already argued that man in general, and more importantly the Daoist sages, should be somewhere in-between Heaven and everyday man. A person in "whom neither Heaven nor man is victor over the other, this is what is meant by the True Man."[96] I have also argued that the works of the Daoist classics are aimed at preparing people for a responsiveness to the world around them that recognizes both the dangers and importance of language as necessities. In all these senses there is an important place for the nonplace of the in-between or interval. As Derrida states regarding time, one of the ongoing focal points of the discussion, and I have to quote at length:

> It is because of *differance* that the movement of signification is possible only if each so-called "present" element, each element appearing on the scene of presence, is related to something other than itself, thereby keeping within itself the mark of the past element, and already letting itself be vitiated by the mark of its relation to the future element, this trace being related no less to what is called the future than to what is called the past, and constituting what is called the present by means of this very

> relation to what it is not: what it is absolutely not, not even a past or a future as a modified present. An interval must separate the present from what it is not in order for the present to be itself, but this interval that constitutes it as present must, by the same token, divide the present in and of itself, thereby also dividing, along with the present, everything that is thought on the basis of the present, that is, in our metaphysical language, every being, and singularly substance or the subject. In constituting itself, in dividing itself dynamically, this interval is what might be called *spacing*, the becoming-space of time or the becoming-time of space (*temporization*).[97]

In my view this interval, the between that is itself nothing, not just as difference, but also as time-related difference, as *spacing*, or as *trace*, is an important aspect of Daoist thinking. Apart from *frayage* (breaching), Derrida also mentions the French word *brisure* in connection to *trace*. *Brisure* means both "joint" and "break," and thus is both what brings things together and what sets them apart. *Brisure* can thus mean both what is split, fractured, or broken, and yet it also means "hinge," "joint," as in the hinge that connects two parts.[98] All these words—differance, hinge, brisure, spacing, and trace—point to the same thing: that interminable process of the play of differences, and that is also what Daoism points to. As Zhuangzi puts it: "[A]ll the ten thousand things are what they are, and thus they enfold each other."[99] This is also the way I read the cook Ding passage of Chapter 3 of the *Zhuangzi*. Cook Ding says that his skill is really about finding the spaces in-between where things are joined: "At that joint there is an interval, and the chopper's edge has no thickness; if you insert what has no thickness where there is an interval, then [. . .] there is ample room to move the edge about."[100]

So there are many similarities based on a nonmetaphysical reading of Derrida and Daoism, and even the style in which they proceed is sometimes similar. This (Derridean) style of playing with words is also found with Zhuangzi, and it is one of the aspects that make Derrida closer to Zhuangzi than to Laozi. When we look at the form and style of the Daoist classics, their inherent fluidity means that they can be seen to function as Derridean texts from the start. They were not first original works which later suffered from diverse interpretations; they arose exactly as the result of diverse interpretations. Readers were implicated in the genealogy of the work from the start, and it is often difficult to see what is commentary and what belongs to the apparent authors themselves. And their constant revolving around certain words without ever getting there is similar to Derrida's evading style. But we will see more of this connection when we start to focus on what Heidegger, Derrida, Laozi, and Zhuangzi seem to consider the most important thing in thinking: language.

LANGUAGE IN COMPARISON

> This breaking up of the word is the true step back on the way of thinking.[101]

As argued before, the idea that language is in some way constitutive for our understanding of the world is readily found in Heidegger, Derrida, and Daoism. Although I argue that Daoism shares the criticism toward certain forms of language, we should not thereby expect that the classical Daoist texts are totally not influenced by logo- and/or phonocentrism. In many instances we can find in the Daoist texts the same phonocentrism that especially Derrida saw functioning in the Western languages, the idea that speaking is somehow closer to meaning than writing. For example, in the *Zhuangzi* Chapter 6, the woman "crookback" is asked how she heard the way. Not just the fact that this part specifically mentions *hearing* the way (*dao*) more than twice, the woman also describes it in the following terms:

> I hear it from Inkstain's son, who heard it from Bookworm's grandson, who heard it from Wide-eye, who heard it from Eavesdrop, who heard it from Gossip, who heard it from Singsong, who heard it from Obscurity, who heard it from Mystery, who heard it from what might have been Beginning.[102]

In this tale we can read a steady digression from exclamation and speaking as being closer to the meaning of "what might have been Beginning" to seeing and to writing, which are only secondary. It thus gives us the same phonocentric digression from the oral to the visual. The translation of this passage by Wing-tsit Chan corroborates this idea as he translates or rather interprets the first person mentioned in it as the "son of Writing the Assistant (for writing is no more than an aid)."[103] In general, even though they are written works, there is an emphasis on speaking and hearing throughout the Daoist texts, and in the *Book of Changes*, in the *Appended Words* it is literally said that "writing cannot fully convey the speech, and speech cannot fully convey the meaning."[104] Of course we have to remember that historically, the simple and quite obvious fact that oral language preceded written language in most developments of language around the world is not what Derrida means by this phonocentric bias. The phonocentric fallacy consists in thinking that because of this development oral language is somehow closer to meaning than written language. In seeing this, however, we must also see that the *Daodejing* argues against the possibility that "hearing" is better than "seeing" in getting nearer *dao*.[105] And the *Zhuangzi* argues against the stability of all language, so even though it seems to assert that speaking is closer to the true meaning than writing, it is in the end both speaking and writing that suffer the same provisionality. In fact, every kind of experience functions only because of difference. My claim with regard to the so-called "direct" experiences that Daoists refer to would be that any direct experience is first of all immediately taken up by context, and that is the only way for it to gain meaning, as the notion of iterability has shown. Second, I claim that such "direct" experiences are nothing other than experiences *of* relationality, *of* contextuality, as we saw in the instance where Zhuangzi realized himself to be in a web of relations and then understood that things are ties to each other.

Comparing Heidegger and Derrida on language is itself a difficult task, and comparing their ideas of language to ideas found in classical Chinese language is even more difficult, and can only be done indirectly, for numerous obvious reasons. However, if we compare Heidegger's and Derrida's use of language with classical Chinese language, we must be aware that we are making a couple of interpretations of either. First of all, it will be my interpretation of both Heidegger's and Derrida's thinking as presented. Second, since there seems to be no consensus on a theory of classical Chinese, it will be a case of comparing this interpretation with some of the interpretations of classical Chinese. These latter interpretations, as the preceding chapter has shown, are far from coherent and do present conflicting views. There are, however, views of classical Chinese which are close to Heidegger and Derrida, and since these views are important contenders in the ongoing debates on classical Chinese, I use them to reinforce the nonmetaphysical reading that I am presenting. I agree with Hansen that "[t]he linguistic school that sinologists take to be orthodox assumes that all written languages must be transcriptions of spoken language."[106] This orthodoxy in linguistics led to either a bias against classical Chinese as inferior to the alphabetic languages, which were supposed to be a truer transcription of the phonetic, the spoken language, or else it led to the position mentioned earlier, that is a defense of the idea that classical Chinese is equally a transcription of spoken language, and therefore not that different from Indo-European languages. This orthodoxy, as we have seen, is challenged with regard to Western languages by Heidegger and Derrida, as well as by Ames, Hansen, and others with regard to classical Chinese.

Heidegger, although a definite proponent of the voice and the spoken word, does not necessarily subscribe to the orthodoxy just by this preference. Both written language and spoken language are equally originary:

> The word of language sounds and resounds in the spoken word, shines and clears itself in the written image. Sound and writing are certainly something sensible (*Sinnliches*), but the sensible in which a sense or meaning (*Sinn*) sounds and appears.[107]

The quotation of note 1 of this chapter conveys a similar thought, in that it does not matter whether a dialogue is "written or spoken or neither." Although much emphasis is often put on Heidegger's notions of hearing (*hören*) and belonging (*gehören*) and other related notions, we should not forget Heidegger's equal insistence on language as showing (*zeigen*), and his writings on paintings, or art, that betray the "visual" aspect of his thought.

What remains for us is to see that the metaphysical meaning or the propositional, representational sense of language is but one of many possible ones. Heidegger's idea is that another way of seeing language, as "Saying" (*Sage*), as his poetic thinking tries to do, is more conducive to thinking beyond the confines of metaphysics. This Saying guards the necessary ambiguity of language, its differential and metaphorical nature. As such it seems awkward to our metaphysically trained minds. This Saying, as Heidegger says,

> must always pass through the essential ambiguity (*Mehrdeutigkeit*) of the word and its turn of phrase. The ambiguity of saying by no means consists in a mere accumulation of significations that arise arbitrarily. It resides in a play that, the richer it unfolds, remains all the more rigorously maintained in a concealed rule. Via the latter, the ambiguity plays in the balance of scales whose oscillations we rarely experience. This is why saying remains bound to a supreme law. This law is the freedom that frees us for the ever playful jointure of never resting transformation. The ambiguity of those words that "arise like flowers" (Hölderlin, "Bread and Wine") is the garden of the wilderness in which growth and nurturance are attuned to one another out of an incomprehensible intimacy.[108]

The vagueness, ambiguity, or polysemy inherent in language is also most persistently noticed by Laozi and Zhuangzi, and their thinking thus takes vagueness seriously, and not just in language. Steve Coutinho has argued for seeing this vagueness as a productive force in Daoist thinking. We see this vagueness employed by Laozi and Zhuangzi in their efforts to relate their processual way of thinking.[109] Coutinho finds vagueness at work in the notions of the penumbral, transformations between opposites, growth and decline, and, especially important for our inquiry, in the language of paradoxes and contradictions. This means that both Laozi and Zhuangzi did not subscribe to the orthodoxy in their time regarding language, but sought to convey a different understanding of using language.

That Derrida does not subscribe to the orthodoxy in linguistics that was mentioned earlier is I hope by now clear. The multiple shifts in terminology of Derrida suggest that language is forever provisional. The great import of Daoism with regard to language seems to be that, especially in the *Zhuangzi*, it is not only understood that language guides behavior, and that it is prescriptive, but that it is so only imperfectly, and that language itself can and will come back to haunt its own ideas. This however is not to say that language should be abolished, but like Derrida, Laozi and Zhuangzi are aware that while *dao* is ineffable, and words do not really say anything, they are nonetheless needed and continue to defy our ambitions (or those of the stricter Confucians seeking a final rectification of names) to tie them down. Language, or rather words, are like the statues of Daedalus, in that they will not stay put, but will start to run around as soon as created. Where Plato was always looking for a way to tie these words down, and thus fix their meaning, for Derrida and Zhuangzi it is important to acknowledge the constant shifts and to be skilful in playing with this phenomenon of language, and to continually stay aware of it. For Zhuangzi this is especially so when he explicitly mentions and uses "spillover words." As Graham describes it, Zhuangzi "uses words not like a philosopher but like a poet, sensitive to their richness, exploiting their ambiguities, letting conflicting meanings explode against each other in apparent contradiction."[110] The idea of both Zhuangzi and Derrida seems to be not so much that language is useless and to be discarded, but that we should use it to its utmost possibilities and thereby rethink its normal usage from a different standpoint. By letting words "explode" against each other, that is by exploiting the fullest range of meanings of any term, by bringing out ambiguities and inconsistencies, Zhuangzi and Derrida show us how language is not up to the promise of pure medium, and how we are trapped in a way because we have to use language, meaning we are always in a web of signification and can only operate from within this web. If this is understood as possibility, then Heidegger, Derrida, and Daoism advocate a use of language that seeks to explore it to its fullest possibilities, and this with full awareness of its dangers and limitations, rather than discard it. Again as Graham puts it, speaking of Zhuangzi (but the passage could equally well apply to Derrida):

> In one of his many aspects he is himself a true sophist, fascinated by the subversion of received opinions and intoxicated by the plunge which imperils rationality in the course of discovering its possibilities. He is also, even in the flow of reason itself, a poet who changes course as new insights explode, elliptical even when most logical.[111]

Language, or writing in the Derridean sense, is constitutive of our experience in the world. We have seen that Derrida's "nothing outside the text" means that our lives revolve around structures of signification. Being in these webs of signification means we are thus relational at our core and revolve around language or discourse. We are then in a very real way dia-logos. In Chinese thinking Ames has put this point forward in a similar way:

> [. . .] we are nothing more or less than the ongoing and sedimenting aggregate of these various levels of discourse: what we say and hear, what our countenances express and how it affects others, what our formal behaviors communicate and what they precipitate, what our body language and gestures indicate and how they are interpreted, what our voices and songs convey and how others are prompted to respond to them. As such, we are the organisms that in our doings and undergoings emerge discursively out of these performances of ourselves in community."[112]

What emerges in the Daoist way of thinking is this idea of the ever-ongoing formation of our experiences by forces inside and outside. What both Daoists and Derrida do is to find ways of appreciating this ongoing process of *dao* or of differance. In this context I must also remind the reader that in Chapter 3 I already argued that the *Zhuangzi* says that things "are ties to each other," meaning that everything is related in differential webs, and that language is also such a web, existing only because of and by this relationality. Like Derrida, Zhuangzi, according to Watson, "rejects the conventional values of words as well, deliberately employing them to mean the opposite of what they ordinarily mean in order to demonstrate their essential meaninglessness. When a writer does this, he of course invites misunderstanding, no matter how dazzling the literary effects he achieves."[113] But equally like Derrida, the strategic provocation employed by Zhuangzi is not about the total meaninglessness of words but about the mistake of assigning dogmatically fixed meanings. Zhuangzi is aware of the need for words, and equally welcomes misunderstandings as possibilities to upset the orthodoxy of fixed meaning, so he looks for a similar soul, who "has forgotten words, so I can have a word with him."[114]

Such a person is aware of the provisionality of language, has forgotten the idea that words have fixed meanings, and is therefore a suitable candidate for dialogue. Essentially, both Derrida and Zhuangzi are aware that there is no way they can ever permanently escape the workings of language, and thus they want to break up the rigidity of the workings of the ways of thinking in which they were brought up.

Does Zhuangzi really suggest not speaking and returning to a state of nature? In my opinion, as I have shown, this view is wrong. What then is the nature of *wuwei* and *ziran*? These notions should, as I have explained earlier, not be understood as being against language per se. Heidegger, Derrida, Laozi, and Zhuangzi have all argued against the commonsense notion of language and its possibilities, against its literal interpretations, yet in my view none of them have argued against language per se. It is thus a different idea of language and its possibilities that is put forward, an idea that challenges metaphysical notions of presence, of reference and representation. The importance of language lies exactly in the fact that it is our vehicle for thinking, but that metaphysical (or Confucian) language prohibits certain ways of thinking and tends to make artificial distinctions. It is thus not a question of leaving the vehicle behind, but of understanding how it functions, what it does and can do, in seeing our relation to language differently. As Heidegger says:

> What if the language of metaphysics and metaphysics itself, whether it is that of the living or of the dead god, in fact constituted, *as* metaphysics, that limit which prevents a transition over the line, i.e., the overcoming of nihilism? If this were the case, would not crossing the line then necessarily have to become a transformation of our saying and demand a transformed relation to the essence of language?[115]

Aside from the fact that this statement (rightly, I think) suggests that nihilism is only a function and problem of still thinking within the metaphysical structure, it also means that we should leave behind language as the discourse of representation; we no longer talk *about* the world in propositional statements, but we should rather return to the language of Saying (*Sage*), which speaks *from* Being. Derrida might see this as an impossible and rather nostalgic approach, but Heidegger is well aware that all language, including his own, is subject to the restrictions and dangers inherent in language:

> [. . .] the word itself already reveals something (known) and thereby conceals that which should be brought into openness in thoughtful

> Saying. This difficulty can not be removed by anything, indeed even the attempt to do so already means the failure to appreciate all Saying of Being. This difficulty must be undertaken and understood in its essential belonging (to thinking Being.)[116]

Language might be considered an obstacle, yet it is a necessary obstacle and as such a possibility of which we must be aware, and which we must not shun to employ to its fullest. I have so far mostly agreed with Hansen, but on this point I think in direct contradistinction to Hansen, who says that Daoists seek to "remove language,"[117] that they rather seek an awareness of the artificiality of language and of the need to nevertheless turn that artificiality against itself, making it "explode" by deconstructing it. Understood in this sense, a different thinking approach to language becomes necessary. In Heidegger's words: "The point is not to listen to a series of propositions, but rather to follow the movement of showing."[118] Saying (*Sagen*) is showing (*Zeigen*). As Ames and Hall have argued, in Daoism this awareness of the fact that *ming* 名 (language as naming) *ming* 命 (commands) was furthered by the realization that seeking to close off this naming in a system of fixed reference is not the way to do justice to the ongoing process.[119] Or, in the words of Jullien: "The issue, then, is to consider the heart of language: to invent a speech that can baffle its condition as language and break its mold; a speech that frees itself from the factitious oppositions we usually project onto language and thereby lifts us outside the unilaterality of point of view; a speech that is not blocked in any direction but articulates the eternal transition of things."[120] Another way of saying this is that we should not consider ourselves as subjects who master the world by language, in fact we do not even master language itself, we just try to follow what it says and explore its possibilities with an awareness of its provisional, prescriptive and performative functions. In Heidegger's thought, it is language which speaks, not us.[121]

That such a reading as I am presenting is not alone, could for example be glanced from Youru Wang's idea of a liminology of language in Chan Buddhism.[122] I do not quite agree with his coinage of the term *liminology*, which sounds and is presented as if one could turn deconstruction into a theory or a method, which could then be applied, something neither Heidegger nor Derrida would agree with.[123] However, the important point of Wang's article on language in Chan Buddhism is that he explains how Chan Buddhists do not so much seek an experience that would transcend language, they rather seek to de-limit language, in other words, to free language from its artificial boundaries. Those boundaries are found in our case in the metaphysical way of thinking, which has set language within the subject–object distinction, seeing it as a tool or medium for our use, and thus preventing other ways of thinking about language their place. This I think is what gets to the heart of what Chapter 1 of the *Daodejing* is trying to convey in its paradoxical way. Do not follow language as representing, as propositional, as if you were a subject using language as an object, but listen closely and follow what is being said or hinted at. Not only the first, but also the final Chapter 81 of the *Daodejing* suggests this:

> True words are not beautiful;
> Beautiful words are not true.
> A good man does not argue;
> He who argues is not a good man.
> A wise man has no extensive knowledge;
> He who has extensive knowledge is not a wise man.[124]

The representational and propositional attitude to language and wisdom is not the attitude of the Daoist.

The same goes for the *Zhuangzi*, which is full of messages of a similar kind, like the passages in Chapter 2 which regard the acceptability or non-acceptability of propositional language as superficial and wrongheaded, and claim that following *dao* overcomes this duality by not adhering to fixed representational schemes. Following any fixed representational or propositional scheme "obscures" or "hides" *dao* by installing artificial ideas of right and wrong.[125]

In Chan Buddhism the direct, uncontrolled, and paradoxical sayings of the masters are used as tools to bring us out of the dogmatic slumber of propositional thinking. The paradox is a tool to make us see that metaphysical language with its insistence on strict meaning is wrongheaded, and this is to make us see language differently. The Kōans of Chan Buddhism thus, although in the first place aimed at enlightenment, further function to keep us on guard against relying on propositional language and thus on propositional thinking. To this extent Chan Buddhism is similar to what Heidegger and Derrida try to convey.

I argue then that the so-called "ineffability" of *dao* does not lead us to a transcendental signified in whatever form, which would just be unattainable, but that this *dao* nevertheless functions as the negative space between, and as such seems to be the lubricant which keeps the whole process running smoothly. Many commentators have perceived what they thought to be a great irony, that the Daoists who were proclaiming to get rid of language, who were saying that words cannot convey the meaning, nevertheless wrote and did so very eloquently, using the full richness of the language at their disposal. If my interpretation is right, then there really is no irony. Daoists wrote since they perceived the necessity of language, and they valued language highly, but they did write against a certain type and use of language, which is exactly the kind of language that conceptualizes an ultimate reality behind appearances, and they proceeded to argue that there was another way we could think of language.

As Derrida has put it, any largely "nonphonetic writing breaks the noun apart. It describes relations and not appellations."[126] This brings me back to the difference between performative and constative language. Hall and Ames say: "The performative function of language reflected in the normative implications of *shi* and *fei* means that naming (*ming*) a world, we are commanding (*ming*) this world into being."[127] A danger in understanding language this way lies in the fact that through language we seem to master the world. The Chan masters in their paradoxical use of language seem to be doing nothing more than mastering or overcoming language, exactly in their so-called free use of it. Yet here we could find a difference with Derrida and Heidegger, who say that it is language which speaks, remains beyond the grasp of man, and exactly therefore frustrates all attempts at reappropriation. Youru Wang, precisely in coining the term *liminology*, seems to agree with this extraordinary mastering of language. But in Daoism I think this attitude is not found that easily. Zhuangzi argues that the meaning of words is never fixed, so even what he says himself slips away.[128] And in the *Daodejing* it is said that both the named *and* the nameless together are "obscure," and the general mistrust of language is here never superseded; any kind of naming is subject to the same forces. It is not hereby argued that language has no function, but that its appropriateness is provisional. In the words of Heidegger: "Names, words in the broadest sense, have no a priori fixed measure of their significative content. Names, or again their meanings, change with transformations in our knowledge of things, and the meanings of names and words always change according to the predominance of a specific line of vision toward the thing somehow named by the name."[129] It is also therefore that the distinction between literal language and metaphorical language is usually not acknowledged in Daoism. That would lead us to say that in Daoism metaphorical language is valued in itself. Yet even such a statement falls short of understanding that the whole distinction between literal and metaphorical language itself rests on the assumption that the former would somehow convey reality better, whereas the latter would be derivative and parasitic on this literal language. The point here is that the idea of literal language can only exist on the assumption that reality (at least ideally) can be fully determined in a univocal way. Even Confucius' rectification of names does not suggest going as far as this, especially if we take into account Xunzi's acknowledgment that "[n]ames have no intrinsic appropriateness, [and] [. . .] no intrinsic reality."[130] Naming is based on conventions, and although some names can be good, they must not be thought to be permanently good. Even though the processuality of *dao* admits of a certain constancy, language must remain alert to follow the changes that occur. What has to be meant by the statement that in the *Daodejing* and *Zhuangzi* literal and metaphorical language cannot be separated is that such an assumption of a fixed reality and fixed references to it are not part of the Daoist outlook.[131] The distinction itself does not arise in the first place, or, in the Heideggerian terminology of Michael Heim:

> [. . .] where "beings" have not yet been determined on the basis of a highest being, there can as yet be no strictly "metaphorical" way of speaking and thinking. It is only with us [the West], where the tradition of rationalism is dominant, that we may speak of "metaphor" or literally "bringing over" (Greek *metapherein*) one kind of being to illuminate another kind of being.[132]

The metaphor is impossible to circumvent, and that is also what leads Heidegger, Derrida, and the Daoists to the conclusion that all language is provisional, there is no literal language. As Derrida has shown in "White Mythology,"[133] the light metaphor is one of the most pervasive metaphors in Western philosophy. The light metaphor is meant to take us to the "real" meaning beyond metaphor, but, as Derrida shows, such a move to an unmediated presence is impossible. Heidegger, as we have seen, also does not subscribe to the light metaphor. *Lichtung*, or clearing, is a space in which light is being let in. So it would seem Heidegger does work with this metaphor. Yet we must remember that the star was Heidegger's favorite light metaphor. The star is light, but light *in* darkness, arising out of darkness. And the *Lichtung* is only such in the surrounding darkness. Thus Heidegger stays true to the idea that unconcealing only happens within concealing.

Similarly, in Daoism, when something is profound, it retreats into darkness. It becomes vague, obscure, "and yet there are images within it,"[134] and that suggests that Daoists were aware of the same interplay of light and darkness. In the *Zhuangzi* Chapter 2 mentions, after a lot of talk involving "clarity" or "illumination," that this is really to be understood as "Shaded Light" (*Pao Kuang* 葆光).[135] Graham translates this as referring to a star, thus reaffirming the light-in-darkness idea.[136] Coutinho's insistence on vagueness functions in the same vein. The penumbra, the in-between of light and darkness, is an important feature of Coutinho's argument and is also found in Ziporyn's study of Guo Xiang.[137] I could go on with examples, but the point has been made: meaning only ever arises in-between differences, so we must now move on and see where this in-between could be located.

"BEYOND" THE INVERSION OF OPPOSITES

The sorting which evens things out.[138]

The inversion of opposites or the negative approach we have been talking about in Heidegger, in Derrida, and in Daoism, must be recognized as a stage. Yet this stage is not something to be overcome in a dialectic *Aufhebung* of the Hegelian kind. Heidegger and Derrida, as well as Laozi and Zhuangzi, make it very clear that the stage of inversion, although a stage, is *always* a necessary stage. There is no position beyond it where we can rest on our laurels; there is always the danger of reappropriation into metaphysical structures, in fixed meanings, and in fact we are never totally beyond such structures. As Derrida puts it:

> To counter this simple alternative [the mere inversion of opposites], to counter the simple choice of one of the terms or one of the series against the other, we maintain that it is necessary to seek new concepts and new models, an *economy* escaping this system of metaphysical oppositions. [. . .] If we appear to oppose one series to the other, it is because from within the classical system we wish to make apparent the noncritical privilege naively granted to the other series by a certain structuralism. Our discourse irreducibly belongs to the system of metaphysical oppositions. The break with this structure of belonging can be announced only through a *certain* organization, a certain *strategic* arrangement which, within the field of metaphysical opposition, uses the strength of the field to turn its own stratagems against it, producing a force of dislocation that spreads itself throughout the entire system.[139]

The metaphysical system is dominant, but we must use it against itself, to see that webs of signification are always and everywhere differing, growing and decaying, altering. Contexts are contexts not as definable perimeters, but are contexts exactly because they can never be defined exhaustively. We are never finished, and that means a constant awareness, a constant repetition of inversion. In my view this is clearest in Derrida and Zhuangzi, who argue extensively for constant guarding and endless provisionality.

As an important point connected to this I would like to say something about the notions of nihilism and the related negativity and/or positivity in Heidegger, Derrida, and Daoism. In doing this I deal with a number of scholars who have compared Heidegger and/or Derrida to Daoism, only to see some similarity in the negative aspects, after which they go on to claim that Daoism provides more solace, or therapeutic value, than Heidegger or Derrida do, by offering a way out of the impasse of writing and metaphysics. Many interpreters have therefore maybe seen that in Daoism the inversion is a stage; they fail, however, to see a similar thing happening in Heidegger and Derrida. Hence the many accusations of nihilism, especially toward Derrida, but to a lesser extent also to Heidegger. Alternatively, my argument is that both Heidegger's and Derrida's thinking show definite signs of overcoming this nihilism in a positive affirmation, and provide equal "solace" to the reader trained in Western ways of thinking. Yet this affirmation is never a third position over and against the simple opposites.

One author exemplary of the kind of reading that proposes Daoism as a "way out" of the nihilism that Heidegger and Derrida seem unable to avoid is Mark Berkson.[140] While to a large extent in agreement with Berkson, I must differ on exactly the point where he gives Zhuangzi the advantage over Derrida. Seeing Zhuangzi in this way, Berkson suggests that the Daoist sage "escapes the perspectivism of human-centered points of view trapped within systems by escaping the systems altogether in a Heaven's-eye view that illuminates all things to show their relativity and ultimate equality."[141] This is exactly the form of mysticism Heidegger showed to be firmly trapped in metaphysical thinking. By perceiving language as a trap, one suggests we must look for a way out of this undesirable trap, a search which Derrida has unmasked as one of the defining features of metaphysics. As Berkson says further on, Derrida "has no positive picture, no way to get out of an infinite play of signifiers."[142] That might be true, but it is only true because Derrida does not *want* to get out, since getting out implies a return to the metaphysical way of thinking he has been trying to undermine. The point is that many like Berkson believe in such a third position outside the realm of metaphysics and its nihilistic opposite, without realizing that this search for a beyond and outside is itself in fact a return to metaphysics, be it as mysticism or otherwise. Heidegger argued against such a return to the framework of metaphysics. And in my view Derrida definitely has the advantage here over Berkson's Zhuangzi. For first of all, the inversion of hierarchy that might lead (but not necessarily) to nihilism is indeed a stage to overcome, something to which Heidegger, Derrida, Laozi, Zhuangzi, and Berkson would agree. It is a stage, aimed at showing how opposites are dependent on each other, how concepts, words and human thinking only function through differences. Yet this overcoming of the hierarchy is neither to establish an inverse hierarchy nor to move completely beyond the opposites into some dialectically conceived third realm. It is rather the realization and recognition of the constant interplay of differences as "all there is" and the affirmation of this "all there is." The realization of a no-beyond means that no absolutes exist, and that goes as well for opposites. No absolute opposites exist, since one side always has traces of the other in itself; there is no purity. In Berkson's view, which seems to be an exponent of the standard view, Zhuangzi proposes a sageliness that goes beyond language. What I have argued is that Derrida realizes that such a position is impossible. Positively, the affirmation consists exactly in dealing with this impossibility of getting beyond language, in using it with full awareness of its dangers and shortcomings, and to not perceive these as dangers and shortcomings, but as possibilities which open up the world to us. It is, as I have argued, not an experience that goes beyond relationality, but an experience and affirmation *of* relationality.

The second point I would make against Berkson is that he is exactly espousing the standard view that has Zhuangzi fleeing the world, or standing somewhere above it, where I have tried to argue that through a different understanding of Zhuangzi's views of language we can argue that he can be seen differently, as espousing a similar view of language, and ultimately of the world, as Derrida—namely, that it is processual, constantly provisional, and that any identity is at least constantly shifting and a product of this process rather than a producer.

There are a number of other scholars who seem to make the same point as Berkson, at least with regard to this aspect of comparison. Robert Magliola, J. J. Clarke, and Michael Saso all argue along similar lines: Derridean deconstruction, and to a lesser extent Heidegger's thinking as well, leave us no way out of the quandary of nihilism, whereas Daoism or Chan/Zen Buddhism take deconstruction one step further to a reinstatement of some essentially blissful or tranquil harmonic position from which to see the world. Magliola suggests that the differential form of Chan Buddhism renders the ongoing process of paradoxes, "trace," somehow blissful since the Buddhist can slide "*at will*"[143] between the logocentric and the deconstructive. Saso thinks the solution lies in transcending the necessary stage of deconstruction in some "intuitive" metaphysical state outside space and time.[144] And Clarke, although highly perceptive and appreciative of the similarities between Daoism and post-modernism, still ends up suggesting that deconstruction "tends to portray the (constructed) world as inherently banal and aimless, and therefore to exude a kind of skepticism that leads to cynicism and even despair rather than to wisdom or spiritual growth."[145] All I am suggesting is that these positions do not so much get stuck in the inversion of metaphysics, but fail to perceive that deconstruction cannot be understood as the negative term of a dialectic process that seeks to overcome metaphysics (since that would mean a return to metaphysics) and that therefore deconstruction itself cannot be overcome through positing some third realm outside space and time. The process is not metaphysics → deconstruction → synthesis in an *Aufhebung* that sees deconstruction as a stage. Derrida's whole point is that the possibility of dialectic thinking and thereby of any *Aufhebung* itself is profoundly challenged by deconstructive ideas. As an example that Zhuangzi thinks in the same way, we could look at the following passage where Zhuangzi speaks of the transformation of things. After describing how everything constantly changes and is in process, he describes the person who understands *dao*:

> He who understands the Way [. . .] is certain to know how to deal with circumstances. And he who knows how to deal with circumstances will not allow things to do him harm. When a man has perfect virtue, fire cannot burn him, water cannot drown him, cold and heat cannot afflict him, birds and beasts cannot injure him. I do not say that he makes light of these things. I mean that he distinguishes between safety and danger, contents himself with fortune or misfortune, and is cautious in his comings and goings. Therefore nothing can harm him.[146]

The sage is not someone who floats beyond the earth, but one who accepts and knows how to deal with change. Especially the last part of this passage shows clearly how earthly, or this-worldly, Zhuangzi's sage is. He is not one who lives in another realm, but one who understands the provisionality and transformation of this realm, affirms it, and deals with it.

If we see therapeutic value in this way, then obviously it is there in Heidegger and Derrida as well, if you know where to look and how to read it. Yet it is a different therapeutic value, one that does not deny or go beyond the problems, but lives with them. That is where the difference between positivity and affirmation comes in. Derrida observes, regarding his own work: "I would say that deconstruction is affirmation rather than questioning, in a sense which is not positive: I would distinguish between the positive, or positions, and affirmation."[147] Affirmation is different from taking a fixed position. In Derrida's view, both getting stuck in the inversion of opposites and thinking there is a way out of them are really (untenable) positions. In fact, affirmation denies the possibility of ever getting stuck in positions exactly because it affirms the danger of thinking in hierarchies. And I have tried to show how in Daoism this also happens. No mysticism in fleeing the world, but "mysticism" that acknowledges the world in all its facets. Heidegger and Derrida do indeed overemphasize the different, the other, yet not in order to merely inverse the hierarchy set up by metaphysics between opposite terms and concepts, but precisely to question that hierarchy itself. Daoism does so too; by saying "keep to the female" it is not advocated to overturn the masculine but to come to some sort of ever-shifting equilibrium that acknowledges the necessity of both opposites.

But is Daoism about reconciling the opposites or differences or about acknowledging them, because acknowledging is what Heidegger and Derrida do, when they say we should remain with the hinge, the lever, at the margin. Here we tread on precarious ground, because in the case of Daoism, something could be said for both. There are passages in the *Daodejing* and some parts of the *Zhuangzi* that seem to advocate some kind of third position, at least for the sage or ruler, whereas other parts of these works, and for example the commentary by Guo Xiang, advocate the process of differentiation purely as itself. And even in Heidegger, we find hints that all his work is mere preparation, waiting for the advent of Being in its true sense, although nobody knows how that may look. Yet I have tried to show how the part that acknowledges the world as it is, is at least equally strong, if not stronger, in most of what Heidegger, Derrida, and the Daoists think. And many of the passages suggesting a third position can also be reinterpreted to fit my nonmetaphysical reading. Therefore the this-worldliness of Daoism is something I see as the dominant trend.

Ames' wider aim has often been to criticize the persistent characterization of Daoism as negative, quietist, and similar interpretations. What we must keep realizing is that Daoism is about both *yin* and *yang*, not one more than the other, in spite of the insistence of mostly the *Daodejing* on the more *yin* aspects of life. As the *Book of Changes* tells us: "The successive movement of yin and yang constitutes the Way (Tao)."[148] In similar vein, Heidegger has explained *logos* as *polemos*. Derrida reduces the overly optimistic conceptuality of Western logic and language, yet finds himself always both inside and outside of metaphysics, or rather maybe in-between metaphysics and its other. What they all have in common is the acknowledgment of the play of different forces that shape and guide (our understanding of) the world.

In Daoism one learns by reducing artificially constructed concepts and rules. In my view, since Daoists still speak, there is no reduction to meaninglessness, there is realization of provisionality of all meaning. This again relates to the use "under erasure" of concepts by Derrida.

So what I have argued for in this chapter is how there can be two ways of reappropriation which Heidegger, Derrida, and Daoism seek to avoid. There is first of all the mere inversion of opposites, which takes the form of blaming Heidegger and Derrida of nihilism, or of saying that Daoism is mystical or a pure return to nature beyond language, or a skepticism or relativism that discredits language. But the second form of reappropriation lies in the fact that many interpreters of Daoism have taken this inversion as a stage to be overcome in a dialectic third position, somewhere and somehow beyond the workings of opposites and of language. To these forms of reappropriation I have tried to counter how Heidegger, Derrida, Laozi, and Zhuangzi are fully aware of the impossibility of such enterprises. And in this sense, my understanding of deconstruction is that it seeks out exactly how the reversal or inversion of hierarchies or opposites remains on the same level as the metaphysical approach in the first place, and that at the same time, deconstruction shows how an overcoming of this dualism can no longer be a Hegelian sublimation. Overcoming metaphysical hierarchies is acknowledging that both sides of any dichotomy are always related and that the play between the two sides is not something we can step outside of. Chi-Hui Chien tries to relate this thinking of difference in the following way: "The double character of Tao, *wu* and *yu*, thus should be understood in terms of 'both one and the other' and 'neither one nor the other.'"[149] In other words, there is no way to get outside the double play of differance or *dao* understood in this way. To sum it up in Derrida's words, deconstruction traces and sets to work "certain marks [. . .] that can no longer be included within philosophical (binary) opposition, but which, however, inhabit philosophical opposition, resisting and disorganizing it, *without ever* constituting a third term, without ever leaving room for a solution in the form of a speculative dialectics."[150]

In order to achieve the disposition that Heidegger, Derrida, and the Daoists are trying to convey, the question remains whether one should not rather try to write in a Daoist way? As a criticism of Western-style scholarship, which has obvious connections to the logocentric tradition of searching for a final truth, this would make sense, but my point is that a similar effect, if we can still speak of "achieving," "dispositions" and "effects," would come from writing in Heideggerian or Derridean fashion, in that such writing also upsets the standard view of language and thus of thinking. In fact, even a more standard version of "writing," like this book, which admittedly follows certain mainly Western structures although it also employs Heideggerian, Derridean, and Daoist influences, could still, if as a work it insists like I do on seeing language and with that thinking in a different way, be able to point or at least guide us to such a changed attitude.

ETHICAL AND POLITICAL IMPLICATIONS

The heavens and the earth are not partial to institutionalized morality.[151]

One of the problems we face if we deny the standard interpretation of Daoism as an escape from the world in a return to nature or a dialectic sublimation, is the question of the ethical and political imports of the thoughts of Heidegger, Derrida, and Daoism. One of the most obvious problems we run into when trying to continue this nonmetaphysical comparison on an ethical level is the lack of an absolute standard. Since there is no ultimate reality, or transcendental signified, relativism and nihilism seem to ensue. How do we compare the Daoist inclinations toward a nonmetaphysical basis for ethical behavior, *wuwei* and *ziran*, toward the "other" in general, not rule-oriented or based on universal, rational, or otherwise foundational principles, but critical of artificial constructs, with Heidegger's *Gelassenheit*, authenticity and *Geviert*, and with Derrida's notions of responsibility, openness, or opening up of power structures which have had and continue to have such influence on our societies?

It is impossible to separate thinking from ethics and politics: Heidegger argued that our way of thinking had become "technological," and Derrida, amongst others, has argued for an understanding of the essential ethical and political implications of so-called "fundamental" research. This means that he argues for an ethical awareness in both science and philosophy. No matter how rational, objective, abstract or remote, or value-free some research might look, and that includes philosophy, there are always ways in which this research has ethical implications. We must in some way be responsibly aware of these implications. And there is no denying that the *Daodejing* is at least in part (also) a political treatise.

In reality, these implications can be seen from the fact that Heidegger (and Nietzsche) have been annexed by the Nazis, Derrida has been accused of being both left-wing and right-wing,[152] and Daoism for its part has been connected with anarchist inclinations for its insistence on *laissez faire* government in the *Daodejing* and freedom in the *Zhuangzi*, but also with the totalitarian system of the legalists.[153] One can take a negative view and reproach all three for failing to provide an ethical system based on their respective philosophies and thus for being open to appropriation by different ethical systems. However, this has often been suggested, and I find it rather simplistic to think it that easy to condemn the three. The relations between the philosophies expounded and political or ethical power systems which have taken over and reinterpreted their ideas, are far from simple and different in each instance.

In the case of Daoism, its incorporation into the legalist despotism by Han Feizi took a parallel approach to it in acknowledging the forces of nature, but suggested that these could be mastered and used by the government to stabilize society.[154] Yet Daoism is at the same time often used in anarchistic arguments for abolishing any and every kind of government. What are we to make of all these accusations and implications? In each case there seems to be an appropriation of the "original" thinkers by others with their own agenda. While the history of these appropriations is not to be denied, it might be more fruitful to return to the "originals" and see whether we can find any ethical positions directly. But we must first of all remember that to criticize certain current systems and theories of morality and politics is not an argument against ethics and politics in itself. The fact that Heidegger, Derrida, and Daoism deconstruct their cultures' respective structural systems of thought, and thereby of ethics, is not a warrant for saying that they therefore do not believe in any ethics.

The ethics and politics of performative language could provide a meeting place for Heidegger, Derrida, and Daoism, as all three are intent on showing how language actually does something to the way the world is perceived and therefore also to the way the world is run. It is undoubtedly so that the metaphysical outlook of the West has, through its functioning in language, created the kind of rationalistic and scientistic view of the world that is dominant, and thereby has also disallowed other views of how the world functions and how we should find our place in it, by excluding such considerations from the framework of meaningful discussion, at least within philosophy. Thinking within such a structure but criticizing it means being open to the charge of irrationality, or nihilism. Once we understand that Heidegger, Derrida, and Daoism try not to get stuck in the inversion of this scheme, another way of seeing their contributions opens up. We should therefore question the longstanding idea that if we acknowledge that there is no constant *dao*, we must therefore discredit all norms. Or, in other words, we must question the idea that if one adheres to a certain form of relativism, all is relative. This plainly is a very superficial understanding of relativism. To argue that "things are ties to each other"[155] does not necessitate the conclusion that there are therefore no standards or norms at all. As I have shown in the case of Derrida, the fact that something is complicated, questioned, and challenged does not necessarily mean that it is therefore to be totally discarded. And the fact that there are patterns of change with some continuity within the process of change tells us that meaning can still arise within the webs of signification, as relational and situational. The performative function, or rather character, of language makes it instantly and of necessity relate to what is outside of it.[156] This means that philosophy is always about its outside, its other, something which again we can see in an ethical way, in the sense that we must take care not to impose, through our use of language, artificial structures on, and thus hindrances to, the development of things from themselves. The views of language that Heidegger, Derrida, and Daoists give us are then already implicated in otherness, and show a responsiveness to and respect for otherness. The performative in language is, in Derrida's terminology, a "yes" to otherness which is located before philosophy, thus in a way outside of it yet constitutive of it.

On the ethical level, notions of letting things take their natural course are readily found both in Heidegger and Daoism. And together with Derrida's idea of responsiveness, all three advocate an attitude of openness to things unfamiliar, a letting be of difference. This in response to the perceived artificiality of the ideas current in their respective times. Thus the Daoists argue against the artificial Confucian standards, which they actually see as an obstacle to the development of natural or unmediated morality. Morality in this unmediated sense will develop of itself, it is *ziran* or spontaneous, without the artificial imposition of rules and regulations. Heidegger argues against the "they" (*Man*) attitude of social conventions and tries to establish how *Gelassenheit* could help us overcome this artificial approach. Derrida searches for ways to affirm otherness and to criticize the dominance of certain power systems. With this he seeks to establish a natural responsiveness to others that is certainly ethical, and reminiscent, as we have seen, of Levinas. Yet a difficulty arises when we start thinking about how far this openness should extend. Should we let things be even if they are harmful to us?[157] It is only Zhuangzi who seems to have no problem with this, since he advocates an affirmation of life in all its aspects.[158] But Heidegger, Derrida, and Laozi do advocate certain restraints of the people. Thus "following nature" inevitably becomes "following certain parts of nature, but not all of nature." The unlearning of conventions, the reducing day by day of knowledge that is artificial, should lead one to spontaneous inclinations, but in how far these spontaneous inclinations are purely natural is dubious, and even more so the question how they can point to an ethical system. Even Derrida had to acknowledge that he was arguing for notions such as democracy and human rights "under erasure," meaning they eventually came from the system he tried to undo. The challenge is to see whether and how these ideals can also be derived from the thinking of Heidegger, Derrida, and the Daoists themselves.

Graham has called the Daoist ideal society a "paternalistic anarchism."[159] This means that the people order themselves by themselves through their own ways, spontaneously, but the ruler has to oversee this and make sure nothing interferes with this spontaneity. That is why it is said in Chapter 17 of the *Daodejing* that the best rulers are invisible; nobody knows more than that they are there.[160] *Wuwei* and *ziran* are effectively two sides of the same coin, in the sense that by acting *wuwei* we are following the *ziran* course of nature. However, in the *Daodejing*, and to a lesser extent in the *Zhuangzi* as well, there is the suggestion of a supervisor overseeing this process and keeping it from degenerating into artificiality. Exactly how this is to be achieved is unclear, though, besides referring back to *wuwei* and *ziran*.

Heidegger and Derrida were very much proponents of an ethical way of life, yet it is equally hard to establish where *Gelassenheit* or the decision to responsibility lead in actual societies. Derrida's ethical ideas stem largely from Levinas' notion of the other. Ethics arises as a direct consequence of an opening toward what is other, both in Heidegger and in Derrida. Since what is other is always inserted into the self, which is constitutive for it, it becomes impossible not to acknowledge the other, and that means a responsiveness that entails a responsibility. This responsibility is direct, not derived from some greater source or origin, but purely as a consequence of the relationality to alterity or difference. In early Heideggerian terminology, Dasein is always *Mitsein*, being-with, and its way of being is *Sorge*, care. The *Geviert* or fourfold of the later Heidegger similarly suggests that we, as mortals, are part of the world and thus have to care for it. In Derrida, responsiveness to the other leads to responsibility for the other. The same happens in Daoism, insofar as no preference is given to the self, and insofar as Daoism suggests we should let all things be what they inherently are. This letting be is then actively a responsibility not to interfere with the natural inclinations of other things. This is indeed an ethical position, yet the problem remains how this can avoid becoming a total "anything goes" in the political sphere. The sages let things be what they are, but "[a]lthough they are quite capable of helping all things (*wanwu*) follow their own course (*ziran*), they would not think of doing so."[161] From the ethical acknowledgment of otherness to political action that helps others is a difficult step, one the Daoist seems not to want to take.

Simon Critchley argues that although there is an ethics in Derrida, and although Derrida definitely has a political agenda, to philosophically connect these seems to pose a problem.[162] The same problem is applicable to Heidegger and to Daoism. Critchley argues that what he calls the "political" and "politics" are two different fields. Philosophy is about the "political"; it can never do, or get implied in, real "politics." Heidegger's ill-conceived rectorate in 1933 serves as an example, and so do the many instances of Daoist political advisors in the *Zhuangzi*. Does this mean that philosophy, or thinking, can only give an ethical foundation, but never move beyond the vagueness of this foundation? It would seem so, since this foundation can apparently be used in politics in very diverse and even opposite directions.

In the Daoist case, the political actions seem to range from advice to the ruler in the *Daodejing* to set up a Daoist state, to the legalist despotism of Han Feizi, to the retreat approach of the *Zhuangzi*, advocating detachment from the world of politics and seeing self-preservation as a good valued above that of the state. Are such diverse interpretations misunderstandings of the real political meaning of Daoism, or is there no such real meaning? My line of argument goes in the second direction; the meaning of these texts at the level of politics can be open, yet the point of this section is to show that although these diverse interpretations are possible, that does not mean that there is no foundation of ethics to be found in Daoism. The foundation is there, but of necessity is vague and open in that it is only openness to otherness. In deconstructive fashion, it just shows that there is always an underlying assumption of otherness inherent in the same, an otherness that prohibits pure identity.

In Daoism, this idea takes a form that is central to the yin-yang cosmology, which is that the mutual influences of opposites are unavoidable and that we therefore had better be in a position to respond to deflections and irregularities. We should not try, as in the West, to assert only one point of view as the best, or to do away with evil altogether, because these views are self-defeating; we must rather acknowledge differences of opinion, and work with these as our basic assumptions. We cannot try to undo the yang side altogether, but must constantly shift within the yin-yang range of options. In Antonio S. Cua's words, "*tao* as a vision of harmony appears to lie in its emphasis on opposites as complements."[163]

Heidegger's Dasein, as we have seen, is fundamentally *Mitsein*, *Sorge*. In his later work, Dasein, or the mortals, form an integral part of the Fourfold (*Geviert*). Dasein comes to be understood from the complex of relations to the heavens, the earth, the divinities, and other mortals. This is comparable to the Daoist individual who only exists as the function of a matrix of relationships, and thus is ever changing, without a fixed core.

Derrida's work is filled with political undertone, and Derrida is noted for having called logocentrism 'ethnocentric' in the sense of Eurocentric, and metaphysics as perpetuating Western power structures.[164] Deconstruction is as much about criticising those power structures as it is about the language in which they thrive. Derrida's more political writings include not just arguments against the more straightforwardly political institutions, but also against academic and publishing institutions. His "decision" or "yes" could be compared to Zhuangzi saying that we should see everything as both "this" and "not this." A realization and affirmation of relationality again ensues, which in Derrida's case means that subjectivity can only be understood as a function of difference, through the workings of differance.

In trying to apply their thinking to politics, one of the implications of Heidegger, Derrida, and Daoism could be the stress on the overcoming of dualistic thinking in which opposites were always constructed in a hierarchical manner. These hierarchies are now overturned, and although this overturning is, as we have seen, but a stage of the process, it should still reveal an approach based more on equality and less on hierarchy. That basis of the necessity of having opposites and differences, and of the affirmation of the equivalence of these differences, is I think as far as Heidegger, Derrida, and the Daoists go in the field of ethics and politics.

CONCLUDING THE COMPARISON

I have shown in this chapter how a nonmetaphysical reading of Daoism can yield fruitful comparisons with Heidegger and Derrida, although obviously important differences remain. I have sought to relieve the protagonists of the charge of nihilism, relativism, and/or skepticism. My argument has been that the inversion of opposites, or the negative approach, is not to be seen as a mere inversion, yet also is not to be sublimated in a dialectic third position, which is what has happened in a lot of interpretations of Daoism. Through a reading of Heidegger and Derrida that discredits these interpretations of Daoism, we can start understanding new possibilities of reading them all that involve an acknowledgment of the interplay of differences and the *in-between* of these differences as their relationality. In doing so, however, we must remain aware of the dangers the proponents themselves point to, especially the danger of language and the ensuing danger in trying to extrapolate an ethics and politics from them. There are ethical implications of their ways of thinking, and we should actively take responsibility for the interpretations we give to these ethical implications.

Conclusion

Many interpretations of Heidegger, Derrida, and Daoism get stuck in the inversion of opposites, since these interpretations do not look beyond their negative approach. This also goes for many comparisons of Heidegger, Derrida, and Daoism. These comparisons get stuck in a sort of negative theology, replacing one fundamental principle with another, which is just vaguer and more ineffable. Throughout this book I have tried to show how neither Heidegger, nor Derrida, nor Laozi and Zhuangzi propose such a negative guiding principle, but instead focus on the inability of everyday language to show us beyond this inversion. While not wanting to get stuck in the inversion, we have to be careful when claiming to go beyond it. Many comparative philosophers seem to argue for some kind of dialectic third position which would somehow sublimate the ongoing processes of difference in a static unity. I have argued that neither Heidegger, nor Derrida, nor the Daoists advocate such a sublimated position. The point is rather to see this third position as an affirmation and realization of the constant play of differences alternatively called Being, differance, or *dao*, which are but a few names that have been given provisionally. My presentation of the proponents of this kind of thinking has hopefully made it clear how this affirmation need not plunge us into a debilitating relativism, but can rather be understood as a productive possibility. By understanding meaning from context and relationality, relativism, nihilism, and skepticism can be avoided. Meaning exists, yet never absolute and never beyond this world.

Similarly, comparative philosophy as a discipline should look at itself in this way. Not content with merely pointing to similarities, it has moved on to pointing to differences, and should move on again to pointing beyond the differences, though not in some overall fusion of horizons, but in acknowledging differences while not succumbing to the charge of absolute relativism that is then leveled against this acknowledging. Like Heidegger and Derrida, and like Laozi and Zhuangzi, it should seek to understand the differences as productive, and to make these differences work to dismantle the system that denies them a valid place. In Clarke's words:

> The benefits lie more in the tensions and differences that prevail and which continue to place Daoism and contemporary philosophical thinking in a creative counterpoint with each other rather than in comforting unison.[1]

Metaphorically speaking, the relations between Heidegger and Laozi on the one hand and Derrida and Zhuangzi on the other can be pictured in the following way. Life is seen as a tree, and a tree grows from the roots, so we need to return to these roots. But where Heidegger sought to find a ground in which the roots were firmly planted through language as Saying, Derrida exposes the roots themselves by wiping away the loose soil that language is made of. *Both* the notions of roots and ground then lose their ultimate values. Similarly, Laozi advocated a return to a primitive, natural way of life, the roots, and sought to establish an ultimate ground for this, *dao,* even if this ground, like Heidegger's, was not to be understood as a metaphysical, transcendent ground. Zhuangzi then shows the ultimate provisionality of such an enterprise in his relativistic or relational approach.

In this book I have tried to show that Heidegger, Derrida, and Daoism can fruitfully be compared on a different level, or a different field, for they are indeed "the sort that roams beyond the guidelines"[2]—or rather, *on* the guidelines, in the margins, on the periphery of our normal everyday thinking. From these margins, we can derive new readings of old terms like *Sein*, logos, differance, trace, and *dao, ziran, wuwei, tian* by different scholars, like Heidegger, Derrida, Guo Xiang, Ames, Hall, Hansen, and others. Taking these seriously (instead of remaining stuck within the guidelines, that is the metaphysical interpretations and the language which perpetuates these interpretations by denying the possibility of thinking otherwise), there will open up a new level of comparison that is nonmetaphysical in inclination. Whether this new reading of Daoism is in fact historically and culturally more accurate must be left open. First of all I am not in a position to judge here, so that must be left to others more qualified. Second and more importantly, my point would be that if it did not fit into our preconceived ideas of the cultural and historical sphere of the ancient Chinese, these preconceived interpretations might themselves stand in need of rereading in the same way. And similarly it has always been my intention to follow Heidegger when he said that we have to think "more Greek" than the Greeks themselves. Heidegger was well aware of the fact that we cannot bridge the gap to any ancient society, and that the real challenge lies in making the ancients speak to us, and in thinking through them in such a way that we can think what they maybe left unthought or what was passed over in the history of subsequent interpretations.

In comparing, the position of language has been extremely important. Not only have I argued that language, understood in a broad way, is an essential feature of our experiences, at least in the sense that experiences only gain meaning through language, but as such, I have argued that the proponents of this comparison do not argue for some position beyond language. In other words, neither Heidegger, nor Derrida, nor Laozi and Zhuangzi argue for transcending language to some pure, direct, and unmediated experience of the "real" world. At the very least our humanity mediates experience, and our languages provide meaning, however provisional. Heidegger, Derrida, and the Daoists are extremely aware of the necessity of language, and all in their own way argue for an opening up of language to its own possibilities, rather than remaining in its limited metaphysical field. Language is not denied, but a certain idea and use of language, the metaphysical or propositional and representational use, is denied dominance and superiority over other avenues. In its place we must seek to use language to its fullest, which will in turn point us to the interplay of differences, or that process we are part of, sometimes called, provisionally, Being, differance, *dao*.

Notes

NOTES TO INTRODUCTION

1. Zweig 1990, 30, my translation.

2. Hölderlin 1966, 70/71 (translation modified) and 1970, 241:

> "Einig zu sein, ist göttlich und gut; woher ist die Sucht denn
> Unter den Menschen, daß nur Einer und Eines nur sei?"

3. See Said 1978.

4. Heidegger 1993, 51; 1962, 76. In this book I work with both original German language works by Heidegger (and others) and English translations, and I refer to these in the following way: If the reference is to an original German language work, the year of publication and page number will appear first, and where possible and available the reference to the work in translation will follow after a semicolon. In general I will follow available translations of Heidegger, unless there is either none available or I do not agree with the translation, in which cases translations will be mine, as will be indicated, and in such cases and others where I find it clarifying, the German original passage will appear in the notes.

5. Heidegger 1999, 35; 1974, 45: "Allein das Selbe ist nicht das Gleiche. Im Gleichen verschwindet die Verschiedenheit. Im Selben erscheint die Verschiedenheit." See also: Heidegger 1994b, 187.

6. Heidegger 1997b, 94; 1971a, 8.

7. See Panikkar's contribution to *Interpreting Across Boundaries* (Larson & Deutsch, eds., 1988), especially 130–136.

8. I do not hereby deny that some comparisons of certain ways of thinking can be comparisons of the metaphysics involved in these ways of thinking, yet I do wish to argue that even such a comparison in itself should not aim at or be led by a supposedly *neutral* metaphysical principle or a dialectical sublimation of the differences.

9. Or, to give the reader a prelude of the Derridean approach adopted later in this book, maybe we should be looking for something different *from* conceptual schemes.

10. The metaphysical interpretation of Daoism is not a specifically Western invention or imposition. Metaphysical interpretations have been found in the Chinese tradition as well, for example in the Wang Bi commentary on the *Daodejing.* Yet my main concern is the domination of the comparative discourse by these metaphysical approaches, and that is why I focus more on the Western interpretations of Daoism, and those by Chinese scholars who seem influenced by these Western interpretations.

11. This book features a number of odd or even nonexistent English words or neologisms, as well as untranslated German, French, and ancient Greek words and neologisms, and further untranslated classical Chinese characters in Romanization. The reader is asked to be patient in this respect and to acknowledge the necessity of my stretching of the English language or resorting to non-English in making my arguments. In reality, I hope to show that these "excursions" are literally part of the argument.

12. Romanization of Chinese characters is according to the now standard Pinyin conversion, except in quotations where the Wade-Giles Romanization is used, so as not to disrupt the original translations.

13. Petzet 1983, 176–177; 1993, 168. Words or sentences in quotations, in square brackets, are mine but in line with the surrounding text.

14. See Quine 1960, especially 22–35, and Quine 1998.

15. See Davidson 1998.

NOTES TO CHAPTER ONE

1. Heidegger 1994b, 43; 1977, 157–158.

2. As we have briefly seen before, *Auseinandersetzung* is one of the key words in Heidegger's thinking and also of this book. A possible translation of *Auseinandersetzung* could be "con-frontation," as it captures most of the meaning of coming together in difference through the hyphen. In most cases I leave it untranslated because it is a word so important that a false translation, or one that does not capture its full and ambivalent meaning, would seem inappropriate. There is, however, discussion and explanation of the word throughout the book. *Wiederholung* is another important word. Usually translated as "repetition," we will see that Heidegger means it to be anything but a mere repeating of what others, in this case the ancient Greeks, have said and thought.

3. Heidegger 1963, 24, my translation.

4. Heidegger 1997b, 134; 1971a, 39.

5. Although "originary" is not a proper English word, it has philosophical use as being different from "original(ly)," which has too many connotations with regard to a possible origin. "Originary" also goes to explain the idea of thinking something through as it engages us, rather than "originally," which would then mean thinking something exactly the way the Greeks, for example, thought it. Heidegger considers this last option to be either impossible or uninteresting, as it has nothing to say to us now.

6. In many of the titles of essays and books by Heidegger the hint to this double notion of *von* is obvious. Also see Heidegger 1996, 313–364: *Brief über den*

Humanismus for a similar reading of the French "de," and Heidegger 1997a: *Was Heisst Denken?*, in which the double meaning of *heissen* and *durch* are expounded in similar fashion.

7. Maly & Emad 1986, 6.

8. Note that Heidegger was already familiar with and thinking about Daoism and other East Asian ways of thinking at the same time as he was working on the ancient Greeks. Yet Greece received more attention overall.

9. Heidegger 1994a, 321–373; 1975, 13–59.

10. Anaximander, taken from Heidegger's *Der Spruch des Anaximander.* See also Kirk & Raven 1957, 106/107.

11. Heidegger 1994a, 322; 1975, 14.

12. Compare for example Heidegger's "Hegel und die Griechen" in Heidegger 1996, 427–444, or "Moira" in Heidegger 1994b, 223–248; 1975, 79–102, or Heidegger 1979–1987, vol. IV, 17.

13. Of course Heidegger will not deny that bringing your own view into interpretations is inevitable. He is hermeneutic enough to recognize and appreciate this, but is looking for a way that will leave what is interpreted stand by itself more.

14. Heidegger 1994a, 322; 1975, 14: "Aber solange eine Übersetzung nur wörtlich ist, braucht sie noch nicht wortgetreu zu sein. Wortgetreu is sie erst, wenn ihre Wörter Worte sind, sprechend aus der Sprache der Sache."

15. Heidegger 1994a, 335; 1975, 25.

16. Heidegger sometimes uses Abgrund, Graben, Kluft, and so on, but the point is always leaving behind (to a certain extent) the hindrances of metaphysics.

17. Translation taken from: Nahm 1964, 39/40. Other translations offer little variation and stick to this interpretation, so this one can serve as representative of the normal, traditional version.

18. Heidegger 1994a, 341; 1975, 30. Heidegger did not make this up himself (see Heidegger 1994a, 340; 1975, 28, where he refers to John Burnet). Heidegger was ambivalent, though, saying he was "inclined" to think only the middle part was from Anaximander, and in *Holzwege* this is the part he focuses on. In the slightly earlier lecture course, though, he focused on the whole fragment.

19. Heidegger 1991, 101.

20. Translation by Kenneth Maly in: Sallis 1993, 231.

21. Heidegger 1975, 57.

22. Heidegger 1994a, 372; 1975, 57.

23. Think of *Geviert* (fourfold) or his explications of what a "thing" is, or of *Welt*, *Auseinandersetzung*, and so on.

24. Heidegger 1994a, 331; 1975, 21/22.

25. See Heidegger 1994a, 357, my translation: "Das je-weilig Anwesende west an, insofern es weilt, weilend ent-steht und ver-geht, weilend die Fuge des Übergangs aus Herkunft zu Hingang besteht. Dieses je weilenden Bestehen des Übergangs ist die fügliche Beständigkeit des Anwesenden. Sie besteht gerade nicht auf dem bloßen Beharren." Also see Heidegger 1975, 43/44.

26. Heidegger 1994a, 369/370; 1975, 55. See also: Heidegger 1961, vol. 1, 27 & 333/334; 1979–1987, vol. I, 22 and vol. II, 78.

27. Heidegger 1994b, 223–248.

28. Heidegger 1994b, 231; 1975, 86.

29. Now published as volume 55 of the *Gesamtausgabe*. Heidegger 1994c.

30. Heidegger 1994b, 208; 1975, 66.

31. For example: Heidegger 1994a, 327; 1975, 18.

32. Heidegger 1994b, 220; 1975, 77: "Ὁ Λόγος wäre, als die lesende Lege gedacht, das griechisch gedachte Wesen der Sage. Sprache wäre Sage. Sprache wäre: versammelndes vorliegen-Lassen des Anwesenden in seinem Anwesen. In der Tat: die Griechen *wohnten* in diesem Wesen der Sprache. Allein sie haben dieses Wesen der Sprache niemals *gedacht*, auch Heraklit nicht." Italics in original.

33. Heidegger 1994b, 263; 1975, 114.

34. Maybe it would be better to leave *das Selbe* untranslated, but as long as we are alert to what is meant, and we remember that "same" does not mean interchangeable or equal, "Same" or "same" will do. Compare Heidegger 1999, 35; 1974, 45: "Allein das Selbe ist nicht das Gleiche. Im Gleichen verschwindet die Verschiedenheit. Im Selben erscheint die Verschiedenheit."

35. Heidegger 1961, vol. 1, 96; 1979–1987, vol. I, 81.

36. Heidegger 1961, vol. 1, 656; 1979–1987, vol. III, 165.

37. Heidegger 1953, 47, German added: "Auseinandersetzung is allem (Anwesendem) zwar Erzeuger . . .," translation modified from Maly & Emad 1986, 41.

38. Ibid: ". . . allem aber (auch) waltender Bewahrer"; translation Maly & Emad 1986, 41.

39. Heidegger 1994b, 269; 1975, 119.

40. Heidegger 1994a, 371; 1975, 56: ". . . der Λόγος, den Heraklit als den Grundzug des Anwesens denkt, die Μοῖρα, die Parmenides als den Grundzug des Anwesens denkt, das Χρεών, das Anaximander als das Wesende im Anwesen denkt, nennen das Selbe. Im verborgenen Reichtum des Selben ist die Einheit des einenden Einen, das Ἓν von jedem der Denker in seiner Weise gedacht."

41. Compare Heidegger 1994a, 8; 1971b, 23: "Das römische Denken übernimmt die griechische Wörter ohne die entsprechende gleichursprüngliche Erfahrung dessen, was sie Sagen, ohne das griechische Wort. Die Bodenlosigkeit des abendländischen Denkens beginnt mit diesem Übersetzen." "Roman thought takes over the Greek words without a corresponding, equally authentic experience of what they say, without the Greek word. The rootlessness of Western thought begins with this translation."

42. Heidegger 1994a, 371; 1975, 57: "Eine blosse Übersetzung soll dieses veranlasst haben? Doch vielleicht lernen wir bedenken, was sich im Übersetzen ereignen kann. Die eigentliche geschickliche Begegnung der geschichtlichen Sprachen ist ein stilles Ereignis. In ihm spricht aber das Geschick des Seins. In welche Sprache setzt das Abend-Land über?"

43. Heidegger 1961, vol. 1, 288, italics in original; 1979–1987, vol. 2, 35.

44. Vetsch 1992, 88, my translation.

45. Heidegger 1961, vol. 1, 329; 1979–1987, vol. 2, 73.

46. Heidegger 1997b, 196; 1971a, 90.

47. Heidegger 1994b, 132, my translation, German added: "Das dichtend Gesagte und das denkend Gesagte sind niemals das gleiche. Aber das eine und

das andere kann in verschiedenen Weisen dasselbe sagen. Dies glückt allerdings nur dann, wenn die Kluft zwischen Dichten und Denken rein und entschieden klafft." See also Heidegger 1994b, 187; 1971b, 218: "Poetry and thinking meet each other in one and the same [*im selben*] only when, and only as long as, they remain distinctly [*entschieden*] in the distinctness [*Verschiedenheit*] of their nature."

48. Heidegger 1994b, 187; 1971b, 218: "Das Selbe lässt sich nur sagen, wenn der Unterschied gedacht wird." Notice again that the translation in English is not *wortgetreu*, as it would have to be: "The Same lets itself be said only if difference is thought."

49. Hölderlin, 1966, 70/71 (translation modified) and 1970, 241: "Einig zu Sein ist göttlich und gut; woher ist die Sucht denn Unter den Menschen, dass nur Einer und Eines nur sei?" Notice that "einig" means at first being at one in the sense of being in agreement, or in harmony, and thus allows and even calls for difference. See the motto of this book.

50. Hölderlin, 1966, 70/71.

51. Heidegger 1993, 148ff; 1962, 188ff.

52. Heidegger 1996, 313; 1998, 239, translation slightly modified.

53. Heidegger 1997b, 31; 1971b, 208.

54. Heidegger 1994a, 62; 1971b, 74.

55. Heidegger 1994a, 62; 1971b, 74. Heidegger indeed saw other arts fundamentally in the same way, and devoted much of his writings to paintings and other artworks.

56. Fóti 1992, 31.

57. This is already an intimation of the closeness of Heidegger's thinking to Derrida's. For deconstruction similarly seeks to upset the "normal" meaning of texts to reveal through reinterpretation of key terms its "other" meaning, although Derrida's deconstruction goes further in taking apparently non-key terms in texts and seeing how they can nonetheless become disruptive of the text if thought through.

58. See Heidegger 1997b, 142–146; 1971a, 45–48.

59. See Heidegger 1997b, 198; 1971a, 92.

60. Heidegger 1997b, 74–75; 1971a, 192, German added.

61. I would rather use the word "polysemy" as a translation of *Mehrdeutigkeit*, as it seems to capture the ideas of Heidegger better, being closer related to language itself and not having the burden of metaphysical history behind it which terms such as ambiguity and equivocality have. We will later see how the notion of polysemy does not go far enough for Derrida.

62. Vetsch 1992, 68, my translation.

63. Heidegger 1984, 68; 1996, 54: "Wo es (. . .) dabei bleibt, das Fremde zurückzuweisen oder gar zu vernichten, geht notwendig die Möglichkeit des Durchgangs durch das Fremde und damit die Möglichkeit der Heimkehr ins Eigene und damit dieses selbst verloren."

64. Heidegger 1984, 67/68; 1996, 54, German added.

65. Vetsch 1992, 80, my translation.

66. See Vetsch 1992, 81.

67. Heidegger 1984, 60/61; 1996, 49, German added.

68. Heidegger 1984, 151; 1996, 121.

69. Heidegger 1984, 177; 1996, 142, italics in original, German added.

70. Heidegger 1996, 338, 1998, 257: "Wir haben noch kaum begonnen, die geheimnisvollen Bezüge zum Osten zu denken, die in Hölderlins Dichtung Wort geworden sind. . . ."

71. Bruns 1989, xx.

72. Heidegger 1996, 319; 1998, 199.

73. Heidegger 1984, 63ff; 1996, 51ff, where Heidegger translates the Greek δεινόν as *das Unheimliche*, his way of dealing with the fact that δεινόν can mean "fearful," "powerful" or "inhabitual" at the same time. Notice that Heidegger openly accepts the fact that his translation is in many ways "incorrect," adding that it might therefore be more "true" (78; 64).

74. Bruns 1989, 9.

75. Bernasconi 1985, 46, italics in original.

76. Heidegger 1984, 130; 1996, 104/105, German added.

77. Heidegger 1984, 76; 1996, 63.

78. Heidegger 1984, 76; 1996, 63, German added.

79. Heidegger 1996, 333; 1998, 254. The inadequate translation of these sentences has been modified, and the German added. In German: "verdeckt die metaphysisch-animalische Auslegung der Sprache deren seinsgeschichtliches Wesen. Diesem gemäß ist die Sprache das vom Sein ereignete und aus ihm durchfügte Haus des Seins. Daher gilt es, das Wesen der Sprache aus der Entsprechung zum Sein, und zwar als diese Entsprechung, das ist als Behausung des Menschenwesens zu denken."

80. Heidegger 1984, 79/80; 1996, 65.

81. Heidegger 1984, 80; 1996, 65/66, German added.

82. Heidegger 1997b, 12; 1971b, 190, German added.

83. Heidegger's "translation" of two lines of Chapter 15 of the *Daodejing*, taken from a letter by Heidegger to Paul Shih-yi Hsiao, reprinted in Parkes 1987, 102–103, translation Graham Parkes.

84. For a detailed discussion of the "fourfold," see Heidegger 1994b: "Das Ding": 157–180; 1971b, 163–186.

85. Not believing in a strict "Turn" or *Kehre* in Heidegger's work, I take "early," and also "later" of the next section in a loose way. The point is only that Heidegger's thinking in his later work is more suitable for comparative philosophy.

86. See Heidegger 1997a, 136.

87. Heidegger 1993, 21; 1962, 43, German added: "sich nur noch im Interesse an der Vielgestaltigkeit möglicher Typen, Richtungen, Standpunkte des Philosophierens in den entlegensten und fremdesten Kulturen bewegt und mit diesem Interesse die eigene Bodenlosigkeit zu verhüllen sucht."

88. Compare Petzet 1983, 176/177; 1993, 168.

89. Heidegger 1988, 108, my translation.

90. Safranski 1994, 310, my translation.

91. Heidegger 1993, 51; 1962, 76.

92. We must remember that *Sein und Zeit* was published in 1927, when "primitive" was still quite a common term that was largely unquestioned, at least

by Heidegger at this time. Maybe the fact that he didn't question this term goes to show that at the time of *Sein und Zeit* Heidegger was not yet fully appreciative of other cultures and their way of thinking.

93. Although there are still many different opinions about Heidegger's Nazi involvement, this is not the time and place to go into them. The only point I wish to make is that by 1945, and maybe even earlier, Heidegger had become increasingly persuaded by the need for an opening up of philosophy to include other cultures.

94. Heidegger 2000, 61; 1972, 55.

95. Heidegger 1988, 214, my translation.

96. Heidegger 1997a, 136.

97. Heidegger 1994b, 43; 1977, 157/158. Heidegger focuses on East Asia and not on India, since he perceived philosophy from India to be too metaphysical. See also note 1 of this chapter.

98. Heidegger 1994b, 269; 1975, 119. See the part of this chapter on Heraclitus for more detail.

99. See for example Levinas 1988 and 1999.

100. Heidegger 1997b, 83–155; 1971a, 1–54.

101. Paraphrased from Prins 1996, 92/93.

102. Heidegger 1992, 32/33; 1991, 15.

103. In what follows in this paragraph, I am paraphrasing Heidegger from a couple of sources, mostly from Heidegger 1994b.

104. See mostly Heidegger 1985. But also, in numerous other works Heidegger talks of *Gelassenheit.*

[105] See for example Heidegger 1994a, 115–208. Also see Heidegger 1983a and 1983b.

106. Heidegger 1977, 44, my translation.

NOTES TO CHAPTER TWO

1. Derrida 1992a, 9/10, italics and French in original. I work mainly with English translations of Derrida's works, so references will be of these translations, unless otherwise stated, and they will be referred to as 'original.' References to articles or other contributions by Derrida in volumes edited or written mainly by others will either be referred by name of editor/author and year of publication, or by: Derrida in: name of editor/author, followed by year of publication (of volume).

2. Although Derrida's criticism is to a large extent aimed at Western philosophy, it is really the metaphysical sensibility that he is arguing against. This metaphysical way of thinking can also be found in parts of the "East," and this is one of the reasons why the categories of East and West are no longer or never have been appropriate. In many instances I shall therefore use the distinction between metaphysical and nonmetaphysical thinking, or between dualistic and nondualistic philosophy, or logocentric and nonlogocentric thinking as my guideline, fully aware that these distinctions must in the end also be deconstructed with equal force.

3. See for example Derrida 2002a.

4. Derrida 2002a, 89.

5. Derrida 2002a, 72.

6. Again, these metaphysical readings have mostly been the Western interpretations, but they can also be found in some Chinese scholars and commentators throughout the history of Chinese thought.

7. Derrida 1976, 10.

8. Culler 1982, 176.

9. For examples, see the contributions of Rorty and Searle in Madison 1993.

10. For the notion of "iterability," see Derrida 1988, and the part on language and translation in this chapter.

11. Indeed, concepts or words, or any sign or mark for that matter, can only function as relative identities because of this iterability, the possibility of repetition and citation is literally vital for the existence of a concept, but we shall have plenty more to do with this so I will not dwell on it here.

12. Derrida 1985, 85.

13. Derrida 1985, 85.

14. Derrida 1985, 87.

15. Derrida in: Kearney 1984, 118, italics in original.

16. Compare for instance Derrida 1988, 115/116, or Derrida 2001a, 15–19. See also Burke 1992, 162–168, and compare for example Cheney 1995, where "postmodernism" as it is understood to function in Humanities departments in the United States, is attacked for its lack of commitment to truth.

17. Wood & Bernasconi 1988, 4, translation slightly modified.

18. Derrida 1989b, 36.

19. See Derrida 2001a.

20. Derrida in: Kearney 1984, 125, italics in original.

21. Derrida 1976, 158, italics in original.

22. Derrida in: Kearney 1984, 123/124, italics in original.

23. For example: Searle's contributions to Madison 1993, 170–188, or Jung 1984 and Ch'ien 1984 for similar claims.

24. Derrida 1988, 148, also see Derrida 1981a, 35/36.

25. Derrida 1988, 137.

26. We can think for example of Nietzsche, Freud, Heidegger, and Gadamer.

27. Derrida 1998, 29.

28. Derrida 1982, 7.

29. See for example Heidegger 1975, 51.

30. Derrida in: Kearney 1984, 110.

31. Derrida 1982, 22, italics in original.

32. Derrida 1982, 22, italics in original.

33. Heidegger 1994a, 366; 1975, 52.

34. Nietzsche 1968, 380.

35. Derrida 1988, 118, see also 127.

36. See quotation of note 7 of this chapter.

37. Derrida 1993b (in Sallis 1993), 163–218.

38. See for example Derrida 1976, 12.

39. Interestingly enough, it is exactly in Chinese language and thinking that there is phono-centrism, but no logocentrism, according to Derrida, as we shall see later.

40. Derrida in: Kearney 1984, 110.

41. See Derrida 1992b for example.

42. This reading is possible, although my own interpretation gives otherness in Heidegger a more prominent place, and seeks to thus establish that Heidegger is closer to Derrida than is usually thought.

43. Derrida 1988, 152–153.

44. Derrida 1988, 136.

45. Derrida 1976, 7, italics in original.

46. Derrida 1982, 11, italics in original.

47. Magliola 1984, 8.

48. Derrida 1982, 5, italics in original.

49. Derrida 1981a, 350, italics in original.

50. Derrida 1981a, 268, italics in original.

51. Directed by Kurosawa Akira, 1950.

52. Odin 1995, 15.

53. Allen, in Madison 1993, 11.

54. Derrida 1982, 315, where Derrida links iterability to the Sanskrit *itara*, which means "other" and thus points to alterity.

55. Derrida 1988, 40, compare also Derrida 1988, 7.

56. Derrida in: Wood & Bernasconi 1988, 5.

57. Of course we know by now that Derrida goes further and says that similarly there is no truth or reality behind the play of differance, but for this particular argument that part of his whole thinking does not seem to matter much.

58. Derrida 1981b, 31, italics in original. (Can we still speak of original?)

59. Derrida 1985, 152.

60. Derrida 2004, 19, italics added.

61. Derrida 1995, 225.

62. Derrida 1992a, 55.

63. Derrida 1995, 374.

64. Derrida 1995, 375.

65. Not just in written language, but even more so in language in a broad sense, when we take Derrida's idea of "writing," as encompassing all sign structures of signification, as a substitute for language.

66. Derrida 1978, 117/118, italics in original.

67. See for example Caputo 1993, Norris 1989.

68. Derrida 1982, 6.

69. Derrida 1982, 11.

70. Derrida 1982, 26.

71. Derrida 1982, 26, italics in original.

72. Derrida 2004, 170.

73. Derrida in: Wood & Bernasconi 1988, 4.

74. Derrida 1992a, 4.

75. Derrida 1992a, 10.

76. Derrida 1992a, 10.

77. Derrida 1992a, 29, italics in original.

78. Derrida 1995, 202. French in original.

79. Heidegger 1963, 24.

80. Derrida 2004, 202/03.

81. Derrida 2004, 242/43.

82. Derrida 1995, 376.

83. Although ethnocentrism is sometimes discussed, and Derrida never hesitates to state that this ethnocentrism should be overcome, there is no rigorous effort on the part of Derrida to make such overcoming real in an encounter with different cultures. Derrida is usually content to just mention the other-than-Western ways of thinking, and then return to his own project, the deconstruction of Western philosophy. For example, see Derrida 1982, 112/113.

84. Spivak in Derrida 1976, lxxxii, italics in original.

85. Derrida 1976, 90.

86. Derrida 1976, 90.

87. Derrida 1976, 91.

88. Derrida in: Kearney 1984, 116/117.

89. Derrida 1976, 92, italics in original.

90. Jung 1984.

91. Derrida 1976, 26, italics in original.

92. Derrida 1992a, 30.

93. Derrida 1981a, 290, italics in original.

94. Derrida 1981a, 292.

95. Derrida 1981a, 295.

96. Derrida 1981a, 296. The "margins of our domestic library" contain "Islamic, Mexican, and Indian mythologies, the Zohar, the Tao Tö King; Empedocles, Nicholas of Cusa, Bruno, Marx, Nietzsche, Lenin, Artaud, Mao Tse'tung, Bataille, etc." They can be read perhaps as the alternative history of philosophy.

97. Derrida 1981a, 357.

98. Derrida 1981a, 356, italics in original.

99. See Derrida 1981a, 347ff.

100. See Derrida 1981a, especially 347–353.

101. Derrida's personal reluctance to delve deeper into this "supplement" is, as we have seen, perhaps explicable. The fact that what is "other" is constitutive for what is "self" does not necessarily mean we know exactly how this "other" functions.

102. Derrida 1994, 89, translation adapted from Hillis Miller 1996, 166.

103. Derrida in: Kearney 1984, 123.

104. See J. Hillis Miller: "Derrida's Others" in Brannigan, Robbins, & Wolfreys 1996, 153–170.

105. Derrida 1993a, 22.

106. Derrida 1993a.

107. Derrida 1989b, 55.

108. Derrida 1989b, 59/60.

109. Oxford English Dictionary website. The original French *déhiscence* has the same botanical background.

110. Derrida 1989b, 62.

111. Derrida & Bennington 1993, 291.

112. Compare for example Levinas 1988 and 1999.

113. Derrida 1982, 26, italics in original.

114. Derrida 1982, 6, italics in original, bold added.

115. Derrida in: Kearney 1984, 124.

116. Derrida 1981a, 252, italics in original.

NOTES TO CHAPTER THREE

1. Ames & Hall 2003, 18.

2. See Hansen 1992, 12–14 for example, or Lau 2001, xxxix/xl.

3. For more discussions concerning the distinction between philosophical and religious Daoism, see for example: Creel 1970, 7–24; Fung Yu-lan 1948, 3; Cleary 1991, xxv and on, Graham 1989, 170–172.

4. Graham 1989, 172.

5. For example: Hansen 1992, 33–54.

6. Fung Yu-lan 1948, 28.

7. Waley 1934, 30.

8. For example, contemporary Chinese scholars like Mou Zongsan and Li Minghui: see Hall & Ames 1998, 222–232.

9. Of course, a lot of generalizations are made here. Western philosophy is anything but this unified view of itself, and there are many dissenting voices within that tradition. Yet it has persisted even through the current onslaughts of postmodernism. It is the same sort of philosophy as has been questioned and attacked by Heidegger and Derrida, as shown in the previous chapters. Daoism is of course equally diverse and not just one unified whole.

10. Hansen 1992, 6/7.

11. Cleary 1991, xxv and on.

12. Giles 1980, 17.

13. *Zhuangzi*, Graham 1981, 57. As I mostly deal with English translations of the classical Chinese works, mainly the *Daodejing* and the *Zhuangzi*, references will be to the title of the work itself; and to indicate from which translation the reference stems, the name of the work will be followed by the translator and year of publication of the translation, and then the page number of this translation. For example: *Zhuangzi*, Watson 2003, 25.

14. *Zhuangzi*, Giles 1980, 42. The biblical resonance is obvious: "In the beginning there was the Word."

15. Legge 1891/1989, 12–18.

16. Legge 1891/1989, 30.

17. See for example Mungello 1992, 186–188.

18. See Cook & Rosemont 1992, 82–91.

19. W. Chan 1963a, 136.

20. W. Chan 1963a, 178.

21. I shall use the personal names Laozi and Zhuangzi in a loose manner, as embodiments of the works that go by their respective names, without however assuming that they were in all cases the actual authors of all that goes in their name.

22. W. Chan 1963a, 183.

23. Creel 1970, 2, italics in original.

24. The point I would make is that neither Confucius nor the *Daodejing* nor the *Zhuangzi* promote any conceptual or metaphysical transcendentality familiar to Western ears.

25. Hall & Ames 1998, 29.

26. For example: Graham 1986, 322–360, 1989, 406–414.

27. Waley 1934, 30/31.

28. Watson 1968, 25; the claim to mysticism is made throughout his introduction.

29. Watson 2003, 3.

30. Fung Yu-lan 1948, 4.

31. Fung Yu-lan 1948, 8/9.

32. Fung Yu-lan 1948, 8.

33. Fung Yu-lan 1975 (1928), 3–23.

34. Lau 2001, xvii.

35. Lau 2001, xvii.

36. Robinet 1999, 135, italics in original.

37. Robinet 1999, 137, italics in original.

38. Schwartz 1975, 65.

39. Schwartz 1985, 197.

40. Schwartz 1985, 192–200.

41. Schwartz 1985, 197.

42. Kaltenmark 1969, 24.

43. Interestingly enough, although I have argued against some of Watson's ideas about Daoism, and in general agree more with Graham, I have since found that Watson's translation of the *Zhuangzi* often much better conveys my reading than Graham's, of which examples follow later.

44. Derrida 2004, 153.

45. Ames & Hall 2003, 83.

46. See for example Clarke 2000, 16 and on.

47. Graham 1989, 199.

48. Whorf 1956, 83/84.

49. See Graham 1989, 389–428 and 1992, 59–83.

50. Graham 1989, 391.

51. Graham 1989, 404.

52. Hansen 1992, 37, italics in original. Obviously this way of seeing language is much closer to Derrida's notion of 'writing,' although there are important differences.

53. Hansen 1992, 34.

54. Hansen 1992, 40.

55. See Hansen 1983, and 1992, 48/49.

56. Hansen 1992, 48.

57. Ames & Rosemont 1998, 38/39.

58. Ames & Hall 2001, 16.

59. Ames & Hall 2001, 17.

60. *Zhuangzi*, Watson 2003, 38.

61. *Zhuangzi*, Graham 1981, 55.

62. Ames 2008, 45.

63. *Zhuangzi*, Graham 1981, 118.

64. That Zhuangzi assents "uneasily" has probably more to do with the fact that this chapter of the book has a strong Yangist flavor, and is thus concerned with the preservation of his personal life, whereas the "later" Zhuangzi is much less concerned with the preservation of his person. See Graham 1981, 117.

65. Ames 2008, 42, italics in original.

66. Although current philosophy of language is moving away from this traditional idea, it nevertheless is still the common view and a view that still functions as orthodox, and is used as such by many comparative philosophers. Part of the argument in this book is to bring current comparative thinking more in line with postmodern criticisms of this orthodoxy.

67. Hall & Ames 1987, 294.

68. Hall & Ames 1987, 264.

69. Hansen 1983, 35, italics in original.

70. Ames & Hall 2003, 45–46.

71. Graham 1981, 107.

72. *Zhuangzi*, Watson 2003, 141.

73. *Daodejing*, Ames & Hall 2003, 198, also see Chapter 81.

74. *Daodejing*, Ames & Hall 2003, 111.

75. *Daodejing*, Ames & Hall 2003, 127.

76. Graham 1989, 410.

77. Graham 1989, 199.

78. *Zhuangzi*, Watson 2003, 46.

79. *Zhuangzi*, Watson 2003, 39.

80. See Wang, Youru 2001 and Wright 1992.

81. Wright 1992, 133, italics in original.

82. *Zhuangzi*, Watson 2003, 35, translation slightly modified.

83. Herrlee Creel suggests that this is the most common translation in his study of the different translations of the opening lines of the *Daodejing*. Creel 1983, 302.

84. Hall & Ames 1998, 235.

85. Hall & Ames 1998, 190.

86. See Robinet 1999, 147/148.

87. Hall & Ames 1987, 12, and 1998, 191/192.

88. Hall & Ames 1998, 193.

89. Graham 1989, 412.

90. Fung Yu-lan 1980, 45, italics in original.

91. Ziporyn 2003, 9.

92. *Zhuangzi*, Watson 2003, 38/39, italics in original.

93. Jullien 2000, 290–291, italics in original.

94. See Jullien 2000, 302–304.
95. Cheng 2002, preface.
96. Neville 2002, 6/7.
97. Neville 2002, 16.
98. Møllgaard 2005, 6.
99. Møllgaard 2005, 17.
100. Møllgaard 2005, 7 and on.
101. Møllgaard 2005, 7, italics in original.
102. It is of course exactly this tendency to establish metaphysical principles, which might seem natural to some, that I am arguing against throughout this book.
103. For example: Graham 1986, 322–360, 1989, 406–414.
104. *Daodejing*, Ames & Hall 2003, 80, italics in original. Other translations have something along the lines of "Being and Non-Being produce each other," for example W. Chan 1963 and Duyvendak 1954.
105. *Daodejing*, Ames & Hall 2003, 91, italics in original.
106. *Daodejing*, Ames & Hall 2003, 139, italics in original.
107. *Daodejing*, Ames & Hall 2003, 130, italics in original.
108. Hall & Ames 1998, 245, italics in original.
109. Hansen 1983, 32.
110. Hansen 1983, 30/31, italics in original.
111. Graham 1991, 287.
112. *Zhuangzi*, Graham 1981, 53.
113. *Zhuangzi*, Graham 1981, 123.
114. Hall & Ames 1998, 250, italics in original.
115. Duyvendak 1954, 9.
116. Creel 1983, 302.
117. *Daodejing*, Duyvendak 1954, 17.
118. Hansen 1992, 50/51, italics in original.
119. *Zhuangzi*, Watson 2003, 104–105.
120. *Zhuangzi*, Watson 2003, 33.
121. *Zhuangzi*, Watson 1968, 156–157.
122. *Zhuangzi*, Watson 2003, 103.
123. Jullien 2000, 321.
124. Jullien 2000, 322, italics in original.
125. See also Jullien 2000, 324, where he says:

> *Zhuangzi* invites us to shift our perspectives, but not in order to lead us into another reality (that is, a reality of another order, either ontological or theological, which might represent the intelligible or the divine). It aims to detach us from the limitations and oppositions in which we contain reality. In other words, the heights it invites us to reach lead to the emancipation of experience—not to a belief in another world. The gesture of going beyond suffices; and transcendence is not objectified into a Truth. And if Zhuangzi comes closest in Chinese Antiquity to the Western aspiration to a sense of the beyond, such a beyond assumes no theoretical consistency for him.

This quote reveals the nonmetaphysical approach by Jullien, yet it also reveals why I am reluctant to make too much use of him, as he does work within the conceptual framework of metaphysics, and as such seems to favor ideas of transcendence; even if his ideas of transcendence are not directed to "another world," they could still be read as supportive of the essentialist or absolutist view which Ames and Hall consider inappropriate as well. See Jullien 2000, 275–332. Overall, though, I think Jullien's views can be understood as propounding a nonmetaphysical view of Daoism.

126. "Gatekeeper" is W. Chan's translation (1963a, 136), also often rendered as border guard or keeper of the pass. Yet the name of the gatekeeper Kuan Yin and the Han Gu Pass are both based on the gateway (*men* 門) character.

127. As in Lau 2001, x, italics added.

128. *Daodejing*, Ames & Hall 2003, 143, italics and Romanizations in original.

129. Ames & Rosemont 1998, 56.

130. Ames & Hall 2003, 59, italics in original.

131. *Yuandao*, Lau & Ames 1998, 117, italics in original.

132. *Yuandao*, Lau & Ames 1998, 93.

133. *Yuandao*, Lau & Ames 1998, 109.

134. *Daodejing*, Ames & Hall 2003, 77.

135. *Daodejing*, Ames & Hall 2003, 158 and 164.

136. *Daodejing*, Ames & Hall 2003, 159.

137. *Daodejing*, Ames & Hall 2003, 90, Chinese Romanization added.

138. *Daodejing*, Ames & Hall 2003, 192, italics in original.

139. W. Chan 1963a, 167.

140. *Daodejing*, Ames & Hall 2003, 106. Moeller 2007, 51, has "undifferentiated," and W. Chan 1963a, 150, has "no distinctions."

141. Although in the following cases of "seeming" different Chinese characters are used for this notion, there nevertheless seems to be a philosophical idea involved which I am trying to convey.

142. One can think of so many other metaphors of vagueness and indeterminacy in both the *Daodejing* and the *Zhuangzi* that it seems superfluous to mention specific examples. Further chapters in the *Daodejing* where the language of "seeming" is used include 20, 41, 45.

143. *Zhuangzi*, Watson 1968, 162, Romanization added.

144. *Zhuangzi*, Watson 1968, 256.

145. *Zhuangzi*, Watson 1968, 257.

146. *Zhuangzi*, Watson 2003, 35.

147. *Zhuangzi*, Watson 1968, 362, Romanization added.

148. For a discussion of vagueness and penumbra in the *Zhuangzi*, see Coutinho 2004.

149. *Yuandao*, Lau & Ames 1998, 133, translation slightly modified.

150. *Zhuangzi*, Watson 2003, 79.

151. *Zhuangzi*, Watson 1968, 120.

152. *Zhuangzi*, Watson 2003, 38.

153. *Zhuangzi*, Graham 1981, 281.

NOTES TO CHAPTER FOUR

1. Heidegger 1997b, 151–152; 1971, 52, translation slightly modified.
2. Derrida 1978, 117.
3. *Zhuangzi*, Watson 2003, 141.
4. As the reader may have noticed, I prefer to translate the Heideggerian "*Ursprünglich*" by "originary" rather than "primordial," but will keep to translations as they have appeared, adding the German when necessary.
5. Jung 1984, 220.
6. For examples of these comparisons, and in general of comparative studies of Heidegger or Derrida with Chinese philosophy, I refer the reader to the bibliography at the end of this book.
7. C. Chang 1975, xv, italics in original.
8. Heidegger 1961, vol. 2, 28; 1979–1987, vol. III, 182.
9. I do so later in this chapter with the notion of "Zeit-Spiel-Raum" or "Zeit-Raum."
10. *Daodejing*, C. Chang 1975, 33. Ames & Hall 2003 translate: "profound efficacy," and Lau 2001 has: "mysterious virtue."
11. Parkes 1984, 354.
12. Parkes 1984, 357.
13. Ames & Hall 2003, 91.
14. Parkes 1984, 361.
15. Although there are no real connections between Nishida and Heidegger, the former was familiar with Sartre and presumably, as is evident for example in Yuasa's contribution to *Heidegger and Asian Thought* (ed. Parkes, 1987), the Kyoto School in general interpreted Heidegger similarly in an existentialist way, mainly because they were only aware of Heidegger's early thought, which they saw as too subjectivistic (see also Mizoguchi's contribution in the same volume).
16. Nishitani 1982, 152.
17. Nishitani 1987, 145–154.
18. Nishitani 1987, 148/49.
19. Jung 1984.
20. While Jung's reading may be excusable if purely based on a rather superficial reading of *Of Grammatology* alone (although even then it is not warranted), between the appearance of *Of Grammatology* in English and Jung's article lies a time span of eight years in which Derrida repeatedly denied and sought to clarify his position regarding "writing" and to defend himself against claims like those of Jung. Some instances include interviews first published in 1982 ("The Almost Nothing of the Unpresentable," now in *Points* . . . Derrida 1995), the "Outwork" of *Dissemination* (Derrida 1981a, especially 3–6), and *Writing and Difference* (Derrida 1978, for example page 22).
21. Beckett paraphrased in Jung 1984, 217.
22. Jung 1984, 226.
23. Jung 1984, 227.
24. See Derrida 1976, 90.
25. Ch'ien 1984, especially 382/383.

26. L. Zhang 1985.

27. L. Zhang 1985, 395.

28. L. Zhang 1985, 397.

29. L. Zhang 1985, 397.

30. L. Zhang 1985, 397.

31. Dilworth 1990.

32. Dilworth 1990, 9, italics in original.

33. Dilworth 1990, 12.

34. Heidegger 1997b; 1971, 70.

35. Derrida 2002b, 13.

36. See note 4 of Chapter 1.

37. Heidegger 1997b; 1971, 92.

38. *Daodejing*, Ames & Hall 2003, 98. Lau 2001, 23 has: "Who can be muddy and yet, settling, slowly become limpid? Who can be at rest and yet, stirring, slowly come to life?"

39. Letter from Heidegger to Professor Hsiao, quoted in Parkes 1987, 103.

40. Hsiao 1987, 100.

41. Heidegger 1997b, 24/5; 1971b, 202. *Diaphora* is in Greek script in Heidegger's German original.

42. Ivanhoe 2003, xxii, italics in original.

43. Heidegger 2000, 78/79; 1972, 71, German added.

44. Examples abound in the *Daodejing*: chapters 1, 4, 14, 15, 21, to name a few.

45. Heidegger 1989, 371–388.

46. Ames & Lau 1998, 13–19.

47. Heidegger 1989. Although Heidegger wrote the *Beiträge* around and between 1937 and 1939, this work was not published during his life, and only appeared in the *Gesamtausgabe* in 1989. It is however of great importance in understanding Heidegger's turn toward thinking Being from itself, or rather from *Ereignis*, instead of from Dasein.

48. Heidegger 2000; 1972, 21.

49. Ruin, in Dreyfus & Wrathall 2005, 365.

50. Compare Heidegger 1989, 407ff on *Ereignis* as *Kehre*.

51. Heidegger 1989, 260, italics in original. Translation taken from Richard Polt, in Dreyfus & Wrathall 2005, 381, German added.

52. Heidegger 1989, 26, my translation, German added.

53. Heidegger 1989, 73, my translation, German added. In German: "Das Ereignis ist die sich selbst ermittelnde und vermittelnde Mitte, in die alle Wesung der Wahrheit des Seyns im voraus zurückgedacht werden muß."

54. Heidegger 1989, 50, my translation.

55. Leung 1998.

56. *Zhuangzi*, Watson 2003, 79.

57. *Zhuangzi*, Graham 1981, 87, italics added.

58. W. Chan 1963a, 196.

59. Heidegger 1993, 32–33; 1962, 55–56.

60. Heidegger 1994c, 141–147.

61. Heidegger 1994c, 145.

62. Other chapters conveying the same message are 34 and 62.

63. Heidegger 1989, 265, my translation, italics in original, German added.

64. Heidegger 2000; 1972, 3.

65. Heidegger 2000; 1972, 3.

66. Heidegger 1997b; 1971, 66/67.

67. Heidegger 1997b; 1971, 57.

68. In the Watson 2003 translation. Graham 1981 has "Going rambling without a destination," which conveys a similar thought.

69. Heidegger 1985, 64, italics in original.

70. Heidegger 1996, 407, 408/9; 1998, 308, 309, italics in original, German added.

71. Heidegger 1989, 251, my translation, Da-sein in original, other German added.

72. Heidegger 1989, 251, my translation, German added.

73. *Zhuangzi*, Graham 1981, 53, pinyin Romanization added.

74. *Daodejing*, Ames & Hall 2003, 112, pinyin Romanization added.

75. Ames & Hall 2003, 59 and 57.

76. Heidegger 1997b, 261; 1971, 129, only *wëgen* appears in italics in the German original, German in square brackets added.

77. Heidegger 1996, 411; 1998, 311.

78. *Daodejing*, especially chapters 18, 19, and 38.

79. *Daodejing*, Ames & Hall 2003, 151, pinyin Romanization in original.

80. See Heidegger 2000, 71–72, 1972, 65.

81. See for example Pöggeler on trace in Heidegger, in Parkes 1987, 70, or Heidegger's frequent mentions of things like "the secret of Being" and "the originary call."

82. In the *Daodejing* there are hints that could be understood as pointing to a source of which we can only perceive the traces, in a negative theology fashion. Although these hints can also, as I have shown, be read in another way, it is possible to give the metaphysical reading, seemingly in the *Daodejing* and in Heidegger as well. My point would be that the "context" makes the nonmetaphysical readings more plausible.

83. For example in Derrida 1982, 8.

84. *Daodejing*, Ames & Hall 2003, 173, pinyin Romanization in original.

85. *Daodejing*, Ames & Hall 2003, 107.

86. *Zhuangzi*, Watson 2003, 35 and 38.

87. Graham 1989, 228, italics in original.

88. Derrida 1982, 8, also see 13.

89. Derrida 1982, 5, italics in original.

90. Derrida 1981b, 27, italics in original.

91. Foshay 1994, 310.

92. Derrida in: Kearney 1984, 123/124, italics in original.

93. Graham 1989, 190.

94. Ames 2008, 45/46, italics in original, quotation slightly modified.

95. *Daodejing*, Ames & Hall 2003, 77.

96. *Zhuangzi*, Graham 1981, 85.

97. Derrida 1982, 13, italics in original.

98. Derrida 1976, 65.

99. *Zhuangzi*, Watson 2003, 42.

100. *Zhuangzi*, Graham 1981, 64.

101. Heidegger 1997b; 1971, 108.

102. *Zhuangzi*, Graham 1981, 87.

103. *Zhuangzi*, W. Chan 1963a, 196. See also Watson 2003, 79/80, for a similar reading.

104. *Book of Changes*, Shaughnessy 1996, 201.

105. See for example *Daodejing* Chapters 12, 14.

106. Hansen 1992, 34.

107. Heidegger 1983b, 150 and 209. Translation including German by Graham Parkes in Parkes 1987, 70.

108. Heidegger 1996, 423/4; 1998, 320, German added.

109. See Coutinho 2004, especially 122–131 and 153–178 for a fuller explanation of the function of vagueness in Daoism.

110. Graham 1981, 26.

111. Graham 1989, 178.

112. Ames 2008, 45.

113. Watson 1968, 17.

114. *Zhuangzi*, Watson 2003, 141.

115. Heidegger 1996, 405; 1998, 306, italics in original.

116. Heidegger 1989, 83, my translation.

117. Hansen 1992, 229.

118. Heidegger 2000, 2; 1972, 2.

119. See Ames & Hall 2003, 135–136.

120. Jullien 2000, 314.

121. Compare Heidegger 1997b, 11–33, 1971b, 187–210.

122. Wang, Youru 2001.

123. See for example Derrida 1989b, 36. The fact that I do not agree with this term as applying to either Derrida or Daoism says nothing about its possible application in Chan Buddhism though. It might be the fact that it *is* applicable to Chan Buddhism which makes me reluctant to draw too many parallels between Chan Buddhism and Daoism, and between Chan Buddhism and Heidegger and/or Derrida.

124. *Daodejing*, W. Chan 1963a, 175–176.

125. See *Zhuangzi* chapter 2: Watson 2003, 34–36; Graham 1981, 52/3; W. Chan 1963a, 182–184.

126. Derrida 1976, 26.

127. Hall & Ames 1998, 48, italics in original.

128. See for example *Zhuangzi*, Watson 2003, 34–40.

129 Heidegger 1982, 197.

130. *Hsün Tzu*, Watson 1963, 144.

131. An exception to this general rule of seeing language as conventional, which is not only found in Daoism, but in most of Chinese philosophy, seems to be the *Huang-Lao* way of thought, which suggest that "things arise from dao replete with form and name" (Peerenboom 1993, 40, see also 41 and 55–57). My

suggestion is that in this area at least, *Huang-Lao* thought is not on par with the Daoist vision of language as I have presented it in the *Daodejing* and *Zhuangzi.*

132. Heim 1984, 333, italics in original.

133. Derrida 1982, 207–271, especially 266ff.

134. *Daodejing*, Ames & Hall 2003, 107 (ch. 21). Other chapters conveying a similar idea include 6, 14, 15, 41, 45.

135. *Zhuangzi*, Watson 2003, 40.

136. *Zhuangzi*, Graham 1981, 57.

137. Ziporyn 2003.

138. *Zhuangzi*, Graham 1981, 48.

139. Derrida 1978, 22, italics in original.

140. Berkson 1996.

141. Berkson 1996, 108.

142. Berkson 1996, 115.

143. Magliola 1990, 91, italics added.

144. Saso 1990, 56–57.

145. Clarke 2000, 193.

146. *Zhuangzi*, Watson 2003, 105.

147. Derrida in: Salusinszky 1987, 20.

148. *Book of Changes*, W. Chan 1963a, 266.

149. Chien 1990, 45, quotation slightly modified.

150. Derrida 1981b, 42–43, italics in original.

151. *Daodejing*, Ames & Hall 2003, 84.

152. For the accusation of right-wing, see Hogan 1990, 78. Derrida's left-wing inclinations can be read from his own writings.

153. For the legalist interpretation of Daoism, see the writings of Han Feizi in Watson 1964, and Hansen 1992, 344 and on.

154. See Graham 1989, 289.

155. *Zhuangzi*, Graham 1981, 118.

156. If we remember that this outside is always already in "context."

157. We must remember J. S. Mill's principle that the individual is free to do as he or she pleases as long as it does not harm others, an injunction of singular importance in present-day problematics.

158. See the discussions on the transformation and death of people in Chapters 3, 6, and 18 of the *Zhuangzi* for example.

159. Graham 1989, 303.

160. *Daodejing*, Ames & Hall 2003, 101–103.

161. *Daodejing*, Ames & Hall 2003, 178, italics in original.

162. Critchley 1992, especially Chapters 1 and 5.

163. Cua 1981, 129, italics in original.

164. Derrida 1976, 3.

NOTES TO CONCLUSION

1. Clarke 2000, 193.

2. *Zhuangzi*, Graham 1981, 89.

Bibliography

Abe, Masao (1985). *Zen and Western Thought*. Edited by W. R. Lafleur. Honolulu: University of Hawaii Press.

——— (1997). *Zen and Comparative Studies*. Edited by S. Heine. Honolulu: University of Hawaii Press.

Ames, Roger T., ed. (1998). *Wandering at Ease in the Zhuangzi*. Albany: SUNY Press.

Ames, Roger T. (2008). "Paronomasia: A Confucian Way of Making Meaning." In *Confucius Now: Contemporary Encounters with the Analects*. Edited by David Jones. La Salle, IL: Open Court, 37–48.

Ames, Roger T., & David L. Hall, trans. (2003). *Daodejing: Making This Life Significant*. New York: Ballantine Books.

Ames, Roger T., & D. C. Lau (1998). *Yuan Dao: Tracing* Dao *to Its Source*. New York: Ballantine Books.

Ames, Roger T., & Henry Rosemont, Jr. (1998). *The Analects of Confucius: A Philosophical Translation*. New York: Ballantine Books.

Appelbaum, David (1983). "On Turning a Zen Ear." *Philosophy East & West* 33, 2: 115–122.

Baynes, Cary F., trans. (1967). *I Ching: The Book of Changes*. Princeton: Bollington Series.

Berkson, Mark (1996). "Language: The Guest of Reality—Zhuangzi and Derrida on Language, Reality, and Skillfulness." In Kjellberg & Ivanhoe 1996, 97–126.

Bernasconi, Robert (1985). *The Question of Language in Heidegger's History of Being*. London: Macmillan Press.

Bollnow, Otto F. (1987). *Das Wesen der Stimmungen*. Frankfurt: Klostermann.

Boltz, William G. (1985). "The *Lao Tzu* Text that Wang Pi and Ho-shang Kung Never Saw." *Bulletin of the School of Oriental and African Studies* 48, 3: 493–501.

Brannigan, John, Ruth Robbins, & Julian Wolfreys, eds. (1996). *Applying: To Derrida*. London: Macmillan Press.

Bruns, Gerald L. (1989). *Heidegger's Estrangements: Language, Truth, and Poetry in the Later Writings*. New Haven: Yale University Press.

Burke, Séan (1992). *The Death and Return of the Author: Criticism and Subjectivity in Barthes, Foucault and Derrida*. Edinburgh: Edinburgh University Press.

Caputo, John D. (1986). *The Mystical Element in Heidegger's Thought*. New York: Fordham University Press.

——— 1993. "On Not Circumventing the Quasi-Transcendental: The Case of Rorty and Derrida." In Madison 1993, 147–169.

Chan, Alan K. L. (1991). *Two Visions of the Way*. Albany: SUNY Press.

Chan, Wing-tsit (1963a). *A Source Book in Chinese Philosophy*. Princeton, NJ: Princeton University Press.

——— (1963b). *The Way of Lao Tzu (Tao-te Ching)*. Indianapolis, IN: Bobbs-Merrill Company.

Chang, Chung-yuan (1969). *Original Teachings of Ch'an Buddhism*. New York: Pantheon Books.

——— (1975). *Tao, a New Way of Thinking*. New York: Harper & Row.

——— (1977). "The Philosophy of Taoism According to Chuang Tzu." *Philosophy East & West* 27, 4: 409–422.

Cheney, Lynne V. (1995). *Telling the Truth*. New York: Simon & Schuster.

Cheng, Chung-ying (1973). "On Zen (Ch'an) Language and Zen Paradoxes." *Journal of Chinese Philosophy* 1, 1: 77–102.

——— (1990). "A Taoist Interpretation of 'Differance' in Derrida." *Journal of Chinese Philosophy* 17, 1: 19–30.

——— (2002). "Preface." In "Tao and God," special issue, *Journal of Chinese Philosophy* 29, 1: 1–2.

Cheng, Jie-wei (1995). "Deconstruction, Yin-Yang, and Negative Theology." *Journal of Chinese Philosophy* 22, 3: 263–288

Ch'ien, Edward T. (1984). "The Conception of Language and the Use of Paradox in Buddhism and Taoism." *Journal of Chinese Philosophy* 11, 4: 375–399.

Chien, Chi-hui (1990). "'Theft's Way,' A Comparative Study of Chuang Tzu's Tao and Derridean Trace." *Journal of Chinese Philosophy* 17, 1: 31–50.

Ching, Julia, & Willard G. Oxtoby, eds. (1992). *Discovering China: European Interpretations in the Enlightenment*. Rochester: University of Rochester Press.

Clarke, J. J. (1997). *Oriental Enlightenment: The Encounter between Asian and Western Thought*. London: Routledge.

——— (2000). *The Tao of the West: Western Transformations of Taoist Thought*. London: Routledge.

Cleary, Thomas, trans. (1986). *Shobogenzo: Zen Essays by Dogen*. Honolulu: University of Hawaii Press.

——— (1991). *The Essential Tao: An Initiation into the Heart of Taoism Through the Authentic Tao Te Ching and the Inner Teachings of Chuang-tzu*. New York: HarperCollins.

Coltman, Rod (1998). *The Language of Hermeneutics: Gadamer and Heidegger in Dialogue*. Albany: SUNY Press.

Coutinho, Steve (2004). *Zhuangzi and Early Chinese Philosophy: Vagueness, Transformation and Paradox*. Aldershot (UK): Ashgate Publishing Ltd.

Cook, Daniel. J., & Henry Rosemont, Jr. (1992). "The Pre-established Harmony between Leibniz and Chinese Thought." In Ching & Oxtoby 1992, 82–96.

Coward, Harold (1990). *Derrida and Indian Philosophy.* Albany: SUNY Press.

——— & Toby Foshay, eds. (1992). *Derrida and Negative Theology.* Albany: SUNY Press.

Creel, Herrlee G. (1970). *What Is Taoism, and Other Studies in Chinese Cultural History.* Chicago: University of Chicago Press.

——— (1983). "On the Opening Words of the Lao-Tzu." *Journal of Chinese Philosophy* 10, 4: 299–329.

Critchley, Simon. (1992). *The Ethics of Deconstruction.* Oxford: Blackwell Publishers.

Csikszentmihalyi, M., & P. J. Ivanhoe, eds. (1999). *Religious and Philosophical Aspects of the Laozi.* Albany: SUNY Press.

Cua, Antonio S. (1981). "Opposites as Complements: Reflections on the Significance of *Tao.*" *Philosophy East & West* 31, 2: 123–140.

Culler, Jonathan (1982). *On Deconstruction: Theory and Criticism after Structuralism.* Ithaca, NY: Cornell University Press.

Dallmayr, Fred (1993). *The Other Heidegger.* Ithaca, NY: Cornell University Press.

——— (1996). *Beyond Orientalism: Essays on Cross-cultural Encounter.* Albany: SUNY Press.

Dasenbrock, Reed Way, ed. (1989). *Redrawing the Lines: Analytic Philosophy, Deconstruction, and Literary Theory.* Minneapolis: University of Minnesota Press.

Davidson, Donald (1998). "On the Very Idea of a Conceptual Scheme." In Nye 1998, 271–283.

Derrida, Jacques (1976). *Of Grammatology.* Translated by G. C. Spivak. Baltimore: Johns Hopkins University Press.

——— (1978). *Writing and Difference.* Translated by Alan Bass. Chicago: Chicago University Press.

——— (1979). *Spurs, Nietzsche's Styles.* Translated by Barbara Harlow. Chicago: Chicago University Press.

——— (1981a). *Dissemination.* Translated by Barbara Johnson. Chicago: Chicago University Press.

——— (1981b). *Positions.* Translated by Alan Bass. Chicago: Chicago University Press.

——— (1982). *Margins of Philosophy.* Translated by Alan Bass. Chicago: University of Chicago Press.

——— (1985). *The Ear of the Other.* Edited by Christie McDonald. Translated by Peggy Kamuf. Lincoln: University of Nebraska Press.

——— (1986). *Glas.* Translated by John P. Leavey, Jr., & Richard Rand. Lincoln: University of Nebraska Press.

——— (1987). *The Postcard: From Socrates to Freud and Beyond.* Translated by Alan Bass. Chicago: University of Chicago Press.

——— (1988). *Limited Inc.* Evanston, IL: Northwestern University Press.

——— (1989a). *Of Spirit: Heidegger and the Question.* Translated by G. Bennington & R. Bowlby. Chicago: Chicago University Press.

——— (1989b). "Psyche: Inventions of the Other." Translated by Catherine Porter. In Waters & Godzich 1989, 25–65.

——— (1991). *Cinders.* Translated by N. Lukacher. Lincoln: University of Nebraska Press.

——— (1992a). *The Other Heading: Reflections on Today's Europe.* Translated by P. Brault & M. Naas. Bloomington: Indiana University Press.

——— (1992b). "Of an Apocalyptic Tone Newly Adopted in Philosophy." In Coward & Foshay 1992, 25–72.

——— (1993a). *Aporias.* Translated by Thomas Dutoit. Stanford, CA: Stanford University Press.

——— (1993b). "Heidegger's Ear: Philopolemology (Geschlecht IV)." In Sallis 1993, 163–218.

——— (1994). "Fourmis." In *Lectures de la Différence Sexuelle.* Edited by Mara Negron & Anne Berger, 69–102. Paris: Des Femmes.

——— (1995). *Points. . ., Interviews, 1974–1994.* Edited by Elisabeth Weber. Translated by Peggy Kamuf and others. Stanford, CA: Stanford University Press.

——— (1998). *Monolingualism of the Other; or, The Prosthesis of Origin.* Translated by Patrick Mensah. Stanford, CA: Stanford University Press.

——— (2001a). "Deconstructions: The Im-possible." In Lotringer & Cohen 2001, 13–31.

——— (2001b). *On Cosmopolitanism and Forgiveness.* Translated by Mark Dooley & Michael Hughes. London: Routledge.

——— (2002a). *Acts of Religion.* Edited by Gil Anidjar. New York: Routledge.

——— (2002b). *Who's Afraid of Philosophy? Right to Philosophy 1.* Translated by Jan Plug. Stanford, CA: Stanford University Press.

——— (2004). *Eyes of the University: Right to Philosophy 2.* Translated by Jan Plug. Stanford, CA: Stanford University Press.

——— & Geoffrey Bennington (1993). *Jacques Derrida.* Translated by G. Bennington. Chicago: University of Chicago Press.

Deutsch, Eliot, ed. (1991). *Culture and Modernity: East-West Philosophic Perspectives.* Honolulu: University of Hawaii Press.

——— & Ron Bontekoe, eds. (1997). *A Companion to World Philosophies.* Oxford: Blackwell.

Dilworth, David A. (1990). "The Critique of Logocentrism, or (else) Derrida's Dead Line." *Journal of Chinese Philosophy* 17, 1: 5–18.

Dreyfus, Hubert L., & Mark A. Wrathall, eds. (2005). *A Companion to Heidegger.* Oxford: Blackwell Publishing Ltd.

Duyvendak, J. J. L., trans. (1954). *Tao Te Ching.* London: John Murray Ltd.

Farrel, Frank B. (1994). *Subjectivity, Realism, and Postmodernism—The Recovery of the World.* Cambridge: Cambridge University Press.

Faure, Bernard (1993). *Ch'an Insights and Oversights.* Princeton, NJ: Princeton University Press.

Fleming, Jesse (1998). "On Translation of Taoist Philosophical Texts: Preservation of Ambiguity and Contradiction." *Journal of Chinese Philosophy* 25, 1: 147–156.

Foshay, Toby Arvard (1994). "Derrida and Dogen: Denegation and the Liberation of Discriminating Thought." In *Negation, Critical Theory, and Postmodern Textuality*. Edited by Daniel Fischlin. Dordrecht: Kluwer Academic Publishers, 301–320.

Fóti, Veronique M. (1992). *Heidegger and the Poets*. Atlantic Highlands, NJ: Humanities Press International.

Fung, Yu-lan (1928). *Chuang Tzŭ: A New Selected Translation with an Exposition of the Philosophy of Kuo Hsiang*. New York: Gordon Press, 1975.

——— (1948). *A Short History of Chinese Philosophy*. New York: The Free Press/ Macmillan.

——— (1953). *A History of Chinese Philosophy*. Vol. II. Translated by Derk Bodde. Princeton, NJ: Princeton University Press.

Gadamer, Hans Georg (1990). *Wahrheit und Methode*. Gesammelte Werke, Band 1. Tübingen: J. C. B. Mohr.

Geertz, Clifford (1993). *The Interpretation of Cultures*. London: Fontana Press.

Giles, Herbert A. (1980). *Chuang Tzŭ: Taoist Philosopher and Chinese Mystic*. London: Unwin Paperbacks. First published 1889, second edition 1926, reprinted 1961.

Graham, A. C., trans. (1960). *The Book of Lieh-tzŭ*. New York: Columbia University Press, 1990.

——— (1981). *Chuang-Tzu: The Inner Chapters*. London: George Allen and Unwin.

——— (1983). "Taoist Spontaneity and the Dichotomy of 'Is' and 'Ought.'" In: Mair 1983, 3–23.

——— (1986). *Studies in Chinese Philosophy and Philosophical Literature*. Singapore: Institute of East Asian Philosophies.

——— (1989). *Disputers of the Tao: Philosophical Argument in Ancient China*. La Salle IL: Open Court.

——— (1991). "Reflections and Replies." In Rosemont 1991, 267–321.

——— (1992). *Unreason Within Reason: Essays on the Outskirts of Rationality*. La Salle, IL: Open Court.

Granet, Marcel (1934). *La Pensée Chinoise*. Paris: Editions Albin Michel.

Hall, David L., & Roger T. Ames (1987). *Thinking Through Confucius*. Albany: SUNY Press.

——— (1995). *Anticipating China*. Albany: SUNY Press.

——— (1998). *Thinking from the Han*. Albany: SUNY Press.

——— (2001). *Focusing the Familiar: A Translation and Philosophical Interpretation of the* Zhongyong. Honolulu: University of Hawaii Press.

Hansen, Chad (1975). "Ancient Chinese Theories of Language." *Journal of Chinese Philosophy* 2, 3: 245–283.

——— (1983a). "A Tao of Tao in Chuang-tzu." In *Experimental Essays on Chuang-tzu*. Edited by Victor H. Mair, 24–55. Honolulu: University of Hawaii Press.

——— (1983b). *Language and Logic in Ancient China*. Ann Arbor: University of Michigan Press.

——— (1992). *A Daoist Theory of Chinese Thought*. Hong Kong: Oxford University Press.

Hayakawa, S. I., ed. (1959). *Our Language and Our World*. New York: Harper.

Heidegger, Martin (1953). *Einführung in die Metaphysik*. Tübingen: Max Niemeyer. Translated by R. Manheim as *An Introduction to Metaphysics*. New Haven: Yale University Press, 1959.

——— (1961). *Nietzsche* (I & II). Pfullingen: Günther Neske. Translated by D. Farrell Krell as *Nietzsche*. San Francisco: Harper & Row, 1979–1987).

——— (1963). *Was ist das—die Philosophie?* Pfullingen: Günther Neske.

——— (since 1975). *Gesamtausgabe*. (GA). Frankfurt a.M.: Klostermann.

——— (1976). *Was ist Metaphysik?* (GA 9). Frankfurt a.M.: Klostermann.

——— (1977). *Zur Seinsfrage*. Frankfurt a.M.: Klostermann.

——— (1981). *Erläuterungen zu Hölderlins Dichtung*. Frankfurt a.M.: Klostermann [5].

——— (1982). *The Basic Problems of Phenomenology*. Translated by A. Hofstadter. Bloomington: Indiana University Press.

——— (1983a). *Denkerfahrungen*. Frankfurt a.M.: Klostermann.

——— (1983b). *Aus der Erfahrung des Denkens*. Frankfurt a.M.: Klostermann.

——— (1984). *Hölderlin's Hymn »Der Ister«*. (GA 53). Frankfurt a.M.: Klostermann. Translated by W. McNeill & J. Davis as *Hölderlin's Hymn "The Ister."* Bloomington: Indiana University Press, 1996.

——— (1985). *Gelassenheit*. Stuttgart, Günther Neske [8]. Translated by J. M. Anderson & E. Hans Freund as *Discourse on Thinking*. New York: Harper & Row, 1966.

——— (1989). *Beiträge zur Philosophie (vom Ereignis)*. (GA 65). Frankfurt a.M.: Klostermann.

——— (1991). *Grundbegriffe (Sommersemester 1941)*. (GA 51). Frankfurt a.M.: Klostermann.

——— (1992). *Der Satz vom Grund*. Stuttgart: Günther Neske [7]. Translated by R. Lilly as *The Principle of Reason*. Bloomington, IN: Indiana University Press, 1991.

——— (1993). *Sein und Zeit*. Tübingen: Max Niemeyer [17]. Translated by J. Macquarrie & E. Robinson as *Being and Time*. New York: Harper, 1962.

——— (1994a). *Holzwege*. Frankfurt a.M.: Klostermann [7].

——— (1994b). *Vorträge und Aufsätze*. Stuttgart: Günther Neske [7].

——— (1994c). *Heraklit* (GA 55, Frankfurt a.M.: Klostermann [3].

——— (1996). *Wegmarken*. Frankfurt a.M.: Klostermann [3]. Translated by W. McNeill, ed., as *Pathmarks*. Cambridge: Cambridge University Press, 1998.

——— (1997a). *Was Heißt Denken?* Tübingen: Max Niemeyer [5]. Translated by J. Glenn Gray as *What Is Called Thinking?* New York, Harper & Row, 1968.

——— (1997b). *Unterwegs zur Sprache*. Stuttgart: Günther Neske [11]. Translated by P. D. Hertz as *On the Way to Language*. New York: Harper & Row, 1971a.

——— (1999). *Identität und Differenz*. Stuttgart: Günther Neske [11]. Translated by J. Stambaugh as *Identity and Difference*. New York: Harper & Row, 1974.

——— (2000). *Zur Sache des Denkens*. Tübingen: Max Niemeyer [4]. Translated by J. Stambaugh as *On Time and Being*. New York: Harper & Row, 1972.

——— & Eugen Fink (1970). *Heraklit*. Frankfurt a.M.: Klostermann. *Heraclitus Seminar*. Translated by C. H. Seibel as *Heraclitus Seminar*. Tuscaloosa, AL: University of Alabama Press, 1979.

——— & Richard Wisser (1988). *Antwort / Martin Heidegger im Gespräch*. Pfullingen: Günther Neske/ Emil Kettering.

——— (1971b). *Poetry, Language, Thought*. Translated and compiled by A. Hofstadter. New York: Harper & Row.

——— (1975). *Early Greek Thinking*. Translated and compiled by D. F. Krell & F. Capuzzi. New York: Harper & Row.

——— (1977). *The Question Concerning Technology and Other Essays*. Translated and compiled by W. Lovitt. New York: Harper & Row.

——— (1978). *Basic Writings*. Translated and compiled by D. F. Krell. London: Routledge & Kegan Paul.

——— (1985). *Schelling's Treatise on the Essence of Human Freedom*. Translated and compiled by J. Stambaugh. Athens: Ohio University Press.

Heim, Michael (1984). "A Philosophy of Comparison: Heidegger and Lao Tzu." *Journal of Chinese Philosophy* 11, 4: 307–335.

Heine, Steven, & Dale S. Wright, eds. (2000). *The Kōan: Texts and Contexts in Zen Buddhism*. New York: Oxford University Press.

Heine, Steven, & Charles Wei-Hsun Fu, eds. (1995). *Japan in Traditional and Postmodern Perspectives*. Albany: SUNY Press.

Henricks, Robert G. (1983). *Philosophy and Argumentation in Third-Century China: The Essays of Hsi K'ang*. Princeton, NJ: Princeton University Press.

———, trans. (2000). *Lao Tzu's Tao Te Ching*. New York: Columbia University Press.

Hillis Miller, J. (1993). "Derrida's Others." In Madison 1993, 153–170.

Hobart, Mark (2000). *After Culture: Anthropology as Radical Metaphysical Critique*. Yogyakarta: Duta Wacana Press.

Hogan, Patrick C. (1990). *The Politics of Interpretation: Ideology, Professionalism, and the Study of Literature*. New York: Oxford University Press.

Hölderlin, Friedrich (1966). *Poems and Fragments*. Translated by M. Hamburger. London: Routledge & Kegan Paul Ltd.

——— (1970). *Sämtliche Werke und Briefe*. München: Carl Hanser Verlag.

Hsiao, Paul Shih-yi (1987). "Heidegger and Our Translation of the *Tao Te Ching*." In Parkes 1987, 93–103.

Ivanhoe, P. J., ed. (1996). *Chinese Language, Thought, and Culture: Nivison and his Critics*. Chicago: Open Court.

——— (2003). *The Daodejing of Laozi*. Indianapolis, IN: Hackett Publishing Company.

Jullien, François (2000). *Detour and Access: Strategies of Meaning in China and Greece*. Translated by Sophie Hawkes. New York: Zone Books.

Jung, Hwa Yol (1984). "Misreading the Ideogram: From Fenollosa to Derrida and McLuhan." *Paideuma* 13, 2: 211–227.

Kaltenmark, Max (1969). *Lao Tzu and Taoism*. Translated by Roger Greaves. Stanford, CA: Stanford University Press.

Kasulis, Thomas P. (1981). *Zen Action Zen Person*. Honolulu: University of Hawaii Press.

——— (2002). *Intimacy or Integrity: Philosophy and Cultural Difference*. Honolulu: University of Hawaii Press.

Kearney, Richard (1984). *Dialogues with Contemporary Continental Thinkers.* Manchester: Manchester University Press.

Kimmerle, Heinz, ed. (1996). *Das Multiversum der Kulturen.* Amsterdam: Elementa/ Rodopi.

Kirk, G. S., & J. E. Raven (1957). *The Presocratic Philosophers.* Cambridge: Cambridge University Press.

Kjellberg, Paul, & P. J. Ivanhoe, eds. (1996). *Essays on Skepticism, Relativism and Ethics in the Zhuangzi.* New York: SUNY Press.

Kockelmans, Joseph J., ed. (1972). *On Heidegger and Language.* Evanston, IL: Northwestern University Press.

Kohn, Livia, & Michael Lafargue, eds. (1988). *Lao-tzu and the Tao-te-ching.* Albany: SUNY Press.

Lafont, Christina (1994). *Sprache und Welterschliessung: Zur Linguistischen Wende der Hermeneutik Heideggers.* Frankfurt: Suhrkamp. Translated by Graham Harman as *Heidegger, Language and World-disclosure.* Cambridge: Cambridge University Press, 2000.

Larson, Gerald J., & Eliot Deutsch, eds. (1988). *Interpreting Across Boundaries: New Essays in Comparative Philosophy.* Princeton, NJ: Princeton University Press.

Lau, D. C., trans. (2001). *Lao Tzu: Tao te Ching.* Hong Kong: Chinese University Press.

Legge, James (1891). *The Texts of Taoism.* (Reprint, 1989). Singapore: Graham Brash (Pte) Ltd.

Leung, Thomas In-Sing (1998). "Tao and Logos." *Journal of Chinese Philosophy* 25, 1: 131–146.

Levinas, Emmanuel (1988). *Entre-Nous: On Thinking-of-the-Other.* Translated by Michael B. Smith & Barbara Harshav. New York: Columbia University Press.

——— (1999). *Alterity and Transcendence.* Translated by Michael B. Smith. London: Athlone Press.

Lewis, Mark (1999). *Writing and Authority in China.* Albany: SUNY Press.

Lotringer, Sylvère, & Sande Cohen, eds. (2001). *French Theory in America.* New York: Routledge.

Lynn, Richard John (1999). *The Classic of the Way and Virtue: A New Translation of the Tao-te Ching of Laozi as Interpreted by Wang Bi.* New York: Columbia University Press.

Madison, Gary B. (ed.) (1993). *Working Through Derrida.* Evanston, IL: Northwestern University Press.

Magliola, Robert (1984). *Derrida on the Mend.* West Lafayette, IN: Purdue University Press.

——— (1990). "Differentialism in Chinese Ch'an and French Deconstruction: Some Test-cases from the Wu-men-kuan." *Journal of Chinese Philosophy* 17, 1: 87–98.

——— (1997). *On Deconstructing Life-Worlds: Buddhism, Christianity, Culture.* Atlanta: Scholars Press.

Mair, Victor H., ed. (1983). *Experimental Essays on Chuang-tzu.* Honolulu: University of Hawaii Press.

Mall, R. A. (2000). *Intercultural Philosophy.* Lanham, MD: Rowman & Littlefield.

Maly, Kenneth, & Parvis Emad, eds. (1986). *Heidegger on Heraclitus: A New Reading* Lewiston, NY: Edwin Mellen Press,

May, Reinhard (1996). *Heidegger's Hidden Sources.* Translated by Graham Parkes. London: Routledge.

Mehta, J. L. (1976) *Martin Heidegger: The Way and the Vision.* Honolulu: University of Hawaii Press.

Michelfelder, Diane P., & Richard E. Palmer, eds. (1989). *Dialogue and Deconstruction: The Gadamer–Derrida Encounter.* Albany: SUNY Press.

Mistry, Freny (1981). *Nietzsche and Buddhism.* Berlin: De Gruyter.

Mitchell, Donald W., ed. (1998). *Masao Abe: A Zen Life of Dialogue.* Boston: Tuttle Publishing.

Moeller, Hans-Georg, trans. (2007). *Daodejing (Laozi): A Complete Translation and Commentary.* Chicago: Open Court.

Møllgaard, Eske (2005). "Zhuangzi's Notion of Transcendental Life." *Asian Philosophy* 15, 1–18.

Mungello, David E. (1992). "Some Recent Studies on the Confluence of Chinese and Western Intellectual History." In Ching & Oxtoby 1992, 176–188.

Nahm, Milton C. (1964). *Selections from Early Greek Philosophy.* Upper Saddle River, NJ: Prentice-Hall.

Needham, Joseph (1969). *Within the Four Seas: The Dialogue of East and West.* London: Allen & Unwin.

Neville, Robert Cummings (2002). "Daoist Relativism, Ethical Choice, and Normative Measure." *Journal of Chinese Philosoph* 29, 1: 5–20.

Nietzsche, Friedrich (1968). *The Will to Power.* Translated by Walter Kaufmann & R. J. Hollingdale. London: Weidenfeld and Nicolson.

——— (1994). *Werke in drei Bänden.* Köln: Könemann.

Nishida, Kitarō (1987). *Last Writings: Nothingness and the Religious Worldview.* Translated by D. A. Dilworth. Honolulu: University of Hawaii Press.

——— (1988). *Zen no Kenkyū.* Translated by V. H. Viglielmo as *A Study of Good.* New York: Greenwood Press.

——— (1990). *Zen no Kenkyū.* Translated by Masao Abe & Christopher Ives as *An Inquiry into the Good.* New Haven, CT: Yale University Press.

Nishitani, Keiji (1982). *Religion and Nothingness.* Translated by Jan Van Bragt. Berkeley: University of California Press.

——— (1987). "Reflections on Two Addresses by Martin Heidegger." Translated by Graham Parkes. In Parkes 1987, 145–154.

Norris, Christopher (1987). *Derrida.* London: Fontana Paperbacks.

——— (1989). "Philosophy as *Not* Just a 'Kind of Writing': Derrida and the Claim of Reason." In Dasenbrock 1989, 189–203.

Nuyen, A. T. (1995). "Naming the Unnameable: The Being of the *Tao.*" *Journal of Chinese Philosophy* 22, 4: 487–498.

Nye, Andrea, ed. (1998). *Philosophy of Language: The Big Questions.* Oxford: Blackwell Publishers.

Odin, Steve (1995). "Derrida and the Decentered Universe of Ch'an/Zen Buddhism." In Heine & Fu 1995, 1–24.

Olson, Carl (2000). *Zen and the Art of Postmodern Philosophy.* Albany: SUNY Press.

Ownes, Wayne D. (1990). "Radical Concrete Particularity: Heidegger, Lao Tzu, and Chuang Tzu." *Journal of Chinese Philosophy* 17, 2: 235–256.

——— (1993). "Tao and Differance: The Existential Implications." *Journal of Chinese Philosophy* 20, 3: 261–278.

Parkes, Graham (1984). "Intimations of Taoist Themes in Early Heidegger." *Journal of Chinese Philosophy* 11, 4: 353–374.

———, ed. (1987). *Heidegger and Asian Thought.* Honolulu: University of Hawaii Press.

Peerenboom, Randall P. (1993). *Law and Morality in Ancient China: The Silk Manuscripts of Huang-Lao.* Albany: SUNY Press.

Petzet, Heinrich W. (1983) *Auf einen Stern zugehen; Erinnerungen an Martin Heidegger 1929–1976.* Frankfurt: Societäts Verlag. Translated by P. Emad & K. Maly as *Encounters and Dialogues with Martin Heidegger 1929–1976.* Chicago: University of Chicago Press, 1993.

Pöggeler, Otto (1994). *Der Denkweg Martin Heideggers.* Stuttgart: Neske [4]. Translated by D. Magurshak and S. Barber as *Martin Heidegger's Path of Thinking.* Atlantic Highlands, NJ: Humanities Press International, 1987.

Prins, A. W. (1996). "Im Westen nur Neues; Martin Heidegger und die Interkulturellen Auseinandersetzung." In Kimmerle 1996, 77–101.

Quine, W. v. O. (1960). *Word and Object.* Cambridge, MA: Technology Press of the M.I.T.

——— (1998). "Indeterminacy of Translation." In Nye 1998, 259–265.

Radhakrishnan, S., & C. Moore, eds. (1957). *A Sourcebook in Indian Philosophy.* Princeton, NJ: Princeton University Press.

Rapaport, Herman (1991). *Heidegger and Derrida: Reflections on Time and Language.* Lincoln: University of Nebraska Press.

——— (2003). *Later Derrida.* New York: Routledge.

Robinet, Isabelle (1998). "Later Commentaries: Textual Polysemy and Syncretistic Interpretations." In Kohn & Lafargue 1998, 119–142.

——— (1999). "The Diverse Interpretations of the *Laozi.*" In Csikszentmihalyi & Ivanhoe 1999, 127–160.

Rorty, Richard (1979). *Philosophy and the Mirror of Nature.* Princeton, NJ: Princeton University Press.

——— (1991). *Essays on Heidegger and Others.* Cambridge: Cambridge University Press.

Rosemont, Henry, Jr., ed. (1991). *Chinese Texts and Philosophical Contexts: Essays Dedicated to Angus C. Graham.* La Salle, IL: Open Court.

Safranski, Rudiger (1994). *Ein Meister aus Deutschland; Heidegger und seine Zeit.* München: Carl Hanser Verlag.

Said, Edward W. (1978). *Orientalism.* London: Routledge & Kegan Paul Ltd.

——— (1993). *Culture and Imperialism.* New York: Knopf & Random House.

Sallis, John, ed. (1993). *Reading Heidegger: Commemorations.* Bloomington: Indiana University Press.

Salusinszky, Imre (1987). *Criticism in Society: Interviews with Jacques Derrida, Northrop Frye, Harold Bloom, Geoffrey Hartman, Frank Kermode, Edward Said, Barbara Johnson, Frank Lentricchia, and J. Hillis Miller.* New York: Methuen.

Saso, Michael (1990). "Derrida and the Decentered World of K'ou-ch'uan: The Deconstruction of Taoist Oral Semiotics." *Journal of Chinese Philosophy* 17, 1: 51–60.

Schrift, Alan D. (1995). *Nietzsche's French Legacy*. New York: Routledge.

Schwartz, Benjamin (1975). "Transcendence in Ancient China." In *Daedalus* 104, 2: 57–68.

——— (1985). *The World of Thought in Ancient China*. Cambridge, MA: Belknap Press of Harvard University Press.

Searle, John R. (1993). "The World Turned Upside Down." In Madison 1993, 170–188.

Shaughnessy, Edward L. (trans.) (1996). *I-Ching—The Classic of Changes*. New York: Ballantine Books.

Stange, Paul (1991). "Deconstruction as Disempowerment: New Orientalisms of Java." *Bulletin of Concerned Asian Scholars* 23, 3: 51–71.

Stellardi, Giuseppe (2000). *Heidegger and Derrida on Philosophy and Metaphor: Imperfect Thought*. New York: Humanity Books.

Suzuki, Daisetz T. (1961). *Essays in Zen Buddhism* (first, second and third series). New York: Grove Press.

——— (1963). *The Essentials of Zen Buddhism*. Edited by Bernard Phillips. London: Rider & Company.

Vetsch, Florian (1992). *Martin Heideggers Angang der Interkulturellen Auseinandersetzung*. Würzburg: Königshausen & Neumann.

Wagner, Rudolf G. (2000). *The Craft of a Chinese Commentator: Wang Bi on the Laozi*. Albany: SUNY Press.

Waley, Arthur (1968). *The Way and Its Power: A Study of the* Tao Tê Ching *and Its Place in Chinese Thought*. London: George Allen & Unwin Ltd.

Wang, Robin R. ed. (2004). *Chinese Philosophy in an Era of Globalization*. Albany: SUNY Press.

Wang, Youru (2000). "Philosophy of Change and the Deconstruction of Self in the *Zhuangzi*." *Journal of Chinese Philosophy* 27, 3: 345–360.

——— (2001). "Liberating Oneself from the Absolutized Boundary of Language: A Liminological Approach to the Interplay of Speech and Silence in Chan Buddhism." *Philosophy East & West* 51, 1: 83–99.

——— (2003). *Linguistic Strategies in Daoist Zhuangzi and Chan Buddhism*. London: RoutledgeCurzon.

Waters, Lindsay, & Wlad Godzich, eds. (1989). *Reading de Man Reading*. Minneapolis: University of Minnesota Press.

Watson, Burton, trans. (1963). *Hsün Tzu: Basic Writings*. New York: Columbia University Press.

——— (1964). *Han Fei Tzu: Basic Writings*. New York: Columbia University Press.

——— (1968). *The Complete Works of Chuang Tzu*. New York: Columbia University Press.

——— (1999). *The Zen Teachings of Master Lin-chi*. New York: Columbia University Press.

——— (2003). *Zhuangzi: Basic Writings*. New York: Columbia University Press.

Watsuji, Tetsurō (1971). *Climates and Culture: A Philosophical Study*. Translated by Geoffrey Bownas. Tokyo: Kokuseido Press.

Whorf, Benjamin Lee (1956). *Language, Thought, and Reality*. Cambridge, MA: MIT Press.

Wieger, Leon (1940). *Chinese Characters: Their Origin, Etymology, History, Classification, and Significance*. Translated by L. Davrout. Beijing: Ho Chi Press.

Wood, David, ed. (1992). *Derrida: A Critical Reader*. Oxford: Blackwell Publishers.

——— & Robert Bernasconi, eds. (1988). *Derrida and Differance*. Evanston, IL: Northwestern University Press.

Wright, Dale S. (1992). "Rethinking Transcendence: The Role of Language in Zen Experience." *Philosophy East & West* 42, 1: 113–138.

——— (2000). "Kōan History: Transformative Language in Chinese Buddhist Thought." In Heine & Wright 2000, 200–212.

Yeh, Michelle (1983). "The Deconstructive Way: A Comparative Study of Derrida and Chuang Tzu." *Journal of Chinese Philosophy* 10, 2: 95–125.

Zhang, Longxi (1985). "The *Tao* and the *Logos:* Notes on Derrida's Critique of Logocentrism." *Critical Inquiry* 11, 3: 385–398.

Zhang, Xianglong (2004). "Heidegger's View of Language and the Lao-Zhuang View of *Dao*-Language." In R. Wang 2004, 195–214.

Zongqi, Cai (1993). "Derrida and Seng-Zhao: Linguistic and Philosophical Deconstructions." *Philosophy East & West* 43, 3: 389–404.

Ziporyn, Brook (2003). *The Penumbra Unbound: The Neo-Taoist Philosophy of Guo Xiang*. Albany: SUNY Press.

Zweig, Stefan (1990). *Gesammelte Werke in Einzelbänden: Zeiten und Schicksale*. Frankfurt a.M.: S. Fischer Verlag.

Index